MATLAB Blues

MATLAB Blues is an accessible, comprehensive introduction to the MATLAB computer programming language—a powerful and increasingly popular tool for students and researchers. Rosenbaum identifies many of the common mistakes and pitfalls associated with using MATLAB, and shows users how they can learn from these mistakes to be better, happier programmers.

Each chapter systematically addresses one of the basic principles of the programming language, like matrices, calculations, contingencies, plotting, input-output, and graphics, and then identifies areas that are problematic, as well as potential errors that can occur. This not only provides the reader with the fundamental "scales and chords" that a MATLAB programmer needs to know, but also with a series of examples and explanations of how to avoid and remedy common mistakes.

Accompanied by an array of sample code that can be used and manipulated in conjunction with the textbook, this book is a practical, insightful introduction to MATLAB which provides motivation and encouragement to those with little or no background in programming as well as to those with more advanced concerns. It is an invaluable resource for researchers and students undertaking courses in research methods, statistics, and programming.

David A. Rosenbaum is Distinguished Professor of Psychology at University of California, Riverside, USA.

MATLAB Blues

How Behavioral Scientists and Others
Can Learn From Mistakes for Better,
Happier Programming

David A. Rosenbaum

NEW YORK AND LONDON

First published 2020
by Routledge
52 Vanderbilt Avenue, New York, NY 10017

and by Routledge
2 Park Square, Milton Park, Abingdon, Oxon OX14 4RN

Routledge is an imprint of the Taylor & Francis Group, an informa business

© 2020 Taylor & Francis

The right of David A. Rosenbaum to be identified as author of this work has been asserted by him in accordance with sections 77 and 78 of the Copyright, Designs and Patents Act 1988.

All rights reserved. No part of this book may be reprinted or reproduced or utilised in any form or by any electronic, mechanical, or other means, now known or hereafter invented, including photocopying and recording, or in any information storage or retrieval system, without permission in writing from the publishers.

Trademark notice: Product or corporate names may be trademarks or registered trademarks, and are used only for identification and explanation without intent to infringe.

Library of Congress Cataloging-in-Publication Data
Names: Rosenbaum, David A., author.
Title: MATLAB blues : how behavioral scientists and others can learn from mistakes for better, happier programming / David A. Rosenbaum, University of California, Riverside.
Description: Abingdon, Oxon ; New York, NY : Routledge, [2020] | Includes index.
Identifiers: LCCN 2019012220 (print) | LCCN 2019017019 (ebook) |
  ISBN 9780429299094 (Ebook) | ISBN 9781138480537 (hbk) |
  ISBN 9781138480544 (pbk) | ISBN 9780429299094 (ebk)
Subjects: LCSH: MATLAB. | Computer programming. | Quantitative research—Data processing. | Software failures.
Classification: LCC TA345.5.M42 (ebook) | LCC TA345.5.M42 R67 2020 (print) | DDC 510.285/536—dc23
LC record available at https://lccn.loc.gov/2019012220

ISBN: 978-1-138-48053-7 (hbk)
ISBN: 978-1-138-48054-4 (pbk)
ISBN: 978-0-429-29909-4 (ebk)

Typeset in Times New Roman
by Apex CoVantage, LLC

Visit the eResource: www.routledge.com/9781138480544

This book is an incredible resource for both novice and skilled programmers. Coding textbooks will usually describe a correct method for doing various tasks, but we often encounter obstacles or bugs that don't have an obvious solution. *MATLAB Blues* is a treasure trove of practical examples of the kinds of problems that can mire even an expert coder. By working through such examples, either as a standalone or in concert with another instructional book, any programmer will accelerate their journey in the learning of coding skills.

—**Brad Wyble, Associate Professor of Psychology,
Pennsylvania State University, USA**

Professor David Rosenbaum, internationally renowned for his psychological research in the area of Action and Movement Control, delivers another very useful MATLAB volume every psychology and motor control lab should have on its shelves. There are many MATLAB traps for the unwary and the purpose of this book is to help researchers anticipate and avoid many of them. The book is written at a level suited to graduate or postdoctoral psychologists and I fully concur with Prof. Rosenbaum's suggestion that it will be relevant to frequent MATLAB users and not just beginners. I will certainly recommend students in my lab to buy this book now and save hours trying to sort incomprehensible MATLAB errors in the future.

—**Alan Wing, Sensory Motor Neuroscience Lab,
School of Psychology, University of Birmingham, UK**

The many short programming examples in this book are useful for all MATLAB users who want to make most of MATLAB. The programming problems and their elegant solutions are not only easy to comprehend but they are also helpful building blocks for developing one's own MATLAB scripts. The book is useful for beginners and even advanced users of MATLAB who want to learn more about MATLAB by studying concrete and frequently encountered problems that are both interesting and challenging.

—**Rolf Ulrich, Department of Psychology,
University of Tübingen, Germany**

Dr. Rosenbaum's books are "just right" for individuals who do not have prior experience in programming. Most students open the book with a doubtful mind about writing their own code. When finishing the book, they turn into confident individuals who can code and program for their own research. This new book, in particular, teaches students to learn from mistakes, which is the most common pathway of learning. Dr. Rosenbaum is the bravest scientist to share his own mistakes for the benefits of everyone who wants to learn MATLAB.

—**Zheng Wang, Assistant Professor, Department of
Occupational Therapy, University of Florida, USA**

Contents

Preface   x

1   Introduction   1

   1.1   A Problem You Can Learn From: Giving a Variable a Function Name 1
   1.2   Another Problem You Can Learn From: Getting the Enter Key to Stop Crashing Programs 4
   1.3   A Third Example of a Problem Yielding Unexpected Riches: Adding Letters With Quote Marks 5
   1.4   Program Pairs, the Sections They Occupy, and the Importance of %% 6
   1.5   Useful Keystroke Sequences 7
   1.6   MATLAB's Publish Feature 8
   1.7   Disclaimers 10

2   Matrices   11

   2.1   Printing the Value of a Variable in the Command Window 11
   2.2   Adding Elements to the Right Side of a Matrix 12
   2.3   Assigning Values to Indexed Positions 13
   2.4   Giving Variables Acceptable Names 13
   2.5   Deleting Elements From a One-Row Array 14
   2.6   Deleting a Column From a Multi-row Matrix 15
   2.7   Checking the Number of Values in Matrices 17
   2.8   Adding a Matrix to the Bottom of Another Matrix 18
   2.9   Inserting a Column Into a Matrix 19
   2.10   Switching Positions of Elements in a Matrix 20

3   Calculations   23

   3.1   Simple Summing 23
   3.2   Checking Whether Two Matrices Are the Same 24
   3.3   Multiplying Matrices 26
   3.4   Multiplying Matrices Element by Element 28
   3.5   Discovering and Then Taking the Dot Product 29
   3.6   Dividing Matrices 31
   3.7   Raising Values to a Power 32
   3.8   Getting Means 33

viii   *Contents*

    3.9 *Understanding What You "Mean"* 35
    3.10 *Getting Standard Deviations* 37

4 Contingencies   41

    4.1 *Using If Statements* 41
    4.2 *Using For Statements* 44
    4.3 *Checking Values Relative to Cutoffs* 46
    4.4 *Sorting* 51
    4.5 *Using While* 55
    4.6 *Adding to a New Matrix if a Criterion Is Met* 58
    4.7 *Creating a Latin Square Design* 61
    4.8 *Creating a Latin Square for Multiple Groups* 65
    4.9 *Timing Program Completions* 70
    4.10 *Using Find to Save Time* 73

5 Plotting   77

    5.1 *Defining Terms for Plotting* 77
    5.2 *Showing Multiple Curves* 79
    5.3 *Controlling Colors, Point Shapes, Graph Limits, and Standard Error Bars* 81
    5.4 *Adding Power Function Curves, Legends, and Labels for x- and y-Axes* 85
    5.5 *Creating Subplots* 90
    5.6 *Adding Text, a Grid, and a Fitted Exponential Function* 99
    5.7 *Adding Titles and Comparing Power Versus Exponential Functions* 106
    5.8 *Creating Bar Graphs* 109
    5.9 *Controlling Bars for Bar Graphs and xtick Labels* 113
    5.10 *Thinking Clearly While "Bar Hopping"* 116

6 Input-Output   119

    6.1 *Writing to Excel* 119
    6.2 *Writing to Excel With Column Headers Using the array2table Function* 122
    6.3 *Writing Out and Reading Back in a .dlm file* 125
    6.4 *Avoiding Overwriting Existing Files* 126
    6.5 *Formatting Data Printouts* 130
    6.6 *Creating Formatted Data and Headers for Excel* 133
    6.7 *Interacting With Users Via the input Function* 137
    6.8 *Looking for Particular Inputs* 139
    6.9 *Checking Users' Email Addresses* 141
    6.10 *Clicking on Figures and Saving Figures* 143

7 Data Types   147

    7.1 *Using Cells to Concatenate Double and Char Variables* 148
    7.2 *Seeing Cell Contents* 150

- 7.3 *Using Cells to Allow for Tick Labels With Different Numbers of Characters* 152
- 7.4 *Using Cells to Allow for Figure Titles With Different Numbers of Characters per Row* 154
- 7.5 *Assigning Values to Cell Positions* 156
- 7.6 *Putting Structure Elements Into a Matrix* 157
- 7.7 *Creating a Deeply Nested (Three-Tiered) Structure* 159
- 7.8 *Printing Structure Contents* 171
- 7.9 *Using a Structure to Graph a Deeply Nested Structure With Different Kinds of Fields* 173
- 7.10 *Using Fit, Understanding Its Fields* 182

8 Functions 186

- 8.1 *Understanding Size, Length, and Numel* 186
- 8.2 *Discovering Features of Mean* 189
- 8.3 *Messing With a Built-In Function: ginput Loses Crosshairs in david_ginput* 192
- 8.4 *Using Separate Names for Variables and Functions: Avoiding 'Text' as Output for xlsread* 197
- 8.5 *Understanding When Functions Are Not Helpful* 201
- 8.6 *Starting Functions With the Word 'Function'* 203
- 8.7 *Calling Functions Correctly* 205
- 8.8 *Creating and Calling a New Function to Control Ticklabel Formatting* 207
- 8.9 *Creating and Calling a New Function to Draw Arrows* 212
- 8.10 *Calling Programs or Functions Remotely Using Eval* 217

9 Graphics 220

- 9.1 *Ordering Legends* 220
- 9.2 *Showing Legends for Some Curves But Not Others, and Showing Subscripts* 222
- 9.3 *Adding Italics and Symbols to Graphs* 226
- 9.4 *Sequencing Points for Graphs* 228
- 9.5 *Naming Rather Than Numbering Figures, and Filling n-tagons* 232
- 9.6 *Rotating Text, Overlaying Text on Arrows, and More Plotting* 237
- 9.7 *Plotting and Filling in 3D, and Controlling the Camera Angle* 250
- 9.8 *Showing and Then Cropping Images* 257
- 9.9 *Showing Multiple Images and Replacing One of Them* 260
- 9.10 *Keeping Animations From Slowing Down* 264

Index 270

Preface

A good way to learn is to make mistakes. An even better way is to see others falter and learn from *their* blunders. You can learn it's unwise to step on a banana peel by stepping on one and landing on your behind. But seeing someone else fall on their butt is more efficient, at least for you. By seeing the other person's mistake, you can avoid injury yourself, and maybe get a good laugh.

Laughing at others isn't something any of us should be proud of; it's a pretty shameful tendency. For reasons that are unclear to me, that shameful tendency has a German name (*Schadenfreude*). Delighting in others' misfortune reflects an aggressive side that most of us have, probably inherited from our ancestors. Though we might not like it, our forebears must have been pretty tough to do whatever they did to enable us now, millennia later, to be here thinking about – of all things – computer programming.

Comedians, for eons, have used Schadenfreude to get others to laugh at them. In slapstick comedy, actors fall off ladders, land in mud, and get pies thrown in their faces, all for laughs at their own expense (or that of their customers, who bought the tickets to watch the burlesque).

In this book, I'm going to be your fall guy. Of course, books about computer programming are not places normally devoted to comedy, but I'll be funny for you, in a sense, occupying the position of a hapless, struggling programmer, showing you how I've fallen off computational ladders, landed in coding mud, and gotten MATLAB pies thrown in my face, all in the service of programming. What do I tolerate such insults? I do the coding I do, warts and all, because I need it for my research, but also because I like puzzles, and I like to learn.

MATLAB (short for Matrix Laboratory) is a technical programming language from Mathworks, a company based in Natick, Massachusetts. I have no commercial ties with Mathworks, nor do I have a beef with them, notwithstanding the title of this book, which is meant to be lighthearted, not dark or menacing in any way.

I'm going to share my programming-related imperfections with you, freely admitting that I have made countless mistakes while programming in MATLAB. My abiding principle is that if you see bloopers that I've made (or in some cases contrived for this presentation), you'll be a bit less likely to make the same mistakes yourself. Seeing that even a so-called expert can err, and seeing how a supposed expert is willing to brush off the dirt on his uniform and step up to the plate again, you'll hopefully be less likely to despair over the boo-boos you'll inevitably commit. Hopefully, you'll go from feeling blue (if you are) to feeling informed and even inspired.[1]

---

1 My philosophy echoes one of the most useful distinctions to come out of psychological research, at least in my opinion as a research psychologist. This is the distinction between *entity* learners and *incremental* learners. Entity learners see their failures as indictments of their genes. Incremental learners see their mistakes as vehicles for better performance. The aim of this book is to help you become an incremental learner, at least when it comes to MATLAB programming. If that mindset generalizes to other pursuits, so much the better. The distinction between entity learners and incremental learners was put forth by Dweck, C. S., & Bempechat, J. (1983). Children's theories of intelligence. In S. Paris, G. Olsen, & H. Stevenson (Eds.), *Learning and Motivation in the Classroom* (pp. 239-256). Hillsdale, NJ: Erlbaum.

How did this book come to be? It arose from my teaching of MATLAB. I've taught several MATLAB classes—first at Penn State University, where I was on the faculty from 1994 to 2016, and then at the University of California, Riverside (UCR), where I have been on the faculty since 2016. To help with my teaching, I first wrote course notes that turned into the first edition of *MATLAB for Behavioral Scientists* (Rosenbaum, 2007). That book was expanded and improved upon with the help of Jonathan Vaughan and Brad Wyble, in *MATLAB for Behavioral Scientists, Second Edition* (Rosenbaum, Vaughan, & Wyble, 2014).[2]

Paul Dukes, who was my editor at the time at Psychology Press and who shepherded the first and second editions of *MATLAB for Behavioral Scientists*, became interested in a possible third edition of the book. As I considered his suggestion, I realized that a more useful product might be a kind of study guide. The contract I signed with Paul was for a book called *Study Guide for MATLAB for Behavioral Scientists*.

As I worked on the new book, pursuing the approach that Paul and I had agreed to, it occurred to me that the title Paul and I had chosen might be improved upon. I thought a work not specifically tied to a particular textbook would have broader appeal, and I came to believe that a title aimed at a broader market would be preferable. So arose the proposal to change the name of the work to *MATLAB Blues*. Happily, Paul agreed, as did his successor as my new editor, Lucy McClune. Lucy encouraged me to provide a subtitle to help folks understand what this book would actually be about. In consultation with her, we settled on *How Behavioral Scientists and Others Can Learn From Mistakes for Better, Happier Programming*.

The material offered here assumes basic knowledge of MATLAB. It happens that the organization of this book follows, more or less, the organization of *MATLAB for Behavioral Scientists, Second Edition*, except that one topic has been brought forward. That topic is generating graphs (the topic of Chapter 9 in the textbook). The reason for advancing the presentation of plotting is to let you get to graphs sooner than you would otherwise. Making professional-level graphs is one of the most attractive features of MATLAB. Once you start making your own graphs, you'll probably be even more motivated than you were before to rev up your programming skills. (The present book also omits a few topics that were covered in the earlier textbook, such as sound generation, which I do little of in MATLAB. Having nothing new to offer beyond what was in the earlier volumes, I chose not to write about sound generation here.)

How should you use this book? If you're using it on your own, I suggest you consult relevant background material such as the book referred to above, or other volumes or websites. You can also take advantage of on-line resources such as MATLAB *Grader* or MATLAB *Onramp* to challenge yourself along the lines those resources promote. Socializing with others who use MATLAB can be useful as well.

The critical feature of the programs presented here is that every one comes in two versions. The first *doesn't* work. The second *does*. The rationale for this scheme is that by focusing on what distinguishes good code from bad, you can get attuned to what makes programs work. Most of the programs I've written and that I've seen others write have at least one bug or typo before the program finally functioned. Confronting programming errors is an integral part of the programming process.

Though the programs here have problems, there are no problems as such for you to solve. I don't assign problems. The reason is that, in my teaching, I have come to see that solving other

---

2 The references for these two books are Rosenbaum, D. A. (2007). *MATLAB for Behavioral Scientists*. Mahwah, NJ: Lawrence Erlbaum Associates, and Rosenbaum, D. A., Vaughan, J., & Wyble, B. (2015). *MATLAB for Behavioral Scientists (Second Edition)*. Routledge/Taylor and Francis Group. The website for the second edition, with code that can be downloaded, is at http://cw.routledge.com/textbooks/matlab/. The website for the present book, with code that can be downloaded is at www.routledge.com/9781138480544

people's programming problems is anathema to most people. I used to give students programming problems such as code with errors to debug, programs with lines or parts of lines missing, or open-ended challenges concerning particular issues to be addressed, such as "Write a program that shows two curves, one red and one blue, associated with negative exponential functions that both start at 21 and end at different asymptotes." I've learned that most students don't get charged up by such challenges. What *does* charge them up is chasing a topic of interest to them. When they have a reason to program, their excitement drives them forward.

Building on my experience, I intend this book to be used for classroom teaching. I have tested it (or drafts of it) in two classes I have taught. In a course taught at UCR in the Fall of 2017 and then again in the Fall of 2018, I asked students to read a chapter in *MATLAB for Behavioral Scientists, Second Edition*, and come to class ready to see new example programs I had drafted. The key feature of the ten or so new programs I showed in each class meeting was that they pertained to the chapter the students had been asked to read. The students and I went through the examples, which I projected onto a screen at the front of the classroom, trying to make sure the students understood the aims of the programs, the problem or problems with the first version, and the solution or solutions in the second version. I tried to get the students to articulate the general principle that each pair of programs illustrated.

A procedural detail is worth mentioning for instructors considering this approach for their teaching. In my classes, after the students and I went through the examples together, I uploaded the code to the class drive so the students could work it on their own. I did not send the code out to the class before or during the lectures because I wanted the students to be with me and with each other during the presentation. Today's rabbit hole, into which modern-day Alices can easily descend, is their laptops.

Once the class ended, I uploaded the code and the students left with the invitation to write whatever code they wished, drawing on the code they had been shown in class to pursue their own interests. I encouraged the students to work singly or in teams, as they preferred. There were some students who liked the lone-wolf method. Others preferred to run with the pack. I let them proceed as they wished, for I have found that forcing less social students to work with others can be like leading horses to water; if they're not thirsty, they just won't drink. Conversely, students who are social butterflies dislike the prospect of fluttering alone.

When the students returned in the next class meeting, they gave presentations about their programming exploits. Each student, or each group of students, shared their lapses followed by their successes. They were encouraged to draw out their classmates about the general principles their programming forays illustrated. I used this as an opportunity to help the students with their *teaching* as well as their *programming*.

A joke at the start of each academic quarter was that if code was written and it didn't fail at first, the students would have to make up something to show a possible error. The joke arose when a student said that I, their professor who presumably knew MATLAB backwards and forwards and had written two books on it, must surely be faking my errors. "Oh no," I protested. "I make mistakes all the time!" As the course went on and the students got to know me better, they became increasingly sure that I had flubbed when I said I did. That I was open and undefensive about it was, of course, the point. All of us make mistakes, and that's OK, especially if we turn the lemons into lemonade.

After the quarter (or semester) ended, the students gave the course and me feedback. I was pleased to see that they liked the course very much. They appreciated the message that it's acceptable to make mistakes, and they were heartened to learn that everyone messes up, even professors. They liked that they could go their own way with the programs they wrote, exploring whatever challenges they wished to pursue.

This freedom to explore turned out to be extremely important to the students. When I taught this course before, giving specific programming problems such as debugging exercises, students felt hemmed in by the approach. Quite a few of them, in those earlier courses, indicated that they actually *hated* the approach and said so in their evaluations. Suitably chastened, I changed things in later versions, using the *wrong-then-right* method and giving students carte blanche to go their own way. They were much happier than their predecessors were, and they definitely learned more.

So happy have I been with this approach that I now feel justified in suggesting to other teachers that they consider using it their own courses. The materials in this book can constitute the lecture materials for a course on MATLAB taught to graduate students, undergraduate students, or, conceivably, high school or even more junior high pupils.

Apropos teaching, I should add that one request I made of the students was that the programs they wrote in any given week not bring in programming techniques that had not yet been introduced in the course. The reason for this proscription against "time-machining," as I called it, was to reduce the chance that more advanced students would snow students who were less far along. All the students, both the more advanced ones and those less so, accepted and appreciated this idea. By extension, in this book I have tried to avoid time-machining, though there is one case (Section 6.2) where I break this rule, just because it would have been really silly not to do so.

As stated above, I believe the approach offered here can prove useful to others teaching programming. This book fills a need related to programming pedagogy. There hasn't really been a resource for in-class teaching of MATLAB. However, with the set of programs offered here, it should be possible to give the kind of structured teaching that students like. To the extent that drama and suspense can enliven lectures, the fact that each pair of programs forms a kind of mini mystery – *Here's a poor injured program. Can we save it?* – may encourage students and, for that matter, faculty, to become more engaged than they would be otherwise.[3]

Many students were engaged in the development of the materials presented here, and I want to thank them. The following students took my course at UCR when I tried out the *MATLAB Blues* approach: Lillian Azer, Alyssa Berger, Chris Chase, Sharon Chee, Josh Dorsi, Jake Elder, Iman Feghhi, Kellan Kadooka, Jenna Klippenstein, Alessandra MacBeth, Seth Margolis, Breanna McGee, Jenna Monson, Preston Mote, Justin Pastore, Kyle Sauerberger, Ashley Stapley, Rebecca Tuckerman, and Floor van den Berg. Some of the code presented here came from a subset of these students. I won't say which snippets came from which ones. Suffice it to say that all the students, one way or the other, helped make the course materials, and so this book, better than it would have been otherwise, and likewise for a faculty colleague, Steve Clark, who audited the course in the Fall of 2018.

I also want to say thanks to those who played a role in the development of the book itself. First, I want to thank Paul Dukes of Psychology Press, who encouraged me to do more with my writing about MATLAB. The content of the present book is what Paul and I agreed to, and I appreciate that when I told Paul about my idea to change the title (at Psychonomics in November 2018), he was on board, at least if my new editor, Lucy McClune, would be as well. I am grateful to Lucy for her support, not just for sanctioning the new title but also for shepherding the book through to publication. My appreciation additionally goes out to Jennifer Fester for copyediting this manuscript. I also thank Sophie Crowe, Marie Louise Roberts, and Abigail Stanley for their help with production of the final work.

---

3 Whether this approach might be applied to other programming languages is an open question. One could imagine the *Blues* term being applied in other contexts – *Python Blues, R Blues*, and so on – with the same pedagogic approach being taken there. Nothing in the present approach makes it singularly suited for MATLAB.

I also want to thank my good friend and collaborator, James Spottiswoode, who patiently listened to me talk about my nascent ideas about this work. While still struggling with how best to frame the material, I shared with James my not-very-satisfying thoughts for a possible title, telling him how I felt that a study guide title fell short. Hearing me say how what I really wanted to achieve was a work about facing and then overcoming challenges in MATLAB programming, James quipped in his high British accent, "Sounds like MATLAB Blues." His idea was brilliant, I thought. It captured what I was trying to achieve. I thanked James for his great suggestion in our conversation and do so here again in print.

Vijay Iyer of Mathworks deserves a thank-you as well. Vijay and I had a phone conversation about this project on December 7, 2018. In his role as a Mathworks marketer (especially for neuroscience), he saw that this could be a welcome resource. I made plain to Vijay that my intent in writing *MATLAB Blues* was not to disparage Mathworks or MATLAB, but instead to help users find solutions more easily. He understood and gave his blessing. "Yes," he admitted, "sometimes getting answers to programming problems in MATLAB can be a bit of a treasure hunt." The treasure-hunt metaphor is apt. I hope Vijay and his Mathworks colleagues will deem this book a treasure, too.

In the planning stages of this work, Brad Wyble, one of my co-authors for the second edition of *MATLAB for Behavioral Scientists*, kindly offered input that helped me reach the final shaping. When it came time to commit to co-authoring the work, Brad decided to focus his energies elsewhere. I accepted his decision. Brad and I remain good friends.

The other co-author of the second edition of *MATLAB for Behavioral Scientists*, Jonathan Vaughan, is no longer with us. Jon succumbed to cancer in the fall of 2014. Jon lived long enough to see publication of the book that he, Brad, and I put together. Jon was a brilliant programmer, a great friend, and a fantastic collaborator on our MATLAB book as well as the scientific research that we did together in the field of human perception and performance. The present work would have been much better if Jon had been able to contribute to it. I have tried to live up to Jon's legacy and dedicate this book to his memory.

Riverside, California
February 22, 2019

1 Introduction

Being able to program is a valuable skill. You know this, of course; it's why you are here. You've probably programmed enough to have some success, but you've probably also gotten the blues when you've worked hard on programs but felt like you were banging your head against a wall. You may have felt frustrated, especially when you knew or believed the programming problem you were having shouldn't be so hard. Perhaps you thought you weren't cut out for this kind of work, that you'd be found out as an impostor.

This book is meant to help you. It's premised on the idea that virtually no one is perfectly suited, from birth, to perform flawlessly in any line of work (or play). Experience builds confidence, and an essential part of experience is error feedback (as well as success feedback).

This book arose from my teaching of MATLAB in several courses (first at Penn State University and then at the University of California, Riverside) and then in two editions of a book I was involved with: *MATLAB for Behavioral Scientists* (Rosenbaum, 2007) and *MATLAB for Behavioral Scientists, Second Edition* (Rosenbaum, Vaughan, & Wyble, 2014).

Though I have taught and written about MATLAB, I have a dirty little secret. Though I have programmed for years, the number of mistakes I have made is vast. In this respect, I'm no different from others who program. Like all or most of them, I have made my fair share of errors – bloopers that were careless or silly or downright stupid, like misspelling a word or leaving out a punctuation mark. Bloopers like these are of little interest, though they can be maddening when they're missed. Other errors have been more interesting and informative. One day it occurred to me that it might be worth sharing them with others. My lapses of thinking or understanding might save others from similar mistakes.

I had another reason for offering a mistake-based treatment. Quite a few of the faux pas I have committed have come up in fairly specialized contexts. I have had various programming needs that I'm pretty sure others have had or will have. Showing the roadblocks I ran into and then overcame may be useful to others as they (you) deal with them. This book is meant to help you with special programming needs you may have, though of course I cannot predict all that you will encounter. In some cases, seeing things I managed to do might kindle in you the thought that you too might try something similar yourself, though you might never have considered it before. For example, seeing that it is possible to have two graphs in a top row and a single graph below them, extending the full width of the two graphs above, might lead you to try something similar. You might not have done so before, but seeing that someone else did so and managed to overcome obstacles in the process may embolden you.

1.1 A Problem You Can Learn From: Giving a Variable a Function Name

To convey the value of this approach, I'd like you to consider an example. The example dives into quite a bit of detail, but I think it's worth reading it to get a broader message.

2 Introduction

In MATLAB, it's possible to read data from Excel spreadsheets and then to carry out analyses and to graph the data in ways that Excel may not easily support. To read in the data, you can use a MATLAB function called `xlsread`. When using `xlsread`, you tell MATLAB the name of the Excel file you want to access, including (optionally) other information about it like the specific spreadsheet(s) you want to read. The latter option is not used below, except implicitly because by default, the spreadsheet that is read in from Excel is spreadsheet number 1. You can also specify which aspects of the data you want to get as outputs from the `xlsread` function. There are three possible aspects: (1) the numerical data; (2) the text; and (3) a combination of data and text (both types together). The word "text" means literal strings such as 'Y' or 'N' for yes/no responses to questions; the quote marks mark these elements as text. A typical command in which all three data types are requested is something like this:

```
[numbers,txt,both]=xlsread('My_Excel_file.xls')
```

The terms on the left of the equal sign are the names of the desired outputs. The exact names don't matter. You could just as well call them Curly, Larry, and Moe. All MATLAB cares about is how many terms are on the left. If there is just one term, the relevant output will be numbers only. If there are two outputs, they will be numbers followed by text. If there are three, the outputs will be numbers, text, and then a combination of the two.[1]

Mindful of the fact that output names can be whatever you want (so long as they obey the rules of variable names in MATLAB), and also mindful of the fact that it's good for variables to have meaningful names, I once wrote a line of code like the following:

```
[numbers,text,both]=xlsread('My_Excel_file.xls')
```

Later in the same program, I tried to plot the numbers in a graph. I wanted to show some text in the graph to highlight features of interest. To achieve this, I used a command whose general format I had used many times before:

```
text(x(i),y(i),text(i)).
```

This command meant, or was supposed to mean, that MATLAB would show, at the ith value of x (along the horizontal axis) and at the ith value of y (along the vertical axis), the ith value of text. I used the variable i to repeat this command for $i = 1$, $i = 2$, and so on. Although I had used the `text` plotting command many times before and had used `xlsread` many times before, in this case I got an error message and was completely baffled by it. The error message said, in so many words, that the `text` feature of plotting graphs in MATLAB was no longer available. This was like learning that electricity would no longer be coming out of the wall socket in my home or that water would no longer be coming out of the tap in my sink. I was confused and frustrated. I thought my computer had been attacked by cyber criminals. I thought, for a few seconds, that I was losing my mind.

To reassure readers familiar with MATLAB who want to know that I know something about MATLAB, note that the actual code that gave rise to this mistake was more complex. The line

---

1 As you probably noticed, different type fonts are used here for different purposes. The book's main text uses Times New Roman. MATLAB code, by contrast, uses Courier New. Also, if you were reading aloud the line of MATLAB code above, you would want to say `[number,text,both]` *gets* `xlsread('My_Excel_file.xls')`. You would not want to say that the values are *equal to* `xlsread('My_Excel_file.xls')`.

with the errant code was buried in many other lines of code; that made the goof hard to spot. Also, the error message I got seemed to bear no relation to anything in the program.

I finally figured out what was wrong. I had used the same word, `text`, for a *variable*, namely, the text (or literal string) elements of the file read in by Excel, and also as a *function*, the utility used with `plot` to place literal strings in a graphics window. Unfortunately, MATLAB did not provide an error message like the following, which would have saved me from considerable consternation:

```
>> Be careful not to use a function word for a variable.
```

There is no such error message in MATLAB. I made it up and dressed it up like a typical MATLAB warning. The actual error message that MATLAB gave was opaque with respect to the actual source of the problem.

So what did I do wrong? I assigned a word reserved for a function in MATLAB to a variable. If you assign data to a variable called `text` and don't use the `text` graphics function while the text variable is still alive (i.e., if the variable hasn't been cleared), you'll be OK; there won't be a problem. But it's better to avoid any such confusion by avoiding function words as variable names. If you think the second output variable of `xlsread` is going to be text (a literal string), it's better not to use that word insofar as `text` is also a MATLAB function. To be safe, use `txt` or `Larry` or some other invented or idiosyncratic term.

Experienced MATLAB users will say they already know this. I did too! But even they, like me, may occasionally falter when it comes to assigning function names to variables. Ideally, Mathworks should automatically create alerts whenever a variable name also happens to be a built-in function. It does so for very common functions like `for` (which is used for `for` loops), as in this example:

```
>> for=1
 for=1
    ↑
Error: The expression to the left of the equals sign is not a
valid target for an assignment.
```

The engineers at Mathworks decided that certain core terms like `for` should not be assignable to variables, but other terms, like `text`, can be.

Undeterred by my bad experience, I decided to turn this lemon into lemonade. I searched the internet on August 8, 2018, and found a request for such a service by one person dated November 9, 2013; there were no follow-ups. However, my further sleuthing turned up a function I didn't associate with this problem. I wrote the following in the Google search bar: "MATLAB make sure variable name not a function." After a fraction of a second, Google suggested a site in MATLAB's documentation. Here is what I found there:

```
exist name returns the type of name as a number. This list
describes the type associated with each value:
```

- `0 — name does not exist or cannot be found for other reasons. For example, if name exists in a restricted folder to which MATLAB® does not have access, exist returns 0.`
- `1 — name is a variable in the workspace.`
- `2 — name is a file with extension .m, .mlx, or .mlapp, or name is the name of a file with a non-registered file extension (.mat, .fig, .txt).`
- `3 — name is a MEX-file on your MATLAB search path.`

4 Introduction

- 4 — `name is a loaded Simulink® model or a Simulink model or library file on your MATLAB search path.`
- 5 — `name is a built-in MATLAB function. This does not include classes.`
- 6 — `name is a P-code file on your MATLAB search path.`
- 7 — `name is a folder.`
- 8 — `name is a class. (exist returns 0 for Java classes if you start MATLAB with the -nojvm option.)`

After reading this documentation, I typed the following into the MATLAB command window:

```
>> exist text
```

The answer I got was

```
ans =
    5
```

In other words, `text` is a built-in MATLAB function. If you care to take the time to use `exist` for every variable you create, you can check whether that variable is a function. If it is, the answer you will get will be 5 (not the most transparent response, but one you can learn to interpret).

Hopefully, the larger point is clear. By reading about a blunder, you'll be unlikely to make it yourself. If you're willing to learn from mistakes – mine, yours, or others' – you'll probably be able to program more happily and effectively.

1.2 Another Problem You Can Learn From: Getting the Enter Key to Stop Crashing Programs

Focusing on flaws can be dispiriting, so let me now share a programming *success*. What I hope to show here is that in addition to laying bare my scars, I also can share some tricks that have served me well. In some cases, they took me many minutes, hours, or even days to figure out. The tricks don't reflect any special deftness on my part. Most of them are pretty mundane and are simply hard to come by because MATLAB, for all its strengths, has all sorts of exceptions and some quirky design features. In addition, the available documentation isn't always as clear or helpful as it might be. Chatter on the internet can help, but sometimes it's less valuable than you might expect. In several cases, when I was unable to find an answer to a question I sent an email to technical help at MATLAB. The experts there – the Mathworks mavens, as I call them – have always been very helpful.

Here is an example. I spent several days trying to figure out how to prevent a MATLAB program from crashing when participants in a study I was setting up hit a key on the keyboard when they shouldn't have. That key wasn't some obscure button that was off in left field. It was the Enter key, one of the most commonly used keys. In the application I was developing, I wanted participants to hit the f key or the j key. These are the two keys that have the special property of having little ridges that people can feel so they don't have to keep looking down at the keyboard to make sure their hands are where they're supposed to be. If any other key was hit, the program moved along, and I was able to provide feedback to the user along the lines of "Sorry, you can only hit the f key or the j key." However, if the Enter key was pressed, the program crashed.

Because the Enter key isn't a weird key that people rarely hit, this was a big concern. I thought about simply warning participants not to press that key, but such advice would only go so far. Telling subjects not to press the Enter key might, ironically, cause them to do it more. (Think about telling people not to think about white bears; this causes them only to think about white bears more than they would otherwise.)

How could I get MATLAB to stop crashing if people pressed the Enter key? Spending more than about one minute on this problem was the last thing I wanted to do, but solving it was something I *had* to do. After concluding that I would be unable to solve the problem myself, I swallowed my pride and wrote to the folks at Mathworks. After some back-and-forth, they provided the solution. The answer was completely unintuitive, though in retrospect it made sense.

It turns out that MATLAB will not crash if the Enter key is pressed and you are using the `ginput` function to gather inputs from the keyboard and you set up logic gates in the right way. You have to set a logic gate to false (or true), and then while that logic gate is false (or true), the keyboard can be checked. If there is input from the keyboard *and* if that input is *not* "empty," then the logic gate can be flipped, whereupon checking for keyboard inputs stops. It turns out that when you hit the Enter key, the value that is returned from the keyboard is [], or "nothing," the empty set. So if the program is instructed to check whether the input is empty, it will keep checking the keyboard if the input is empty; otherwise, the program will go on. The solution, then, inheres in the fact that you need to check whether the keyboard input variable is empty or not empty. The full implementation of these ideas is provided in Problem 6.10.

Don't worry if you don't fully understand all the details of what I've just said, and I won't worry if you honestly don't care about them all right now. The matter will make more sense to you once you delve into the material. If you actually will never care about the inner logic of what it takes to get this to work, you can just adapt the code as you see fit. That is another aim of this book: to provide you with code you can adapt for your own purposes.

1.3 A Third Example of a Problem Yielding Unexpected Riches: Adding Letters With Quote Marks

As stated above, the way I have set up this book is to provide programs that don't work and then do. The rationale for showing programs that don't work is to alert you to traps you might fall into. For example, you might set a variable to zero at the wrong place in a program, or you might not clear a variable (which is not the same thing as setting it to zero) when you should. Seeing how mistakes can arise can reassure you that even experts can err. In addition, seeing slips by others can prime you to avoid them and be on the lookout for similar lapses of your own.

Some errors can reveal *capabilities* of MATLAB that you might not have expected. For example, if you add two literal characters, the letter a in quotes and the letter b in quotes, you can get a numerical sum:

```
>> 'a' + 'b'
ans =
    195
```

Who would have expected such a thing? How can the letters 'a' and 'b' be added and yield a number? The answer turns out to be useful.

Each literal character has a numerical equivalent. This makes sense considering that literal characters are represented by digit strings, just as numbers are. The numerical equivalents can be expressed as so-called double-precision real values:

```
>> double('a')
ans =
    97
```

6   Introduction

```
>> double('b')
ans =
    98
>> double('a') + double('b')
ans =
    195
```

Making the mistake of adding things in quote marks, which a student did in one of my classes, revealed something useful. It turns out that when keyboard inputs are collected with the `ginput` function, the way to determine which key the participant pressed is to reference the double to which the key corresponds (see Problem 6.8). In other words, to check whether the participant typed a or b, a possible approach is to check whether the variable to which the typed input was mapped equals 97, the double for 'a', or 98, the double for 'b'.

1.4   Program Pairs, the Sections They Occupy, and the Importance of %%

You can use this book in a class or with family/friends/colleagues outside a class setting. Some people like to work alone. Others like to work in groups. I think there are advantages to working with, or at least showing your work to, others. Others seeing what you are doing may have suggestions along the way: "Hey, you forgot to put single quote marks around that variable name." "Oh, right," you might reply. It would be good to know you had not erred in vain. You and the person looking over your shoulder may both learn something useful from the mistake.

Regardless of whether you work with others or by yourself, as you use this book you will spend most of your time looking at and working in MATLAB's edit window. The edit window, in contrast to the command window, is where you can write and edit multiple lines of code and save files containing them.

All of the programs written for this book were written in MATLAB's edit window and have the following general structure:

```
%% x.x Topic (unsolved)
% Comments about Program x.x, drawing attention to the error
{... Code that doesn't work ...}

%% x.x Topic (solved)
% Comments about Program x.x, drawing attention to the solution
{... Code that does work ...}
```

As seen above, the first section has a program with a problem. The second section has that same program with the problem solved. That same structure will be used throughout this book.

The word "section" is important here, because in MATLAB, a program or part of a program demarcated by a leading pair of percent signs (%%) has special status. Starting with %% marks the start of a *section* and as such can be clicked, whereupon MATLAB will highlight it in a different color than the background (typically yellow against a white background). The section ends when the next pair of percent signs is encountered or when the program ends. Lines that begin with single percent signs (%) are *comments*. They, like lines that start with double percent signs, are non-executable. So all lines that begin with any number of percent signs is a non-executable comment, but all lines that start with two percent signs are also section starts.

The most useful feature of sections is that they can be run on their own, separate and apart from the larger programs they are part of. This makes it possible to treat each section as a stand-alone program. Considering this possibility, the material offered here has been organized in such a way that every section starts with the same four executable lines of code:

```
clear all
close all
commandwindow
clc
```

The first line, `clear all`, clears all variables. This ensures that all new variables are set up from scratch, allowing you to consider the program in that section entirely on its own without having to keep track of previous values of any of the variables.

The second line, `close all`, closes all figure windows. This ensures that all previously generated graphs and images disappear. Even if there are no open figure windows, it helps to issue the `close all` command as a matter of habit.

The third line, `commandwindow`, automatically opens that window to display all outputs that are to be printed out. It is disconcerting to have to take the extra step of opening the command window when printing is needed. It is easier to do this as a matter of course.

Finally, the fourth line, `clc`, clears the command window. Again, the intent is to allow for a fresh start, ensuring that all previously generated statements are out of the way. Even if there are no statements in the command window, it helps to issue the `clc` command. On occasion, there may actually be previously printed lines that are no longer visible, so this approach is strongly recommended.

You can run the code within a section of a MATLAB program in either of two ways. One is to manually select the section and then evaluate that section alone by clicking on the Run Section icon or by typing Fn-F9 (on the PC). The other way is just to type Ctrl-Enter. If you have clicked somewhere in the section you want to run, the Ctrl-Enter keystroke sequence runs the code for that section. That piece of information can save you a lot of time because manually selecting the code you want to execute can be very time-consuming, not to mention error-prone. Ctrl-Enter, by contrast, is quick and easy, provided again that you have clicked somewhere within the section that you want to run. The programs offered here, within their MATLAB programs, all take advantage of this design feature. I strongly encourage you to put a pair of percent signs (%%) before each program or section you write to take advantage of this convenient fact. Hitting Ctrl-Enter will probably become automatic for you, as it has for me.[2]

1.5 Useful Keystroke Sequences

When you compose your own programs, you'll be able to use a few basic keystroke sequences over and over to help you write, run, and save your programs. Those keyboard sequences are listed here. They may become automatic after you have used them for a

---

[2] There is one disadvantage to clicking a section and hitting Ctrl-Enter as opposed to manually selecting a section and hitting the Run Section icon or typing Fn-F9 (on the PC). Ctrl-Enter will yield errors if they exist, but MATLAB won't tell you where the error is (the line with the first problem MATLAB encounters), nor will it say what the error is. Diagnostic information like this can only be gotten with the Run command or its key sequence equivalent (Fn-F5), which runs the entire program. You can also select the section and use the Run Section command or its keyboard equivalent (Fn-F9) to get diagnostic information if you want it. I have also noted that Ctrl-Enter happily ignores lines of code like this one, which is uninterpretable in MATLAB: y+1=z. So be careful about such instances. You can write y=z-1 but not y+1=z.

while, and I strongly encourage you to learn them because once you do, you will find them immensely useful.

Ctrl-Enter	As just stated, this command runs the section that your cursor is in, provided there is a pair of percent signs (%%) at the start of the section's first line and another pair of percent signs at the start of the line beginning the next section if there is one. The second pair of percent signs can also mark the start of the next section.
Ctrl-r	Turns the selected material from executable code to a comment.
Ctrl-t	Turns the selected material from a comment back to executable code (to uncomment it).
Ctrl-j	Tightens up the right margin of the comment that your cursor is in. Comments start with % or %%, so if you type Ctrl-j while your cursor is in a comment, you won't have to take the time to insert line breaks where you think they'll be needed. If you type Ctrl-a (see below) followed by Ctrl-j, then tightening of the right margin will apply to all of the comments. If you write lots of comments, the amount of time you will save by using Ctrl-j will be enormous.
Ctrl-a	Selects the entire .m file (your executable MATLAB program is or should be saved with the .m suffix).
Ctrl-i	Automatically indents the code so lines of code within for ... end loops, within if ... end loops, and within while ... end loops are indented if the code is set up correctly. The only exception is if those loops are within functions that have their own end statements. Otherwise, if you type Ctrl-a followed by Ctrl-i, the indentation will be applied to the entire .m file. In case you're not sure whether this key sequence is useful, be advised that the author of this book has typed the key sequence Ctrl-a Ctrl-i thousands of times; it is "in his fingers." This four-key sequence is tremendously useful because it automatically indents the entire program and makes the hierarchical structure of your program easy to see.
Fn-F5	Runs the entire .m file and shows what is wrong and where it is wrong if there is an error, in contrast to Ctrl-Enter, which, as said above, is actually more useful than Fn-F5 if you click on sections of code (separated by %%) and want to run just those sections without getting error diagnostics.
Fn-F9	Runs the part of the .m file that is selected and provides informative error feedback if there is a goof, though again Ctrl-Enter is generally easier.
Alt-f-a	Brings up the save-as window.
Alt-tab	Lets you switch windows, for example from the edit window to the command window or vice versa.
Ctrl-0	Brings up the command window. Note that the final character is a zero, not the letter O.
Ctrl-shift-0	Brings up the edit window. Again, that's a zero, not the letter O.

1.6 MATLAB's Publish Feature

As I was preparing this book, I thought I might produce the whole thing with MATLAB's Publish feature. Publish is a handy application that lets you port your code and code output to external media such as HTML or Microsoft Word. I have seen friends and colleagues be surprised and delighted to learn that instead of just running MATLAB programs, they can "publish" programs, too, which means getting nicely formatted output showing the code and output, complete with a table of contents at the beginning. This can be especially helpful when sharing your work with others who don't use MATLAB.

I ultimately decided not to use Publish for this book, however, because it stops working (publishing stops) if a program that is being run encounters an error. MATLAB stops publishing when a program fails, which makes sense, of course, because how could MATLAB publish what it can't compute? Still, this feature of Publish posed a problem for me as I was preparing this book because so much of the code generated errors (by design). Finally, I decided to present the code and output by manually inserting the code and output into Word documents (one per chapter), much as I had done in my two previous books on MATLAB.

Still, Publish is really helpful, so I'll share some problems I encountered using it, aiming to offer tips that may prove helpful to you. First, to generate published output as a Word document rather than HTML (HTML seems to be the default setting), hit the Publish tab in the Editor Window and then, after clicking on the Publish down-arrow tab, go to Edit Publishing Options and next set the Output Publishing Format to doc. Then hit the Publish button to run and simultaneously "publish" the code and output (i.e., put the code and output into a Word document whose name is assigned, by MATLAB, to match the name of the program). Then copy the document or parts you want into whatever masterpiece you are creating.

Second, I lost a fair amount of time when I published a program, then made some changes to it without changing the program name, and then tried publishing it again. I got this spine-tingling error message over and over again as I tried desperately to figure out what was wrong:

```
>> Error using publish (line 144)
The output file "C:\Users\David_A_Rosenbaum\Documents\Dumb Backup Begun
06-01-18\html\MATLAB_BLUES_PROBLEM_SET_1_v9.doc" is not writable.
Error in mdbpublish (line 55)
outputPath = publish(file, options);
Error using open (line 51)
NAME must contain a single character vector.
Error using publish (line 144)
The output file "C:\Users\David_A_Rosenbaum\Documents\Dumb Backup Begun
06-01-18\html\MATLAB_BLUES_PROBLEM_SET_1_v9.doc" is not writable.
Error in mdbpublish (line 55)
outputPath = publish(file, options);
Error using open (line 51)
NAME must contain a single character vector.
```

After doing some research, including finally sending an email to Mathworks, I learned that unlike Microsoft Word, which lets you save a Word document with a given name even if the document is already open, MATLAB takes a different approach. If you publish a program in MATLAB but a publication with the same name is open on your computer, you will get a message like the one above. How much easier it would be if the error message said something like:

```
>> Sorry, you can't Publish a MATLAB program if the output has
the same name as an open output with that same name. Close that
published program and you should be good to go, or update the
name of the program and MATLAB will automatically assign that
new name to a publication and you won't have to worry about
other open publications.
```

1.7 Disclaimers

Disclaimers are statements of limitations, as when a manufacturer tells you the product you bought from them can't do certain things. Here are some disclaimers about this book:

1. *MATLAB Blues* does not cover PsychToolbox, a specialized set of MATLAB programs used for displaying stimuli with more temporal precision than is generally possible with MATLAB alone. PsychToolbox is a world unto itself and takes quite a bit of time to learn.
2. *MATLAB Blues* does not cover graphical user interfaces (GUIs). GUIs, like PsychToolbox, comprise a world unto themselves and also take a long time to learn. Because I do not routinely use GUIs and haven't found the need to cover them in my courses, I have chosen not to include them here.
3. *MATLAB Blues* is not about statistics, though some statistical concepts and quantities are used.
4. *MATLAB Blues* is not concerned with hardware interfaces, such as recording electroencephalograms (EEGs). MATLAB can be used for such purposes, both to record from and activate external devices such as motors, but these topics won't be covered.
5. Concern with programming speed will be minimized. Writing programs that run quickly is an admirable goal, especially when the data sets to be analyzed or produced are very large. You will be shown ways to accelerate your programs in this book, but it turns out that the syntax needed for running programs very quickly can be confusing for many people. Therefore, the philosophy deployed here is that what's most important is that you be as clear as possible about what you want your programs to do and how they should do so. If you write a program to deal with a relatively small data set and don't expect to be dealing with a very large data set in that context again, it is acceptable in my opinion, and in fact *desirable*, to write code that chugs along suboptimally if that is the kind of code you need to fully understand what's happening. Just as it is counterproductive to perform for others while worrying about what they're thinking (the basis for stage fright or "choking"), it is counterproductive to worry that some officious programmer will look over your shoulder and snicker at you for having a few more lines of code than is strictly necessary – for example, for having more variables than you really need to help you keep track of what's going on. MATLAB provides ways of letting you check the efficiency of your code, and it's nice that it does. You can take advantage of that feature if you want to (attending to the little orange lines on the right side of the edit window), but my advice, expressed all through this book, is to be clear as you can be and, if necessary, be more verbose than you think might be ideal. As you get clearer and clearer in your programming, you and your programs will get faster and faster. Be assured, too, that as computing speed increases exponentially, saving a few nanoseconds for a short programming job will hardly be worth the trouble.
6. The MATLAB programming language is vast. There are scores of specialized commands that exist but won't be covered here. My aim is to acquaint you with commands and concepts that I have found useful in my many years of MATLAB programming. My hope is that you will become self-sufficient. I want you to be able to go forth and find functions and capabilities on your own and fix bugs that beset your code that weren't covered here. If you can, this book will have served a useful function.
7. Some material covered in the source book for this one, *MATLAB for Behavioral Scientists, Second Edition*, won't be covered here, as mentioned in the preface.
8. The final disclaimer is that everything that can possibly be disclaimed won't be. ☺

2 Matrices

MATLAB programming uses matrices. These are arrays of values (typically numbers) occupying rows and columns. The number of rows and columns can be as few as 1, and the number of rows needn't be the same as the number of columns, Critically, the number of columns per row must be the same in all rows. This is an essential feature of matrices. Other types of data arrays, covered in Chapter 7, do not have this restriction. Every element of a matrix can be indexed by its row number and column number. When both indices are provided, the row index typically precedes the column index.

2.1 Printing the Value of a Variable in the Command Window

2.1.1 Unsolved Problem Comment

You want to see a listing of the values of x, but none shows up in the command window.

2.1.2 Unsolved Problem Code

```
clear all
close all
commandwindow
clc
x=[1:3];
```

2.1.3 Unsolved Problem Output

2.1.4 Solved Problem Comment

The solution is to omit the semi-colon. Leaving it out tells MATLAB to print the values of x in the command window. By implication, if you want to *suppress* outputs, include semi-colons.

2.1.5 Solved Problem Code

```
clear all
close all
commandwindow
clc
x=[1:3]
```

2.1.6 Solved Problem Output

```
x =
     1     2     3
```

2.2 Adding Elements to the Right Side of a Matrix

2.2.1 Unsolved Problem Comment

You want to see a listing of x and y and then add y to the right side of x, assigning the new concatenated matrix to a new variable z. This doesn't work, however.

2.2.2 Unsolved Problem Code

```
clear all
close all
commandwindow
clc

x=[11 12 13]
y=[21 22 23]
z=[x Y]
```

2.2.3 Unsolved Problem Output

```
x =
    11    12    13
y =
    21    22    23
Undefined function or variable 'Y'.
Did you mean:
>> z=[x y]
```

2.2.4 Solved Problem Comment

As the query from MATLAB implies, the variable Y isn't the same as the variable y. Variable names are case-sensitive.

2.2.5 Solved Problem Code

```
clear all
close all
commandwindow
clc

x=[11 12 13]
y=[21 22 23]
z=[x y]
```

2.2.6 Solved Problem Output

```
x =
    11    12    13
y =
    21    22    23
z =
    11    12    13    21    22    23
```

2.3 Assigning Values to Indexed Positions

2.3.1 Unsolved Problem Comment

You want to assign the values 0, 1, 2, 3, and 4 to a variable called x. But the assignment fails. You get an error message, shown below.

2.3.2 Unsolved Code

```
clear all
close all
commandwindow
clc

x(0:4)=[0:4]
```

2.3.3 Unsolved Problem Output

```
Subscript indices must either be real positive integers or logicals.
```

2.3.4 Solved Problem Comment

Matrix indices must be positive integers. They can't be zero or negative because indices are count values, like house numbers on a city block. There is a house number 1, a house number 2, and so on, but there is no house number 0 (at least in the real world). The indices of x (all column numbers for this one-row matrix) must be changed from 0:4 to 1:5.

2.3.5 Solved Problem Code

```
clear all
close all
commandwindow
clc
x(1:5)=[0:4]
```

2.3.6 Solved Problem Output

```
x =
     0     1     2     3     4
```

2.4 Giving Variables Acceptable Names

2.4.1 Unsolved Problem Comment

You challenge MATLAB to have a non-nerdy variable name but get an error message.

2.4.2 Unsolved Problem Code

```
clear all
close all
```

14 Matrices

```
commandwindow
clc

must_variables_have_nerdy_ names=[-10:.5:10]
```

2.4.3 Unsolved Problem Output

```
Undefined function or variable 'must_variables_have_nerdy_'.
```

2.4.4 Solved Problem Comment

Variable names can't have spaces. They must start with a letter and after that, they can have letters, numerals, or underscore characters but nothing else. As for nerdy or non-nerdy variable names, MATLAB has no understanding of such things. From MATLAB's point of view, a variable name like x or theta is no more or less nerdy than the variable name used here, which is now formed correctly with the underscore character and letters.

2.4.5 Solved Problem Code

```
clear all
close all
commandwindow
clc

must_variables_have_nerdy_names=[-10:.5:10]
```

2.4.6 Solved Problem Output

```
must_variables_have_nerdy_names =
  Columns 1 through 8
      -10      -9.5       -9      -8.5      -8
     -7.5       -7      -6.5
  Columns 9 through 16
       -6      -5.5       -5      -4.5      -4
     -3.5       -3      -2.5
  Columns 17 through 24
       -2      -1.5       -1      -0.5       0
      0.5        1       1.5
  Columns 25 through 32
        2      2.5        3       3.5        4
      4.5        5       5.5
  Columns 33 through 40
        6      6.5        7       7.5        8
      8.5        9       9.5
  Column 41
       10
```

2.5 Deleting Elements From a One-Row Array

2.5.1 Unsolved Problem Comment

Try deleting the 2nd, 5th, and 7th values in a one-row matrix (an array).

2.5.2 Unsolved Problem Code

```
clear all
close all
commandwindow
clc

x=[1 2 3 4 5 6 7 8]
delete(x(2))
delete(x(5))
delete(x(7))
x
```

2.5.3 Unsolved Problem Output

```
x =

     1     2     3     4     5     6     7     8

Error using delete
Invalid or deleted object.
```

2.5.4 Solved Problem Comment

Although you wanted to delete elements, and although MATLAB has a delete function, it's for another application, as can be explored by typing `help delete` in the command line of the command window. A better method is to assign [] to the 2nd, 5th, and 7th elements of x.

2.5.5 Solved Problem Code

```
clear all
close all
commandwindow
clc
x=[1 2 3 4 5 6 7 8]
x([2 5 7])=[];
x
```

2.5.6 Solved Problem Output

```
x =
     1     2     3     4     5     6     7     8
x =
     1     3'    4     6     8
```

2.6 Deleting a Column From a Multi-row Matrix

2.6.1 Unsolved Problem Comment

Try deleting the second column of a two-row matrix. The result is unexpected.

16 Matrices

2.6.2 Unsolved Problem Code

```
clear all
close all
commandwindow
clc

x=[
    11 12 13 14 15 16 17 18
    21 22 23 24 25 26 27 28
    ]
x(1:2)=[]
```

2.6.3 Unsolved Problem Output

```
x =
    11   12   13   14   15   16   17   18
    21   22   23   24   25   26   27   28
x =
    12   22   13   23   14   24   15   25   16   26   17   27
    18   28
```

2.6.4 Solved Problem Comment

MATLAB deleted the first and second element of the matrix, which were, from MATLAB's perspective, the column 1 element of row 1 and the column 2 element of row 2. Next it transformed x to a one-row array. The correct solution is to assign [] to all the rows (indicated with a colon, :), in column 2. Now 13 and 23 are gone.

2.6.5 Solved Problem Code

```
clear all
close all
commandwindow
clc
x=[
    11 12 13 14 15 16 17 18
    21 22 23 24 25 26 27 28
    ]
x(:,2)=[]
```

2.6.6 Solved Problem Output

```
x =
    11   12   13   14   15   16   17   18
    21   22   23   24   25   26   27   28
x =
    11   13   14   15   16   17   18
    21   23   24   25   26   27   28
```

Matrices 17

2.7 Checking the Number of Values in Matrices

2.7.1 Unsolved Problem Comment

You expect the same number of values in two matrices called a_matrix and a_linspace. But that's not what happens. You find that a_matrix has 12 columns, whereas a_linspace has 11 columns. You want both matrices to have 12 columns, but that's not what you get.

2.7.2 Unsolved Problem Code

```
clear all
close all
commandwindow
clc

a_matrix=[0:11]
a_linspace=linspace(0,11,11)
size_of_a_matrix=size(a_matrix)
size_of_a_linspace=size(a_linspace)
```

2.7.3 Unsolved Problem Output

```
a_matrix =
    0    1    2    3    4    5    6    7    8    9   10   11
a_linspace =
  Columns 1 through 8
         0        1.1        2.2        3.3        4.4
       5.5        6.6        7.7
  Columns 9 through 11
       8.8        9.9         11
size_of_a_matrix =
    1    12
size_of_a_linspace =
    1    11
```

2.7.4 Solved Problem Comment

There are 12 integers in the array 0 to 11. No matter however trivial and obvious this is, it turns out that people often goof in such matters. Sometimes you need to use your fingers. There is nothing wrong with that. On the other hand (pun intended), to avoid guesswork about the number of elements in an array, use linspace (or logspace).

2.7.5 Solved Problem Code

```
clear all
close all
commandwindow
clc

a_matrix=[0:11]
a_linspace=linspace(0,11,12)
```

18   *Matrices*

```
size_of_a_matrix=size(a_matrix)
size_of_a_linspace=size(a_linspace)
```

2.7.6 Solved Problem Output

```
a_matrix =
     0     1     2     3     4     5     6     7     8     9    10    11
a_linspace =
     0     1     2     3     4     5     6     7     8     9    10    11
size_of_a_matrix =
     1    12
size_of_a_linspace =
     1    12
```

2.8 Adding a Matrix to the Bottom of Another Matrix

2.8.1 Unsolved Problem Comment

You want to create a matrix called puppy_bunny that consists of a first matrix called puppy and a second matrix beneath it called bunny. The matrix bunny is supposed to have the same number of columns as puppy. This is essential because bunny is supposed to be beneath puppy in the same matrix. In MATLAB, a matrix must always have the same number of columns in every row. You shouldn't have to guess how many elements there are, however. The problem is to find a more convenient and more accurate method of setting the size of bunny so its number of columns agrees with the number of columns that puppy has. You shouldn't have to use your fingers. Indeed, you can't do so reliably when the number is very large. By using your knowledge of the fact that MATLAB keeps track of the number of rows and columns, you should be able to size things up pretty well.

2.8.2 Unsolved Problem Code

```
clear all
close all
commandwindow
clc

cute_puppy=[.25:.5:225.5];
my_guess=410;
cuddly_bunny=linspace(1.25, 988, my_guess);
puppy_bunny=[cute_puppy;cuddly_bunny];
size_of_puppy_bunny=size(puppy_bunny)
```

2.8.3 Unsolved Problem Output

```
Error using vertcat
Dimensions of matrices being concatenated are not consistent.
```

2.8.4 Solved Problem Comment

The number of columns of a matrix, such as one called cute_puppy, can be obtained with the command `size(cute_puppy,2)`. Also, even though it didn't come up in this particular problem, the number of rows of a matrix, such as one called cute_puppy, can be gotten with the command `size(cute_puppy,1)`. The number 1 specifies the number of rows. If the number were 2, the size function would return the number of columns, as indicated above. These numbers make sense from the point of view that rows are generally referred to before columns in MAT-LAB. It should easy for you to remember this if you develop a suitable mnemonic like "Remote Control," "Roman Catholic," "Royal Crown soda," "Riverside California," and so forth.

2.8.5 Solved Problem Code

```
clear all
close all
commandwindow
clc

cute_puppy=[.25:.5:225.5];
actual_length=size(cute_puppy,2);
cuddly_bunny=linspace(1.25, 988, actual_length);
puppy_bunny=[cute_puppy;cuddly_bunny];
size_of_puppy_bunny=size(puppy_bunny)
```

2.8.6 Solved Problem Output

```
size_of_puppy_bunny =
     2   451
```

2.9 Inserting a Column Into a Matrix

2.9.1 Unsolved Problem Comment

You have data from subjects in an experiment. There are just four subjects for now, each with a row of data. The first column per row is each subject's mean proportion correct. The second column per row is each subject's mean reaction time. You want to add a new column to the left of the existing data given the subject number (1 to 4 in this case), but you get an error message. You could ignore the problem and just put in the values by hand, but you'd be in trouble when, later on, you do the study with 100,000 participants.

2.9.2 Unsolved Problem Code

```
clear all
close all
commandwindow
clc

data=[
    .80  789
    .76  654
    .54  367
    .90  888
    ]
data=[[1:size(data,1)] data]
```

20 Matrices

2.9.3 Unsolved Problem Output

```
data =

    0.8          789
    0.76         654
    0.54         367
    0.9          888

Error using horzcat
Dimensions of matrices being concatenated are not consistent.
```

2.9.4 Solved Problem Comment

Use the transpose operator (') to convert a row vector to a column vector or vice versa.

2.9.5 Solved Problem Code

```
clear all
close all
commandwindow
clc

data=[
    .80 789
    .76 654
    .54 367
    .90 888
    ]
data=[[1:size(data,1)]' data]
```

2.9.6 Solved Problem Output

```
data =

    0.8          789
    0.76         654
    0.54         367
    0.9          888
data =

    1       0.8        789
    2       0.76       654
    3       0.54       367
    4       0.9        888
```

2.10 Switching Positions of Elements in a Matrix

2.10.1 Unsolved Problem Comment

You have data from subjects whose participant numbers are in column 1 and whose mean proportion correct values are in column 2. The subjects' mean reaction times are in column 3. You realize that the assignment of data to subjects is wrong. The data from the odd-numbered subjects are in the even-numbered rows, and the data from the even-numbered subjects are in the odd-numbered rows. So the data from subjects 1 and 3 are in rows 2 and 4, whereas the data from subjects 2 and 4 are in rows 1 and 3. You could fix this by hand, of course, just by cutting and pasting, but if you had 100,000 subjects you'd be in trouble. You need a reliable and hopefully simple way to get the data from the odd-numbered subjects into the odd-numbered rows and vice versa. The first attempt doesn't yield the desired result. The data from subjects 2 and 4 are eliminated, which is not what you want.

2.10.2 Unsolved Problem Code

```
clear all
close all
commandwindow
clc

data=[
    2 .80 789
    1 .76 654
    4 .54 367
    3 .90 888
    ]
data(1:2:end,:)=data(2:2:end,:);
data(2:2:end,:)=data(1:2:end,:)
```

2.10.3 Unsolved Problem Output

```
data =

        2        0.8        789
        1        0.76       654
        4        0.54       367
        3        0.9        888
data =

        1        0.76       654
        1        0.76       654
        3        0.9        888
        3        0.9        888
```

2.10.4 Solved Problem Comment

Use temporary variables to momentarily "park" data. Having done that, you can have data be organized correctly going forward (so you don't always have to refer to temp_data). This is done here by checking that temp_data is organized properly, by then deleting data, and then by assigning temp_data to data.

2.10.5 Solved Problem Code

```
clear all
close all
commandwindow
clc
```

22 Matrices

```
data=[
    2 .80 789
    1 .76 654
    4 .54 367
    3 .90 888
    ]
temp_data=data;
temp_data(1:2:end,:)=data(2:2:end,:);
temp_data(2:2:end,:)=data(1:2:end,:)
clear data
data=temp_data
```

2.10.6 Solved Problem Output

```
data =
            2          0.8          789
            1         0.76          654
            4         0.54          367
            3          0.9          888
temp_data =
            1         0.76          654
            2          0.8          789
            3          0.9          888
            4         0.54          367
data =
            1         0.76          654
            2          0.8          789
            3          0.9          888
            4         0.54          367
```

3 Calculations

MATLAB is used for technical computing, so performing calculations is core to those programming with MATLAB. Understanding how to perform calculations in MATLAB is critical, but some unexpected hurdles can come your way. Seeing what they are can help you avoid them.

3.1 Simple Summing

3.1.1 Unsolved Problem Comment

You are interested in taking the sum of two matrices to check that two data matrices are the same if the sum of their differences is zero. You test this on a toy problem, considering two small arrays, X and Y. X runs from −10 to 10 in steps of 1. Y runs from 10 to −10 in steps of −1. You assume that the sum of X and Y will definitely be zero. However, when you write a program to check this, instead of getting a single number for the sum, you get as many numbers as there are elements in the arrays.

3.1.2 Unsolved Problem Code

```
clear all
close all
commandwindow
clc
X=linspace(-10,10,11)
Y=linspace(10,-10,11)
X+Y
```

3.1.3 Unsolved Problem Output

```
X =
   -10   -8   -6   -4   -2    0    2    4    6    8   10
Y =
    10    8    6    4    2    0   -2   -4   -6   -8  -10
ans =
     0    0    0    0    0    0    0    0    0    0    0
```

3.1.4 Solved Problem Comment

Each of the two matrices X and Y is of size(1,n). That is, they each have 1 row and n = 11 columns. Adding two arrays actually entails element-by-element summing. You can get a single sum by applying the sum function to the array of added elements, as shown here. The code after

24 Calculations

the line with `sum(X+Y)` is designed to take the sum of X' and Y', that is, the sum of X transposed and Y transposed, so X and Y are both of size (n, 1), or n rows and 1 column each. The output shows that addition with + is element by element regardless of whether the elements occupy more than 1 column per row or more than 1 row per column.

3.1.5 Solved Problem Code

```
clear all
close all
commandwindow
clc

X=linspace(-10,10,11)
Y=linspace(10,-10,11)
X+Y
sum(X+Y)
X'+Y'
sum(X'+Y')
```

3.1.6 Solved Problem Output

```
X =
    -10    -8    -6    -4    -2     0     2     4     6     8    10
Y =
     10     8     6     4     2     0    -2    -4    -6    -8   -10
ans =
      0     0     0     0     0     0     0     0     0     0     0
ans =
      0
ans =
      0
      0
      0
      0
      0
      0
      0
      0
      0
      0
      0
ans =
      0
```

3.2 Checking Whether Two Matrices Are the Same

3.2.1 Unsolved Problem Comment

Continuing your line of thought from the previous problem, you think that if two matrices are the same, subtracting one from the other should yield a sum of zero. To challenge yourself in regard to this belief, you create two matrices X and Y whose difference, X − Y, is in fact zero, but X and Y are clearly different. This helps you realize that if the total difference between two matrices is zero, that doesn't imply that the two matrices are the same. You come to this realization after generating the code below, but you are still having the problem of getting an output that implies two matrices are identical.

3.2.2 Unsolved Problem Code

```
clear all
close all
commandwindow
clc

X=[1 2 3 4]
Y=[-5 2 3 10]
X-Y
sum(X-Y)
```

3.2.3 Unsolved Problem Output

```
X =
     1     2     3     4
Y =
    -5     2     3    10
ans =
     6     0     0    -6
ans =
     0
```

3.2.4 Solved Problem Comment

You think there *must* be a way to test whether two matrices are identical in MATLAB. Someone at Mathworks must have developed a function for this! You enter the following phrase into Google: "test whether two matrices are the same in MATLAB." You find that you can use the `isequal` function and do so here. It is fine to use the internet to find solutions to problems you run into that you suspect others have solved, though it's also advisable to do so only after you have thought things through for yourself. Note that the `isequal` function, the function that can be used to check that two matrices are the same, returns a Boolean (true/false) value. That's why ans (short for answer) is flagged in the command window as type `logical`. For logical tests, zero is shorthand for false, and 1 is shorthand for true. In this case, the `isequal` test applied to the original arrays X and Y yields a zero or false, which is good. To check that `isequal` yields a 1 or true when applied to two arrays that are known to be identical, clear Y and then assign X to Y, so Y must equal X. Now the output is 1 or true, as expected. The bottom line is, use `isequal` to test whether matrices are the same.

3.2.5 Solved Problem Code

```
clear all
close all
commandwindow
clc
```

26   Calculations

```
X=[1 2 3 4]
Y=[-5 2 3 10]
isequal(X,Y)
clear Y
Y=X
isequal(X,Y)
```

3.2.6   Solved Problem Output

```
X =
     1     2     3     4
Y =
    -5     2     3    10
ans =
  logical
    0
Y =
     1     2     3     4
ans =
  logical
    1
```

3.3   Multiplying Matrices

3.3.1   Unsolved Problem Comment

To develop a model, you want to get the products of the squared values in common positions in R and S. In other words, you want R(1, 1) squared times S(1, 1) squared, R(1, 2) squared times S(1, 2) squared, etc. To check your understanding, you create the matrices R and S, having each one consist of random integers. R gets 1 row and 5 columns of randomly ordered integers from the set [1 ... 9]. S is derived similarly, though S is drawn from 1 through 19 and has 5 rows and 1 column rather than 1 row and 5 columns. You expect 5 numbers but instead get 25. You wonder why, and you wonder whether there is some way to get just the 5 numbers you want.

3.3.2   Unsolved Problem Code

```
clear all
close all
commandwindow
clc

R=randi(9,1,5)
S=randi(19,5,1)
size(R)
size(S)
T=(R.*S).^1
```

3.3.3   Unsolved Problem Output

```
R =
     2     9     3     6     5
```

```
S =
    4
    2
    9
   18
    3
ans =
    1     5
ans =
    5     1
T =
    8    36    12    24    20
    4    18     6    12    10
   18    81    27    54    45
   36   162    54   108    90
    6    27     9    18    15
```

3.3.4 Solved Problem Comment

Instead of carrying out the multiplication you intended, you actually did matrix multiplication. You can get just the 5 numbers of interest by having R and S be the same size and doing element-wise column-by-column multiplication.

3.3.5 Solved Problem Code

```
clear all
close all
commandwindow
clc

R=randi(9,1,5)
S=randi(19,1,5)   % not (19,5,1), which it was before
size(R)
size(S)
T=(R.*S).^1
```

3.3.6 Solved Problem Output

```
R =
    4     5     6     6     2
S =
    1    16     7    12    16
ans =
    1     5
ans =
    1     5
T =
    4    80    42    72    32
```

28   Calculations

3.4 Multiplying Matrices Element by Element

3.4.1 Unsolved Problem Comment

You are preparing to do an analysis in which values in A are each multiplied by values in corresponding positions in B. Think of the A values as scores on tests and the B values as objective difficulty levels of the tests. You want to give students more credit for scores that are more difficult. When you multiply A by B using the * command, you get an error message. You have set this up as a toy problem to make sure your computation is correct for when you later apply the procedure to matrices with scores from thousands of real students. You realize you're not quite ready to unleash your program on the students. They deserve correct scoring, and you want nothing less.

3.4.2 Unsolved Problem Code

```
clear all
close all
commandwindow
clc

A=[1:10]
B=[21:30]
C=A*B
```

3.4.3 Unsolved Problem Output

```
A =
     1     2     3     4     5     6     7     8     9    10
B =
    21    22    23    24    25    26    27    28    29    30
Error using  *
Inner matrix dimensions must agree.
```

3.4.4 Solved Problem Comment

You were attempting element-wise multiplication, and such multiplication applied to multi-element matrices requires the characters .* rather than the single character * without the preceding period. In the previous problem, * was actually preceded by a period when needed. You may not have noticed that, but now realize how important such tiny differences make.

3.4.5 Solved Problem Code

```
clear all
close all
commandwindow
clc

A=[1:10]
B=[21:30]
C=A.*B
```

Calculations 29

3.4.6 Solved Problem Output

```
A =
     1     2     3     4     5     6     7     8     9    10
B =
    21    22    23    24    25    26    27    28    29    30
C =
    21    44    69    96   125   156   189   224   261   300
```

3.5 Discovering and Then Taking the Dot Product

3.5.1 Unsolved Problem Comment

To practice your skills, you try the same basic calculation as in the last problem with the same matrix A and another matrix BB. Oddly, when you run the version of the program that backfired before, that same basic code now works. Mysteriously, the answer you get is just one number. You stare at the number for a while and wonder what it could be. After much thought, you hypothesize that it is the sum of the products of A and BB. That is, you hypothesize that the first element of A is multiplied by the first element of BB, the second element of A is multiplied by the second element of BB, and so on, and then all of the products are summed. You think, "Gee, that computation could be useful if I wanted to give each student a single score, taking into account the difficulty or the points of each test, or if I wanted to get the sum of the products of two comparable matrices for some other reason." You generate code to test this hypothesis. At first it sparks an error, either because of a profound mathematical error that you are the first person in history to discover, or because of a silly typo.

3.5.2 Unsolved Problem Code

```
clear all
close all
commandwindow
clc

A=[1:10]
BB=[21:30]'
CC=A*BB
new_CC=A.*BB'
new_cC=sum(new_C)
diff_between_CC_and_new_CC=CC-new_CC
```

3.5.3 Unsolved Problem Output

```
A =
     1     2     3     4     5     6     7     8     9    10
BB =
    21
    22
    23
    24
    25
```

30   Calculations
```
        26
        27
        28
        29
        30
CC =
        1485
new_CC =
    21    44    69    96   125   156   189   224   261   300
Undefined function or variable 'new_C'.
```

3.5.4 Solved Problem Comment

The error stemmed from forgetting that variable names are case-sensitive. Your mind may have been on math, but if you make a low-level mistake, MATLAB won't forgive you. Notice that multiplication of multi-element matrices with just * yields the sum of the products of the corresponding elements (unless the matrices have structures that don't allow this). You can get the same result with dot multiplication. The dot product is the sum of the products of elements in analogous positions. The dot product of two matrices is a measure of the similarity of the matrices (or the vectors corresponding to those matrices). All of the following commands do the same thing as `new_CC=A.*BB'`: `D=dot(A,BB); E=dot(BB,A); F=dot(A,BB').`

3.5.5 Solved Problem Code

```
clear all
close all
commandwindow
clc
A=[1:10]
BB=[21:30]'
CC=A*BB
new_CC=A.*BB'
new_CC=sum(new_CC)
diff_between_CC_and_new_CC=CC-new_CC
D=dot(A,BB)
E=dot(BB,A)
F=dot(A,BB')
```

3.5.6 Solved Problem Output

```
A =
     1     2     3     4     5     6     7     8     9    10
BB =
    21
    22
    23
    24
    25
    26
    27
```

```
        28
        29
        30
CC =
        1485
new_CC =
        21    44    69    96   125   156   189   224   261   300
new_CC =
        1485
diff_between_CC_and_new_CC =
        0
D =
        1485
E =
        1485
F =
        1485
```

3.6 Dividing Matrices

3.6.1 Unsolved Problem Comment

You have two matrices A and D. A has 1 row and 5 columns. D has 5 rows and 1 column. You want to divide the elements of A by the corresponding elements of D. When you run the program, you get an error message.

3.6.2 Unsolved Problem Code

```
clear all
close all
commandwindow
clc

A(1,1:5)=[101:100:501]
D(1:5,1)=[1:5]
V=A/D
size(V)
```

3.6.3 Unsolved Problem Output

```
A =
   101   201   301   401   501
D =
        1
        2
        3
        4
        5
Error using /
Matrix dimensions must agree.
```

32   Calculations

3.6.4   Solved Problem Comment

Element-wise division, like element-wise multiplication, requires a period. Element-wise division is denoted by slash period (./).

3.6.5   Solved Problem Code

```
clear all
close all
commandwindow
clc

A(1,1:5)=[101:100:501]
D(1:5,1)=[1:5]
V=A./D
size(V)
```

3.6.6   Solved Problem Output

```
A =
   101    201    301    401    501
D =
     1
     2
     3
     4
     5
V =
           101          201          301          401          501
          50.5        100.5        150.5        200.5        250.5
        33.667           67       100.33       133.67          167
         25.25        50.25        75.25       100.25       125.25
          20.2         40.2         60.2         80.2        100.2
ans =
     5     5
```

3.7   Raising Values to a Power

3.7.1   Unsolved Problem Comment

You know that the time to complete a task generally decreases as the task is practiced more. In addition, you know that the rate of improvement decreases with practice. There is a lot of improvement in the first trial, a bit less improvement in the second trial, still less in the third trial, and so on. You want to model this type of change by saying that your dependent variable, which you call performance_time, is a function of the number of trials raised to the minus alpha power. Your code doesn't give this result, however. It gives something weird: performance time *increases* rather than *decreases* as the number of trials grows.

3.7.2   Unsolved Problem Code

```
clear all
close all
```

```
commandwindow
clc

n_trials=8;
trial=[1:n_trials];
alpha=-1/2;
performance_time=trial.^-alpha
```

3.7.3 Unsolved Problem Output

```
performance_time =
          1        1.4142      1.7321        2      2.2361
     2.4495        2.6458      2.8284
```

3.7.4 Solved Problem Comment

Raising a nonnegative number like trial to a *positive* value causes it to grow. Raising a nonnegative value like trial to a *negative* power causes it to shrink. The problem was that alpha was negative – a result of thinking about raising trial to a negative power. When the minus sign was put before alpha in the last line, the exponent became positive, causing the performance time to rise rather than fall. Remember that raising a value to a negative power is the same as putting that value in the denominator and then raising it to that same (now positive) power. The larger the denominator, the smaller the ratio. Also remember that the denominator can't be zero. Dividing by zero is undefined. It is meaningless to say how many zeros there are in some number (in the numerator).

3.7.5 Solved Problem Code

```
clear all
close all
commandwindow
clc

n_trials=8;
trial=[1:n_trials];
alpha=1/2;
performance_time=trial.^-alpha
```

3.7.6 Solved Problem Output

```
performance_time =
          1       0.70711     0.57735      0.5     0.44721
     0.40825     0.37796     0.35355
```

3.8 Getting Means

3.8.1 Unsolved Problem Comment

In the program shown here, you have pseudo-data with three rows. The data concern the benefits of three different training methods. Each row has the benefit for that condition (10, 20, or 30) plus values drawn at random from a normal (bell-shaped or Gaussian) distribution, just to add

34 Calculations

randomness to the values, as in real data. The term "Gaussian" refers to the mathematician Carl Gauss, who invented the equation for the normal curve. All the Gaussian values are scaled by the same standard deviation, sdev=1. You want to compute the mean of the values in the first row, the mean of the values in the second row, and the mean of the values in the third row. Instead, you get means of the 10 columns.

3.8.2 Unsolved Problem Code

```
clear all
close all
commandwindow
clc

benefit=[10 20 30];
sdev=1;
n_subjects=10;
data=[
    benefit(1) + randn(1,n_subjects).*sdev;
    benefit(2) + randn(1,n_subjects).*sdev;
    benefit(3) + randn(1,n_subjects).*sdev;
    ]
mean(data)
```

3.8.3 Unsolved Problem Output

```
data =
  Columns 1 through 8
        9.07        9.4489        8.5349        9.4153        10.422
9.6351        10.556        10.946
       18.803       19.576       19.972       20.099       18.254
21.272        19.332        17.457
       30.05        30.463       30.251       29.842       29.58
30.332        28.798        29.266
  Columns 9 through 10
       11.326       8.8098
       22.259       21.856
       28.651       30.424
ans =
  Columns 1 through 8
       19.308       19.829       19.586       19.785       19.419
20.413        19.562        19.223
  Columns 9 through 10
       20.745       20.363
```

3.8.4 Solved Problem Comment

The built-in function mean can take as an input argument the dimension of the matrix to which the mean function applies—either dimension 1 (rows) or dimension 2 (columns). By default, mean is taken over rows, so by default the input argument is 1. If you want column means for the variable data, you should use mean(data,2). Another approach, which relies on the default argument of 1 for rows and which is implicit when the argument is not given, is to compute the mean of the transpose of the matrix (the matrix name followed by an apostrophe).

3.8.5 Solved Problem Code

```
clear all
close all
commandwindow
clc
benefit=[10 20 30];
sdev=1;
n_subjects=10;
data=[
    benefit(1) + randn(1,n_subjects).*sdev;
    benefit(2) + randn(1,n_subjects).*sdev;
    benefit(3) + randn(1,n_subjects).*sdev;
    ]
mean(data,2)
mean(data')
```

3.8.6 Solved Problem Output

```
data =
  Columns 1 through 8
       7.9142           9.8857           9.7341          10.853           9.7446
10.116           10.891           10.778
      19.443          20.024          19.435          20.098          20.047
20.825           17.842           21.552
      31.232          30.084          30.518          28.426          29.505
28.426           30.039           28.96
  Columns 9 through 10
      12.053          10.686
      21.053          19.814
      31.306          31.789
ans =
      10.266
      20.013
      30.029
ans =
      10.266           20.013           30.029
```

3.9 Understanding What You "Mean"

3.9.1 Unsolved Problem Comment

Gaining confidence in your MATLAB programming, you decide to work on a program that calculates means from scratch. You do this to make sure you really understand what is happening computationally when you use MATLAB's built-in mean function. Your aim is to check the values you come up with against values provided by MATLAB's built-in function. Unfortunately, your code doesn't yield averages that match the means from MATLAB, which suggests either

36   Calculations

that there is an error in the mean function from MATLAB, or that something is wrong with your code. Of course, conceivably, both are wrong.

3.9.2   Unsolved Problem Code

```
clear all
close all
commandwindow
clc
benefit=[10 20 30];
sdev=1;
n_subjects=10;
data=[
    benefit(1) + randn(1,n_subjects).*sdev;
    benefit(2) + randn(1,n_subjects).*sdev;
    benefit(3) + randn(1,n_subjects).*sdev;
    ]
MATLAB_mean=mean(data')
average_row_1=sum(data(1,:))./size(data,1);
average_row_2=sum(data(2,:))./size(data,1);
average_row_3=sum(data(3,:))./size(data,1);
YOUR_mean=[average_row_1 average_row_2 average_row_3]
```

3.9.3   Unsolved Problem Output

```
data =
  Columns 1 through 8
       8.784           10.88          10.436         11.156         10.136
8.5137         9.8921          11.016
      20.644          20.648          21.515         20.034         21.71
20.857         20.309          20.584
      30.118          29.797          30.106         31.641         30.991
29.7           29.973          28.159
  Columns 9 through 10
      11.184          10.406
      20.788          19.99
      30.761          32.24
MATLAB_mean =
       10.24          20.708          30.349
YOUR_mean =
      34.134          69.026          101.16
```

3.9.4   Solved Problem Comment

Remember that when the size function has the number 1 as its argument, it uses the number of rows, whereas when the size function has the number 2 as its argument, it uses the number of columns. In the code above, the average was taken over the number of rows, not the number of columns. When this is corrected, your mean and the mean obtained with MATLAB's mean function are the same.

3.9.5 Solved Problem Code

```
clear all
close all
commandwindow
clc

benefit=[10 20 30];
sdev=1;
n_subjects=10;
data=[
    benefit(1) + randn(1,n_subjects).*sdev;
    benefit(2) + randn(1,n_subjects).*sdev;
    benefit(3) + randn(1,n_subjects).*sdev;
    ]
MATLAB_mean=mean(data')
average_row_1=sum(data(1,:))./size(data,2);
average_row_2=sum(data(2,:))./size(data,2);
average_row_3=sum(data(3,:))./size(data,2);
YOUR_mean=[average_row_1 average_row_2 average_row_3]
```

3.9.6 Solved Problem Output

```
data =
  Columns 1 through 8
      10.648         9.8112         10.109         8.2594         10.273
10.105        10.727         10.961
      19.609         19.455         21.09          19.05          20.88
19.981        18.06          21.117
      29.887         30.203         29.399         30.632         30.63
29.359        28.11          30.828
  Columns 9 through 10
       9.699         10.23
      20.454         21.05
       31.1          29.679
MATLAB_mean =
      10.082         20.074         29.983
YOUR_mean =
      10.082         20.074         29.983
```

3.10 Getting Standard Deviations

3.10.1 Unsolved Problem Comment

Now do the same for the standard deviation. The command `std(data')` gives the standard deviation based on MATLAB's built-in standard deviation function applied to the transpose of `data`. The penultimate output line gives the value based on MATLAB's built-in standard deviation function. The ultimate output line gives the value computed by the homegrown code. The two lines should match, but they don't.

38 Calculations

3.10.2 Unsolved Problem Code

```
clear all
close all
commandwindow
clc

benefit=[10 20 30];
sdev=1;
n_subjects=10;
data=[
    benefit(1) + randn(1,n_subjects).*sdev;
    benefit(2) + randn(1,n_subjects).*sdev;
    benefit(3) + randn(1,n_subjects).*sdev;
    ]
average_row_1=sum(data(1,:))./size(data,2);
average_row_2=sum(data(2,:))./size(data,2);
average_row_3=sum(data(3,:))./size(data,2);

MATLAB_std=std(data')

standard_dev_row_1=(sum((data(1,:)-average_row_1))^2);
standard_dev_row_1=standard_dev_row_1/((size(data,2))-1);
standard_dev_row_1=standard_dev_row_1^.5;

standard_dev_row_2=(sum((data(2,:)-average_row_2)).^2);
standard_dev_row_2=standard_dev_row_2/((size(data,2))-1);
standard_dev_row_2=standard_dev_row_2^.5;

standard_dev_row_3=(sum((data(3,:)-average_row_3)).^2);
standard_dev_row_3=standard_dev_row_3/((size(data,2))-1);
standard_dev_row_3=standard_dev_row_3^.5;

YOUR_std=[ standard_dev_row_1  standard_dev_row_2  standard_dev_row_3]
```

3.10.3 Unsolved Problem Output

```
data =
  Columns 1 through 8
       9.0816         8.9775         9.1494        11.313         10.73
   9.5225         9.9315         9.429
      21.865        19.781        22.714        19.955        19.756
  18.775        19.455        20.995
      31.814        28.875        30.587        31.051        29.732
  29.776        30.453        28.924
  Columns 9 through 10
       9.8155        12.27
      20.721        18.841
      29.861        31.479
```

```
MATLAB_std =
       1.0859        1.2818        1.0026
YOUR_std =
   5.9212e-16    5.9212e-15    2.3685e-15
```

3.10.4 Solved Problem Comment

The problem arose from misplacement of parentheses. The three places where this happened have comments.

3.10.5 Solved Problem Code

```
clear all
close all
commandwindow
clc

benefit=[10 20 30];
sdev=1;
n_subjects=10;
data=[
    benefit(1) + randn(1,n_subjects).*sdev;
    benefit(2) + randn(1,n_subjects).*sdev;
    benefit(3) + randn(1,n_subjects).*sdev;
    ]
% mean(data);
average_row_1=sum(data(1,:))./size(data,2);
average_row_2=sum(data(2,:))./size(data,2);
average_row_3=sum(data(3,:))./size(data,2);

MATLAB_std=std(data')

standard_dev_row_1=sum((data(1,:)-average_row_1).^2); % difference here
standard_dev_row_1=standard_dev_row_1/((size(data,2))-1);
standard_dev_row_1=standard_dev_row_1^.5;

standard_dev_row_2=sum((data(2,:)-average_row_2).^2); % difference here
standard_dev_row_2=standard_dev_row_2/((size(data,2))-1);
standard_dev_row_2=standard_dev_row_2^.5;

standard_dev_row_3=sum((data(3,:)-average_row_3).^2); % difference here
standard_dev_row_3=standard_dev_row_3/((size(data,2))-1);
standard_dev_row_3=standard_dev_row_3^.5;

YOUR_std=[ standard_dev_row_1   standard_dev_row_2
standard_dev_row_3]
```

3.10.6 Solved Problem Output

```
data =
  Columns 1 through 8
       8.3052         10.135         9.9766        8.8945         10.49
10.243         8.036         9.1685
       21.373         19.457        20.941        20.624         17.224
19.409        20.035         20.182
       30.454         28.863        29.438        28.925         28.3
30.302        28.604         30.551
  Columns 9 through 10
       9.6077         10.089
       18.491         20.534
       29.024         29.064
MATLAB_std =
     0.85424         1.2386        0.80562
YOUR_std =
     0.85424         1.2386        0.80562
```

4 Contingencies

Here's a question I ask my students: what's the difference between a computer and a calculating machine? Both kinds of devices help with calculation, and both kinds of devices can have screens and keyboards, but what's the difference? Here's a hint: the answer is a word with just two letters.

When I present the question to students in my MATLAB class, they often sit there, stumped. I then give another hint: "If you think about it, you'll figure it out."

If they *still* don't know the answer, the final clue I give them is that this very sentence has the answer.

The answer is "if." That was the first word of the last sentence. Computers can carry out different operations depending on the conditions in effect at the time. Calculators can't do that, regardless of whether they are electronic or mechanical (as in an abacus). Calculators can't deal with contingencies (if-then branching operations). Computers can. The programs that computers run tell them how to do so.

This chapter is about contingencies in MATLAB. Understanding how to work with contingencies in the MATLAB programming environment will help you do much, much more with your computer than you can with an abacus and that you can do with MATLAB, poorly understood.

4.1 Using If Statements

4.1.1 Unsolved Problem Comment

You have scores from n_students in a class and you want to have the entire class move on to one of two training methods—training method 1 if the mean score for the class is less than or equal to a criterion score, or training method 2 if the mean score for the class is greater than the criterion score. (Notice that all the bases are covered here. One option is <= and the other is >. If the only options were < and >, there could be problems if the = case were present and missed.) Because student number 4 has proven to be highly representative of the class as a whole, you set that student's score as the criterion. To make sure your method works, you write a test program to check it, generating pseudo-data based on a normal distribution (a bell-shaped curve) with an expected value, mu, and a standard deviation, sigma. A problem arises.

4.1.2 Unsolved Code

```
clear all
close all
commandwindow
clc
```

42 Contingencies

```
mu=80;
sigma=5;
n_students=20;
most_typical_student=4;
scores=mu + randn(n_students,1)*sigma
criterion=scores(most_typical_student)
average_score=mean(scores)
if average_score>criterion
    training_method==1
else
    training_method==2
end
```

4.1.3 Unsolved Output

```
scores =
       81.158
       77.036
       85.475
       81.818
       86.793
        81.83
       83.586
       83.003
       87.951
       66.605
       82.957
       81.555
       74.419
       77.588
       79.774
       76.918
       89.507
       81.869
        83.49
       73.144
criterion =
       81.818
average_score =
       80.824
Undefined function or variable 'training_method'.
```

4.1.4 Solved Problem Comment

The if statement requires ==, but assignments of values to variables require = even if the program assignment occurs within an if . . . end contingency. There's another hidden take-home message here as well. If it said training_method=1 or training_method=2 in the preceding program, the outcome would have been wrong. Take a moment to check why before reading on; it's because the inequality was backward. This error was inserted as a reminder that if a program runs, that doesn't mean its outcome is correct.

4.1.5 Solved Problem Code

```
clear all
close all
commandwindow
clc

mu=80;
sigma=5;
n_students=20;
most_typical_student=4;
scores=mu + randn(n_students,1)*sigma
criterion=scores(most_typical_student)
average_score=mean(scores)
if average_score<=criterion
    training_method=1
else
    training_method=2
end
```

4.1.6 Solved Output

```
scores =
        69.752
        82.271
        85.946
        79.038
         79.19
        83.561
        84.671
        85.286
        80.581
        82.238
         73.53
        85.637
        79.315
        81.761
        81.712
        84.272
        83.635
        71.355
        84.534
        81.873
criterion =
        79.038
average_score =
        81.008
training_method =
     2
```

4.2 Using For Statements

4.2.1 Unsolved Problem Comment

In the first problem, the entire class was assigned one training method or another. Now the aim is to assign each student to the training method that is right for him or her. You want an individual student either to move to training method 1 if his or her score equals or falls below the criterion, or to move to training method 2 if his or her score exceeds the criterion. The `for` loop can be used here. The students' scores and training method they are assigned are listed in `scores_plus`. Unfortunately, the program fails.

4.2.2 Unsolved Code

```
clear all
close all
commandwindow
clc

mu=80;
sigma=5;
n_students=20;
most_typical_student=4;
scores= mu + randn(n_students,1)*sigma
criterion=scores(most_typical_student)
for si=1:n_students
    if scores(si)<criterion
        training_method=1;
    else
        training_method=2;
    end
    scores(si)=[scores(si) training_method];
    scores
end
scores
```

4.2.3 Unsolved Output

```
scores =
        80.524
        73.812
        81.952
        80.815
         82.58
        79.152
        88.974
        81.913
        72.462
        71.856
         72.03
          79.4
```

```
         74.454
         89.506
         83.925
         79.184
         80.579
         75.194
         68.545
         74.866
criterion =
         80.815
```
In an assignment A(:) = B, the number of elements in A and B must be the same.

4.2.4 Solved Problem Comment

The assignment scores(si)=[scores(si) training_method] wouldn't work because scores(si) has just one column whereas [scores(si) training_method] has two. Also, note that in the working program below, [scores(si) training_method] is assigned to a new variable, scores_plus. It wouldn't help to say scores(si,:)= [scores(si,1) training_method]; The reason is that the output would still have one column, not the two that are required.

4.2.5 Solved Code

```
clear all
close all
commandwindow
clc

mu=80;
sigma=5;
n_students=20;
most_typical_student=4;
scores= mu + randn(n_students,1)*sigma
criterion=scores(most_typical_student)
for si=1:n_students
    if scores(si)<criterion
        training_method=1;
    else
        training_method=2;
    end
    scores_plus(si,:)=[scores(si,1) training_method];
end
scores_plus
```

4.2.6 Solved Output

```
scores =
         80.011
         80.066
```

```
            73.872
            78.772
            79.268
            76.961
            80.293
            86.616
            81.843
            67.39
            74.675
            82.561
            82.534
            72.365
            86.748
            78.788
            78.125
            76.983
            82.288
            76.905
criterion =
            78.772
scores_plus =
            80.011              2
            80.066              2
            73.872              1
            78.772              2
            79.268              2
            76.961              1
            80.293              2
            86.616              2
            81.843              2
            67.39               1
            74.675              1
            82.561              2
            82.534              2
            72.365              1
            86.748              2
            78.788              2
            78.125              1
            76.983              1
            82.288              2
            76.905              1
```

4.3 Checking Values Relative to Cutoffs

4.3.1 Unsolved Problem Comment

The aim of this program is to assign students to groups based on the decile of their score. Students in the lowest decile (the lowest 10%) should be assigned to group 1, students in the next lowest decile should be assigned to group 2 (the second-lowest 10%), and so on. The aim is to create a matrix called scores_plus_plus that has three columns: a student's score, his or her training method, and his or her decile.

Contingencies

One approach to this problem would be to explicitly list the bounds of each decile range, saying, in effect, if such and such score is in such and such decile range, then assign it to that decile range. But that approach would take more typing than thinking and would not easily generalize to other fractions such as octiles (1/8's) or quartiles (1/4's).

A more versatile approach is taken here. Every student is initially assigned to the decile_group whose identifier is NaN, or not a number. Then, every student's decile group is reset upwards as much as possible based on the highest cutoff that student's score exceeds.

Still, a problem arises. For the particular scores used, the decile to which one score is assigned is NaN, or not a number. Something is wrong. What is it? (By the way, the solution is not to change the numbers to find a set of numbers for which the problem goes away.)

4.3.2 Unsolved Code

```
clear all
close all
commandwindow
clc

n_students=20;
scores_plus =[
    88.8551    2.0000
    81.1064    2.0000
    93.6519    2.0000
    78.5192    2.0000
    82.8215    2.0000
    87.9131    2.0000
    93.6462    2.0000
    81.5178    2.0000
    76.0487    1.0000
    84.0169    2.0000
    73.4005    1.0000
    78.6308    2.0000
    81.3593    2.0000
    87.4478    2.0000
    87.1857    2.0000
    79.8622    2.0000
    84.6197    2.0000
    78.3936    1.0000
    83.3056    2.0000
    89.5765    2.0000
    ]

for si=1:n_students
    decile_group=NaN;
    for decile=0:9
        cutoff(decile+1)=min(scores_plus(:,1)) + ...
            ((decile*.1)*(max(scores_plus(:,1))-min(scores_plus(:,1))));
        if scores_plus(si,1)>cutoff(decile+1)
            decile_group=decile+1;
        end
```

48   *Contingencies*

```
        scores_plus_plus(si,:)=[scores_plus(si,:) decile_group];
    end
end
cutoff
scores_plus_plus
```

4.3.3   Unsolved Output

```
scores_plus =
        88.855          2
        81.106          2
        93.652          2
        78.519          2
        82.822          2
        87.913          2
        93.646          2
        81.518          2
        76.049          1
        84.017          2
         73.4           1
        78.631          2
        81.359          2
        87.448          2
        87.186          2
        79.862          2
         84.62          2
        78.394          1
        83.306          2
        89.576          2
cutoff =
  Columns 1 through 8
         73.4        75.426        77.451        79.476        81.501
   83.526       85.551       87.576
  Columns 9 through 10
        89.602        91.627
scores_plus_plus =
        88.855          2            8
        81.106          2            4
        93.652          2           10
        78.519          2            3
        82.822          2            5
        87.913          2            8
        93.646          2           10
        81.518          2            5
        76.049          1            2
        84.017          2            6
         73.4           1          NaN
        78.631          2            3
        81.359          2            4
        87.448          2            7
```

```
    87.186           2              7
    79.862           2              4
    84.62            2              6
    78.394           1              3
    83.306           2              5
    89.576           2              8
```

4.3.4 Solved Problem Comment

The mistake was that one of the scores equaled a cutoff but that contingency was not covered in the code as a possibility. It can be covered by simply changing > to >=.

As an aside, don't worry about "breaking promises" to MATLAB. It's OK to assign a student to the first decile group and then, an instant later, to assign that same student to the second decile group, and so on. It's fine to force MATLAB to reassign values iteratively. That was the trick used here to avoid typing all the upper and lower bounds for each decile range.

4.3.5 Solved Code

```
clear all
close all
commandwindow
clc

n_students=20;
scores_plus =[
    88.8551    2.0000
    81.1064    2.0000
    93.6519    2.0000
    78.5192    2.0000
    82.8215    2.0000
    87.9131    2.0000
    93.6462    2.0000
    81.5178    2.0000
    76.0487    1.0000
    84.0169    2.0000
    73.4005    1.0000
    78.6308    2.0000
    81.3593    2.0000
    87.4478    2.0000
    87.1857    2.0000
    79.8622    2.0000
    84.6197    2.0000
    78.3936    1.0000
    83.3056    2.0000
    89.5765    2.0000
    ]
for si=1:n_students
    decile_group=NaN;
    for decile=0:9
        cutoff(decile+1)=min(scores_plus(:,1)) + ((decile*.1)*(max(scores_plus(:,1))-min(scores_plus(:,1))));
```

```
            if scores_plus(si,1)>=cutoff(decile+1)
                decile_group=decile+1;
            end
            scores_plus_plus(si,:)=[scores_plus(si,:) decile_group];
        end
end
cutoff
scores_plus_plus
```

4.3.6 Solved Output

```
scores_plus =
         88.855              2
         81.106              2
         93.652              2
         78.519              2
         82.822              2
         87.913              2
         93.646              2
         81.518              2
         76.049              1
         84.017              2
          73.4               1
         78.631              2
         81.359              2
         87.448              2
         87.186              2
         79.862              2
          84.62              2
         78.394              1
         83.306              2
         89.576              2
cutoff =
  Columns 1 through 8
         73.4           75.426          77.451          79.476         81.501
83.526         85.551          87.576
  Columns 9 through 10
         89.602          91.627
scores_plus_plus =
         88.855              2              8
         81.106              2              4
         93.652              2             10
         78.519              2              3
         82.822              2              5
         87.913              2              8
         93.646              2             10
         81.518              2              5
         76.049              1              2
         84.017              2              6
          73.4               1              1
```

78.631	2	3
81.359	2	4
87.448	2	7
87.186	2	7
79.862	2	4
84.62	2	6
78.394	1	3
83.306	2	5
89.576	2	8

4.4 Sorting

4.4.1 Unsolved Problem Comment

The aim of this program is to generalize the last program beyond deciles. Instead of decile_group, the aim is to have n_tile_group, where instead of .1, there can be a different basic_proportion defining the group. Another aim is to sort the scores by the ranges they occupy. You'd like to have the results appear in scores_plus_plus_sorted.

4.4.2 Unsolved Code

```
clear all
close all
commandwindow
clc

n_students=20;
basic_proportion=.05;
n_tiles=basic_proportion;
scores_plus =[
    88.8551    2.0000
    81.1064    2.0000
    93.6519    2.0000
    78.5192    2.0000
    82.8215    2.0000
    87.9131    2.0000
    93.6462    2.0000
    81.5178    2.0000
    76.0487    1.0000
    84.0169    2.0000
    73.4005    1.0000
    78.6308    2.0000
    81.3593    2.0000
    87.4478    2.0000
    87.1857    2.0000
    79.8622    2.0000
    84.6197    2.0000
    78.3936    1.0000
    83.3056    2.0000
    89.5765    2.0000
    ]
```

52 Contingencies

```
scores_plus_plus=[];
for si=1:n_students
    n_tile_group=NaN;
    for n_tile=0:n_tiles-1
        cutoff(n_tile+1)=min(scores_plus(:,1)) + ...
            ((n_tile*basic_proportion)*(max(scores_plus(:,1))-
min(scores_plus(:,1))));
        if scores_plus(si,1)>=cutoff(n_tile+1)
            n_tile_group=n_tile+1;
        end
        scores_plus_plus(si,:)=[scores_plus(si,:) n_tile_group];
    end
end
scores_plus_plus
scores_plus_plus_sorted=sortrows(scores_plus_plus,2)
```

4.4.3 Unsolved Output

```
scores_plus =
        88.855                  2
        81.106                  2
        93.652                  2
        78.519                  2
        82.822                  2
        87.913                  2
        93.646                  2
        81.518                  2
        76.049                  1
        84.017                  2
         73.4                   1
        78.631                  2
        81.359                  2
        87.448                  2
        87.186                  2
        79.862                  2
         84.62                  2
        78.394                  1
        83.306                  2
        89.576                  2
scores_plus_plus =
     []
Error using matlab.internal.math.sortrowsParseInputs>legacyParseCOL
(line 106)
Column sorting vector must contain positive integers between 1 and
the number of columns in the first
argument.
Error in matlab.internal.math.sortrowsParseInputs (line 29)
    [col,colProvided] = legacyParseCOL(col,n,in2);
Error in sortrows (line 60)
    [col, nanflag, compareflag] =
matlab.internal.math.sortrowsParseInputs(A,varargin{:});
```

4.4.4 Solved Problem Comment

The problem lay with n_tiles=basic_proportion, even though the error message was about cutoff. This happens often. An error message actually stems from something wrong before the content that is referred to in the error message itself. The problem with saying n_tiles=basic_proportion is that you then have .05 divisions rather than an integer number of divisions. By saying n_tiles=1/basic_proportion, you have 20 divisions given that $1/.05 = 20$. Now a test is provided to ensure that n_tiles is an integer.

Another take-home message is that `sortrows` is a useful function. The argument it can take specifies the column used for sorting the rows. In this case, that column was column 3. The negative sign of that value specified that the rows were to be sorted in descending order. If the sign of the value were positive, the rows would be sorted in ascending order.

4.4.5 Solved Code

```
clear all
close all
commandwindow
clc

n_students=20;
basic_proportion=.05;
n_tiles=1/basic_proportion;
if rem(n_tiles,1)~=0
    disp('Oops. n_tiles is not an integer')
    disp('Hit ctrl-c to quit and fix the program.')
    pause
end
scores_plus =[
    88.8551    2.0000
    81.1064    2.0000
    93.6519    2.0000
    78.5192    2.0000
    82.8215    2.0000
    87.9131    2.0000
    93.6462    2.0000
    81.5178    2.0000
    76.0487    1.0000
    84.0169    2.0000
    73.4005    1.0000
    78.6308    2.0000
    81.3593    2.0000
    87.4478    2.0000
    87.1857    2.0000
    79.8622    2.0000
    84.6197    2.0000
    78.3936    1.0000
    83.3056    2.0000
    89.5765    2.0000
    ]
```

54 *Contingencies*

```
scores_plus_plus=[];
for si=1:n_students
    n_tile_group=NaN;   % default assignment
    for n_tile=0:n_tiles-1
        cutoff(n_tile+1)=min(scores_plus(:,1)) + ...
           ((n_tile*basic_proportion)*(max(scores_plus(:,1))-min(scores_plus(:,1))));
        if scores_plus(si,1)>=cutoff(n_tile+1)
            n_tile_group=n_tile+1;
        end
        scores_plus_plus(si,:)=[scores_plus(si,:) n_tile_group];
    end
end
scores_plus_plus
scores_plus_plus_sorted=sortrows(scores_plus_plus,-3)
```

4.4.6 Solved Output

scores_plus =

88.855	2
81.106	2
93.652	2
78.519	2
82.822	2
87.913	2
93.646	2
81.518	2
76.049	1
84.017	2
73.4	1
78.631	2
81.359	2
87.448	2
87.186	2
79.862	2
84.62	2
78.394	1
83.306	2
89.576	2

scores_plus_plus =

88.855	2	16
81.106	2	8
93.652	2	20
78.519	2	6
82.822	2	10
87.913	2	15
93.646	2	20
81.518	2	9
76.049	1	3
84.017	2	11

```
      73.4              1              1
    78.631              2              6
    81.359              2              8
    87.448              2             14
    87.186              2             14
    79.862              2              7
     84.62              2             12
    78.394              1              5
    83.306              2             10
    89.576              2             16
scores_plus_plus_sorted =
    93.652              2             20
    93.646              2             20
    88.855              2             16
    89.576              2             16
    87.913              2             15
    87.448              2             14
    87.186              2             14
     84.62              2             12
    84.017              2             11
    82.822              2             10
    83.306              2             10
    81.518              2              9
    81.106              2              8
    81.359              2              8
    79.862              2              7
    78.519              2              6
    78.631              2              6
    78.394              1              5
    76.049              1              3
      73.4              1              1
```

4.5 Using While

4.5.1 Unsolved Problem Comment

How long will it take for an investment to double? Have the program continue while the investment has not yet doubled. In this first, unsolved, case, be prepared to wait a long, long time. Remember that Ctrl-c (on the PC) and Command-c (on the Mac) lets you break out of program executions that go on longer than you want.

4.5.2 Unsolved Code

```
clear all
close all
commandwindow
clc

interest_rate=.04;
t=1;
```

56 Contingencies

```
money(t)=1;
finance_record(1,1:2)=[t money(t)];
money_doubled=false;
while money_doubled==false
    t=t+1
    money(t)=money(t-1)*(1+interest_rate);
    if money(t)==2*money(1)
        money_doubled=true;
    end
    finance_record(t,1:2)=[t money(t)];
end
finance_record
```

3.5.3 Unsolved Output

[What appears in the command window is not reproduced here. It is an endless series of printouts of the form `t = `, followed on the next line by whatever value of t MATLAB is up to at that point. This salvo was finally stopped with Ctrl-c on my PC laptop.]

3.5.4 Solved Problem Comment

The program ran forever because the condition that was needed to break out of the `while` loop was that the money had to *equal* 2 times the original investment: `money(t)==2*money(1)`. This going-on-forever problem was changed by changing `==` to `>=`, so now it reads `if money(t)>=2*money(1)`. The broader message is that when programming with respect to contingencies, plan for *all* contingencies!

4.5.5 Solved Code

```
clear all
close all
commandwindow
clc

interest_rate=.04;
t=1;
money(t)=1;
finance_record(1,1:2)=[t money(t)];
money_doubled=false;
while money_doubled==false
    t=t+1
    money(t)=money(t-1)*(1+interest_rate);
    if money(t)>=2*money(1)
        money_doubled=true;
    end
    finance_record(t,1:2)=[t money(t)];
end
finance_record
```

4.5.6 Solved Output

```
t =
    2
t =
    3
t =
    4
t =
    5
t =
    6
t =
    7
t =
    8
t =
    9
t =
    10
t =
    11
t =
    12
t =
    13
t =
    14
t =
    15
t =
    16
t =
    17
t =
    18
t =
    19
finance_record =
         1           1
         2        1.04
         3      1.0816
         4      1.1249
         5      1.1699
         6      1.2167
         7      1.2653
         8      1.3159
         9      1.3686
        10      1.4233
        11      1.4802
```

58 Contingencies

```
12      1.5395
13       1.601
14      1.6651
15      1.7317
16      1.8009
17       1.873
18      1.9479
19      2.0258
```

4.6 Adding to a New Matrix if a Criterion Is Met

4.6.1 Unsolved Problem Comment

You have a matrix of data, called M, and you want to put rows of data that satisfy a criterion into a new matrix called good_M. A row of M is considered good if the value in *any* of its columns equals or exceeds a criterion, such as criterion = 7. You run the program, expecting good_M to be smaller than or equal in size to M. The matrix good_M can't be bigger than M, but it is. What's wrong?

4.6.2 Unsolved Code

```
clear all
close all
commandwindow
clc

M = [
    4       7       1       7
    4       3       6       2
    10      7       8       7
    7       1       5       8
    10      1       6       6
    10      10      9       3
    1       6       6       5
    5       10      1       9
    8       7       6       3
    4       6       7       7
    ]
criterion=7;
good_M=[];
for ri=1:size(M,1)
    for ci=1:size(M,2)
        if (M(ri,ci)>=criterion)
            good_M=[good_M; M(ri,:)];
        end
    end
end
M
good_M
size_of_M=size(M)
size_of_good_M=size(good_M)
```

4.6.3 *Unsolved Output*

```
M =
     4     7     1     7
     4     3     6     2
    10     7     8     7
     7     1     5     8
    10     1     6     6
    10    10     9     3
     1     6     6     5
     5    10     1     9
     8     7     6     3
     4     6     7     7
M =
     4     7     1     7
     4     3     6     2
    10     7     8     7
     7     1     5     8
    10     1     6     6
    10    10     9     3
     1     6     6     5
     5    10     1     9
     8     7     6     3
     4     6     7     7
good_M =
     4     7     1     7
     4     7     1     7
    10     7     8     7
    10     7     8     7
    10     7     8     7
    10     7     8     7
     7     1     5     8
     7     1     5     8
    10     1     6     6
    10    10     9     3
    10    10     9     3
    10    10     9     3
     5    10     1     9
     5    10     1     9
     8     7     6     3
     8     7     6     3
     4     6     7     7
     4     6     7     7
size_of_M =
    10     4
size_of_good_M =
    18     4
```

4.6.4 Solved Problem Comment

The rows of M kept being added to good_M every time one of the columns of an M row met criterion. A way to break out of this is to use the `break` command or to create a logic gate such that the matrix good_M can only be added to if a column value meets criterion *and* that row has not yet been represented in good_M. Using the logic gate requires more code than the one-word `break`, and you might want to write that code to check your understanding of logic gates. The main idea, however, is only to let a row of M be added to good_M if that row of M hasn't yet been added to good_M.

4.6.5 Solved Code

```
clear all
close all
commandwindow
clc
M = [
    4   7   1   7
    4   3   6   2
    10  7   8   7
    7   1   5   8
    10  1   6   6
    10  10  9   3
    1   6   6   5
    5   10  1   9
    8   7   6   3
    4   6   7   7
    ]
criterion=7;
good_M=[];
for ri=1:size(M,1)
    for ci=1:size(M,2)
        if (M(ri,ci)>=criterion)
            good_M=[good_M; M(ri,:)];
            break   % break out of the for loop if you got here.
        end
    end
end
M
good_M
size_of_M=size(M)
size_of_good_M=size(good_M)
```

4.6.6 Solved Output

```
M =
    4   7   1   7
    4   3   6   2
    10  7   8   7
    7   1   5   8
    10  1   6   6
```

```
         10        10         9         3
          1         6         6         5
          5        10         1         9
          8         7         6         3
          4         6         7         7
M =
          4         7         1         7
          4         3         6         2
         10         7         8         7
          7         1         5         8
         10         1         6         6
         10        10         9         3
          1         6         6         5
          5        10         1         9
          8         7         6         3
          4         6         7         7
good_M =
          4         7         1         7
         10         7         8         7
          7         1         5         8
         10         1         6         6
         10        10         9         3
          5        10         1         9
          8         7         6         3
          4         6         7         7
size_of_M =
         10         4
size_of_good_M =
          8         4
```

4.7 Creating a Latin Square Design

4.7.1 Unsolved Problem Comment

Here is a program to create a Latin square. Recall (or be informed) that a Latin square is, according to Google Dictionary, "an arrangement of letters or symbols that each occur n times in a square array of n^2 compartments such that no letter appears twice in the same row or column." As Google Dictionary goes on to say, "a Latin square [is] used as the basis of experimental procedures in which it is desired to control or allow for two sources of variability while investigating a third."

A typical context where Latin squares are used is that, in a psychology experiment, you have a matrix where each row is for a participant and each column is the trial the participant goes through: column 1 is trial 1, column 2 is trial 2, and so on. With a Latin square, each condition is represented equally often per trial, so you can be reasonably sure any effect of condition isn't an artifact of trial number (e.g., a reflection of practice or fatigue).

The program below creates a Latin square and then a mirror image of that Latin square beneath it. It then puts the subject number at the start of each row in a matrix called `design`. The program is faulty, however. It says that some subjects are given condition 0 in some columns, but there is no condition 0.

62 Contingencies

4.7.2 Unsolved Code

```
clear all
close all
commandwindow
clc

n_subjects=6;    % should be the same as n_conditions for Latin square
n_conditions=6;  % should be the same as n_subjects for Latin square
for si=1:n_subjects
    if si==1  % subject 1
        order(si,1:n_conditions)=randperm(n_conditions);
    else  % subject > 1
        for ci=1:n_conditions-1
            order(si,ci)=order(si-1,ci+1); % inherit the condition from above and to the right
        end
        order(si,ci)=order(si-1,1);   % inherit the first condition from the last subject
    end
end
order
reversed_order=order(:,end:-1:1)
combined_order=[order;reversed_order]
design=[[1:size(combined_order,1)]' combined_order]
```

4.7.3 Unsolved Output

```
order =
     5     1     3     6     2     4
     1     3     6     2     5     0
     3     6     2     5     1     0
     6     2     5     1     3     0
     2     5     1     3     6     0
     5     1     3     6     2     0
reversed_order =
     4     2     6     3     1     5
     0     5     2     6     3     1
     0     1     5     2     6     3
     0     3     1     5     2     6
     0     6     3     1     5     2
     0     2     6     3     1     5
combined_order =
     5     1     3     6     2     4
     1     3     6     2     5     0
     3     6     2     5     1     0
     6     2     5     1     3     0
     2     5     1     3     6     0
     5     1     3     6     2     0
     4     2     6     3     1     5
     0     5     2     6     3     1
```

```
           0      1      5      2      6      3
           0      3      1      5      2      6
           0      6      3      1      5      2
           0      2      6      3      1      5
design =
           1      5      1      3      6      2      4
           2      1      3      6      2      5      0
           3      3      6      2      5      1      0
           4      6      2      5      1      3      0
           5      2      5      1      3      6      0
           6      5      1      3      6      2      0
           7      4      2      6      3      1      5
           8      0      5      2      6      3      1
           9      0      1      5      2      6      3
          10      0      3      1      5      2      6
          11      0      6      3      1      5      2
          12      0      2      6      3      1      5
```

4.7.4 Solved Problem Comment

The error lay in the command `order(si,ci)=order(si-1,1);`. The column index to the left of the equal sign was wrong. It is changed here to `order(si,n_conditions)= order(si-1,1);`.

4.7.5 Solved Code

```
clear all
close all
commandwindow
clc

n_subjects=6;    % should be the same as n_conditions for Latin square
n_conditions=6;  % should be the same as n_subjects for Latin square
for si=1:n_subjects
    if si==1    % subject 1
        order(si,1:n_conditions)=randperm(n_conditions);
    else    % subject > 1
        for ci=1:n_conditions-1
            order(si,ci)=order(si-1,ci+1); % inherit the condition
from above and to the right
        end
        order(si,n_conditions)=order(si-1,1); % inherit the first
condition from the last subject
    end
end
order
reversed_order=order(:,end:-1:1)
combined_order=[order;reversed_order]
design=[[1:size(combined_order,1)]' combined_order]
```

64 Contingencies
4.7.6 Solved Output

```
perm_order =
     1     1     4     6     1     3     5     2
     1     2     6     1     3     5     2     4
     1     3     1     3     5     2     4     6
     1     4     3     5     2     4     6     1
     1     5     5     2     4     6     1     3
     1     6     2     4     6     1     3     5
     2     1     2     1     6     5     3     4
     2     2     1     6     5     3     4     2
     2     3     6     5     3     4     2     1
     2     4     5     3     4     2     1     6
     2     5     3     4     2     1     6     5
     2     6     4     2     1     6     5     3
     3     1     2     6     3     4     1     5
     3     2     6     3     4     1     5     2
     3     3     3     4     1     5     2     6
     3     4     4     1     5     2     6     3
     3     5     1     5     2     6     3     4
     3     6     5     2     6     3     4     1
     4     1     4     6     5     2     1     3
     4     2     6     5     2     1     3     4
     4     3     5     2     1     3     4     6
     4     4     2     1     3     4     6     5
     4     5     1     3     4     6     5     2
     4     6     3     4     6     5     2     1
     5     1     1     5     3     6     4     2
     5     2     5     3     6     4     2     1
     5     3     3     6     4     2     1     5
     5     4     6     4     2     1     5     3
     5     5     4     2     1     5     3     6
     5     6     2     1     5     3     6     4
     6     1     4     3     5     1     2     6
     6     2     3     5     1     2     6     4
     6     3     5     1     2     6     4     3
     6     4     1     2     6     4     3     5
     6     5     2     6     4     3     5     1
     6     6     6     4     3     5     1     2
     7     1     5     2     3     4     1     6
     7     2     2     3     4     1     6     5
     7     3     3     4     1     6     5     2
     7     4     4     1     6     5     2     3
     7     5     1     6     5     2     3     4
     7     6     6     5     2     3     4     1
     8     1     5     1     6     4     2     3
     8     2     1     6     4     2     3     5
     8     3     6     4     2     3     5     1
     8     4     4     2     3     5     1     6
     8     5     2     3     5     1     6     4
     8     6     3     5     1     6     4     2
```

9	1	1	6	4	2	3	5
9	2	6	4	2	3	5	1
9	3	4	2	3	5	1	6
9	4	2	3	5	1	6	4
9	5	3	5	1	6	4	2
9	6	5	1	6	4	2	3
10	1	5	1	2	4	3	6
10	2	1	2	4	3	6	5
10	3	2	4	3	6	5	1
10	4	4	3	6	5	1	2
10	5	3	6	5	1	2	4
10	6	6	5	1	2	4	3
11	1	1	5	4	2	6	3
11	2	5	4	2	6	3	1
11	3	4	2	6	3	1	5
11	4	2	6	3	1	5	4
11	5	6	3	1	5	4	2
11	6	3	1	5	4	2	6
12	1	4	2	5	6	3	1
12	2	2	5	6	3	1	4
12	3	5	6	3	1	4	2
12	4	6	3	1	4	2	5
12	5	3	1	4	2	5	6
12	6	1	4	2	5	6	3

4.8 Creating a Latin Square for Multiple Groups

4.8.1 Unsolved Problem Comment

The aim of this program is to create a more general program to generate Latin squares for several groups (n_groups >= 1) and several subjects (n_subjects >= 1) per group. The previous program was more restrictive, being limited to just one group.

A further aim is to add a constraint: all the subjects within a group must have distinct orders. This limits the number of subjects that can be tested per group. On the other hand, subjects in different groups can have the same orders.

The program produces an output matrix, called perm_order, whose columns are group number, subject number, first condition tested, second condition tested, all the way up to sixth condition tested. The problem with the program is that you can't be sure if all the subjects within a group have unique orders. You could look hard at the output and hope you spot errors, but if you did, you'd have to run the program and check again. If this went on several times, you might get tired and miss a repeat. The difficulty of the problem would grow with the number of conditions and subjects.

4.8.2 Unsolved Code

```
clear all
close all
commandwindow
clc
```

66 Contingencies

```
full_design=[];
n_subjects=6;
n_conditions=6;
n_groups=12;
perm_order=[];
for gi=1:n_groups
    new_group_OK=false;
    while new_group_OK==false
        for si=1:n_subjects
            if si==1
                order(si,1:n_conditions)=randperm(n_conditions);
            else
                for ci=1:n_conditions-1
                    order(si,ci)=order(si-1,ci+1);
                end
                order(si,n_conditions)=order(si-1,1);
            end
        end
        new_group_OK=true;
        group_column(1:n_subjects)=gi;
        subject_column=[1:n_subjects];
        perm_order=[perm_order; full_design;[group_column'
subject_column' order]];
    end
end
perm_order
```

4.8.3 Unsolved Output

```
perm_order =
     1     1     3     2     1     4     5     6
     1     2     2     1     4     5     6     3
     1     3     1     4     5     6     3     2
     1     4     4     5     6     3     2     1
     1     5     5     6     3     2     1     4
     1     6     6     3     2     1     4     5
     2     1     2     6     4     5     3     1
     2     2     6     4     5     3     1     2
     2     3     4     5     3     1     2     6
     2     4     5     3     1     2     6     4
     2     5     3     1     2     6     4     5
     2     6     1     2     6     4     5     3
     3     1     5     1     2     6     4     3
     3     2     1     2     6     4     3     5
     3     3     2     6     4     3     5     1
     3     4     6     4     3     5     1     2
     3     5     4     3     5     1     2     6
     3     6     3     5     1     2     6     4
     4     1     6     5     2     3     4     1
     4     2     5     2     3     4     1     6
```

4	3	2	3	4	1	6	5
4	4	3	4	1	6	5	2
4	5	4	1	6	5	2	3
4	6	1	6	5	2	3	4
5	1	4	2	3	6	1	5
5	2	2	3	6	1	5	4
5	3	3	6	1	5	4	2
5	4	6	1	5	4	2	3
5	5	1	5	4	2	3	6
5	6	5	4	2	3	6	1
6	1	5	4	2	1	6	3
6	2	4	2	1	6	3	5
6	3	2	1	6	3	5	4
6	4	1	6	3	5	4	2
6	5	6	3	5	4	2	1
6	6	3	5	4	2	1	6
7	1	4	1	5	2	3	6
7	2	1	5	2	3	6	4
7	3	5	2	3	6	4	1
7	4	2	3	6	4	1	5
7	5	3	6	4	1	5	2
7	6	6	4	1	5	2	3
8	1	1	4	3	6	5	2
8	2	4	3	6	5	2	1
8	3	3	6	5	2	1	4
8	4	6	5	2	1	4	3
8	5	5	2	1	4	3	6
8	6	2	1	4	3	6	5
9	1	3	5	4	2	1	6
9	2	5	4	2	1	6	3
9	3	4	2	1	6	3	5
9	4	2	1	6	3	5	4
9	5	1	6	3	5	4	2
9	6	6	3	5	4	2	1
10	1	5	2	6	4	1	3
10	2	2	6	4	1	3	5
10	3	6	4	1	3	5	2
10	4	4	1	3	5	2	6
10	5	1	3	5	2	6	4
10	6	3	5	2	6	4	1
11	1	1	3	5	2	4	6
11	2	3	5	2	4	6	1
11	3	5	2	4	6	1	3
11	4	2	4	6	1	3	5
11	5	4	6	1	3	5	2
11	6	6	1	3	5	2	4
12	1	1	3	2	4	6	5
12	2	3	2	4	6	5	1
12	3	2	4	6	5	1	3
12	4	4	6	5	1	3	2

| 12 | 5 | 6 | 5 | 1 | 3 | 2 | 4 |
| 12 | 6 | 5 | 1 | 3 | 2 | 4 | 6 |

4.8.4 Solved Problem Comment

This program checks that all the subjects within a group have distinct orders.

4.8.5 Solved Code

```
clear all
close all
commandwindow
clc

full_design=[];
n_subjects=6;
n_conditions=6;
n_groups=12;
perm_order=[];
for gi=1:n_groups
    new_group_OK=false;
    while new_group_OK==false
        match=0;
        for si=1:n_subjects
            if si==1
                order(si,1:n_conditions)=randperm(n_conditions);
            else
                for ci=1:n_conditions-1
                    order(si,ci)=order(si-1,ci+1);
                end
                order(si,n_conditions)=order(si-1,1);
            end
        end
        % check to make sure the proposed order for this subject
        % doesn't repeat a previous order within this group
        if si>1
            for a=1:size(order,1)-1
                for b=2:size(perm_order,1)
                    if a==b(:,2:end)
                        match=match+1;
                        break
                    end
                end
            end
        end
        if match==0
            new_group_OK=true;
            group_column(1:n_subjects)=gi;
            subject_column=[1:n_subjects];
```

```
            perm_order=[perm_order; full_design;[group_column'
                subject_column' order]];
        end
    end
end
perm_order
```

4.8.6 Solved Output

```
perm_order =
    1    1    6    4    2    3    1    5
    1    2    4    2    3    1    5    6
    1    3    2    3    1    5    6    4
    1    4    3    1    5    6    4    2
    1    5    1    5    6    4    2    3
    1    6    5    6    4    2    3    1
    2    1    4    5    3    2    1    6
    2    2    5    3    2    1    6    4
    2    3    3    2    1    6    4    5
    2    4    2    1    6    4    5    3
    2    5    1    6    4    5    3    2
    2    6    6    4    5    3    2    1
    3    1    6    1    4    5    3    2
    3    2    1    4    5    3    2    6
    3    3    4    5    3    2    6    1
    3    4    5    3    2    6    1    4
    3    5    3    2    6    1    4    5
    3    6    2    6    1    4    5    3
    4    1    3    6    5    4    2    1
    4    2    6    5    4    2    1    3
    4    3    5    4    2    1    3    6
    4    4    4    2    1    3    6    5
    4    5    2    1    3    6    5    4
    4    6    1    3    6    5    4    2
    5    1    4    2    5    1    6    3
    5    2    2    5    1    6    3    4
    5    3    5    1    6    3    4    2
    5    4    1    6    3    4    2    5
    5    5    6    3    4    2    5    1
    5    6    3    4    2    5    1    6
    6    1    5    2    6    4    3    1
    6    2    2    6    4    3    1    5
    6    3    6    4    3    1    5    2
    6    4    4    3    1    5    2    6
    6    5    3    1    5    2    6    4
    6    6    1    5    2    6    4    3
    7    1    6    1    3    2    5    4
    7    2    1    3    2    5    4    6
    7    3    3    2    5    4    6    1
    7    4    2    5    4    6    1    3
```

70   Contingencies

7	5	5	4	6	1	3	2
7	6	4	6	1	3	2	5
8	1	6	1	5	2	3	4
8	2	1	5	2	3	4	6
8	3	5	2	3	4	6	1
8	4	2	3	4	6	1	5
8	5	3	4	6	1	5	2
8	6	4	6	1	5	2	3
9	1	5	3	2	4	6	1
9	2	3	2	4	6	1	5
9	3	2	4	6	1	5	3
9	4	4	6	1	5	3	2
9	5	6	1	5	3	2	4
9	6	1	5	3	2	4	6
10	1	5	2	3	6	1	4
10	2	2	3	6	1	4	5
10	3	3	6	1	4	5	2
10	4	6	1	4	5	2	3
10	5	1	4	5	2	3	6
10	6	4	5	2	3	6	1
11	1	6	1	5	2	4	3
11	2	1	5	2	4	3	6
11	3	5	2	4	3	6	1
11	4	2	4	3	6	1	5
11	5	4	3	6	1	5	2
11	6	3	6	1	5	2	4
12	1	2	6	1	3	5	4
12	2	6	1	3	5	4	2
12	3	1	3	5	4	2	6
12	4	3	5	4	2	6	1
12	5	5	4	2	6	1	3
12	6	4	2	6	1	3	5

4.9   Timing Program Completions

4.9.1   Unsolved Problem Comment

You are curious to know how long it takes to run a program that assigns rows of M to good_M if the sum of columns 2 and 3 exceeds criterion_sum. The larger the value of n_rows (the number of rows), the longer it should take, but how does the actual solution time depend on the value of n_rows?

Use the `tic ... toc` construct to find out. The program prints out the matrix `summary` each time it completes generation of random numbers for successively larger numbers of rows. Because it always prints out the entire `summary` matrix, it includes NaN for each column per row that is not yet completed. This lets you watch in real time as the NaNs get successively replaced by row numbers and total times. The first attempt has a problem, however. All of the times are the same.

4.9.2   Unsolved Code

```
clear all
close all
```

```
commandwindow
clc
rows_per_M=5000.*[1:5];   % the rows_per_M will be 5,000, 10,000,
20,000, ..., 60,000
final_row_numbers_per_M=size(rows_per_M,2); % or 5 in this
instance
columns_per_M=4;
columns_per_summary=2;
max_randi=10;
criterion_sum=5;
summary(1:final_row_numbers_per_M,1:columns_per_summary)=NaN;
for nri=1:final_row_numbers_per_M
    tic
    M=randi(max_randi,rows_per_M(nri),columns_per_M);
    good_M=[];
    for ri=1:rows_per_M(nri)
        if M(ri,2)+M(ri,3)>=criterion_sum
            good_M=[good_M; M(ri,:)];
        end
    end
    M;
    good_M;
    size_of_M=size(M);
    size_of_good_M=size(good_M);
    summary(nri,1:2)=[nri tic]
end   % for nri=1:size(n_rows,2)
```

3.9.3 Unsolved Output

```
summary =
           1    1.1595e+12
           2    1.1595e+12
         NaN           NaN
         NaN           NaN
         NaN           NaN
summary =
           1    1.1595e+12
           2    1.1595e+12
           3    1.1595e+12
         NaN           NaN
         NaN           NaN
summary =
           1    1.1595e+12
           2    1.1595e+12
           3    1.1595e+12
           4    1.1595e+12
         NaN           NaN
summary =
           1    1.1595e+12
           2    1.1595e+12
```

72 Contingencies

```
          3    1.1595e+12
          4    1.1595e+12
          5    1.1595e+12
```

4.9.4 Solved Problem Comment

The way to record the passage of time in MATLAB is not `tic ... tic`. It is `tic ... toc`.

4.9.5 Solved Code

```
clear all
close all
commandwindow
clc
rows_per_M=5000.*[1:5];   % the rows_per_M will be 5,000, 10,000, 15,000, 20,000, 25,000
final_row_numbers_per_M=size(rows_per_M,2); % or 5 in this instance
columns_per_M=4;
columns_per_summary=2;
max_randi=10;
criterion_sum=5;
summary(1:final_row_numbers_per_M,1:columns_per_summary)=NaN;
for nri=1:final_row_numbers_per_M
    tic
    M=randi(max_randi,rows_per_M(nri),columns_per_M);
    good_M=[];
    for ri=1:rows_per_M(nri)
        if M(ri,2)+M(ri,3)>=criterion_sum
            good_M=[good_M; M(ri,:)];
        end
    end
    M;
    good_M;
    size_of_M=size(M);
    size_of_good_M=size(good_M);
    summary(nri,1:2)=[nri toc];
end  % for nri=1:size(n_rows,2)
summary
```

4.9.6 Solved Output

```
summary =
          1        0.1775
        NaN           NaN
        NaN           NaN
        NaN           NaN
        NaN           NaN
```

```
summary =
            1         0.1775
            2         0.41128
          NaN           NaN
          NaN           NaN
          NaN           NaN
summary =
            1         0.1775
            2         0.41128
            3         0.62911
          NaN           NaN
          NaN           NaN
summary =
            1         0.1775
            2         0.41128
            3         0.62911
            4         0.85321
          NaN           NaN
summary =
            1         0.1775
            2         0.41128
            3         0.62911
            4         0.85321
            5         1.2255
summary =
            1         0.1775
            2         0.41128
            3         0.62911
            4         0.85321
            5         1.2255
```

4.10 Using Find to Save Time

4.10.1 Unsolved Problem Comment

Continuing with the task of assigning rows of M to good_M if the sum of column 2 and 3 exceeds criterion_sum, you've seen that the time to check the rows of M grows pretty quickly with the number of rows. If it took 1.1639 seconds to run through 5 * 5,000 = 25,000 rows of data, one shudders to think how long it would take to run through 250,000 rows or 2,500,000 rows. The shuddering would intensify with the number of added rows.

The present program illustrates this problem by enlarging the number of rows. To be able to show results rather than wait "forever" for results to materialize, the line `rows_per_M=5000.*[1:5];` is changed to a larger set of numbers but not one that gets as large as 250,000.

When you run the program, the first time will come up pretty quickly, but then it will take a long time for the second time to come up, a still longer time for the third time to come up, and so on. You could sit around waiting for the third time to come up, and you could wait even longer for the next time to come up, but clearly the times would get intolerably long if the numbers got much larger. Feel free to interrupt the output if your patience wears thin.

74 Contingencies

4.10.2 Unsolved Code

```
clear all
close all
commandwindow
clc

rows_per_M=10000.*[1:5];   % the rows_per_M will be 10,000, 20,000, ...,
50,000;
final_row_numbers_per_M=length(rows_per_M);  % or 5 in this instance
columns_per_M=4;
columns_per_summary=2;
max_randi=10;
criterion_sum=5;
summary(1:final_row_numbers_per_M,1:columns_per_summary)=NaN;
for nri=1:final_row_numbers_per_M
    tic
    M=randi(max_randi,rows_per_M(nri),columns_per_M);
    good_M=[];
    for ri=1:rows_per_M(nri)
        if M(ri,2)+M(ri,3)>=criterion_sum
            good_M=[good_M; M(ri,:)];
        end
    end
    M;
    good_M;
    size_of_M=size(M);
    size_of_good_M=size(good_M);
    summary(nri,1:2)=[nri toc]
end  % for nri=1:size(n_rows,2)
```

4.10.3 Unsolved Output

```
summary =
             1       0.44327
           NaN           NaN
           NaN           NaN
           NaN           NaN
           NaN           NaN
summary =
             1       0.44327
             2        1.0801
           NaN           NaN
           NaN           NaN
           NaN           NaN
summary =
             1       0.44327
             2        1.0801
```

```
                    3          1.7067
                  NaN            NaN
                  NaN            NaN
summary =
                    1        0.44327
                    2         1.0801
                    3         1.7067
                    4         7.6402
                  NaN            NaN
summary =
                    1        0.44327
                    2         1.0801
                    3         1.7067
                    4         7.6402
                    5         20.283
```

4.10.4 Solved Problem Comment

Fortunately, there is a MATLAB command that circumvents the "long wait" problem. That command is find. The find command is used here. Let it run and you will see how much more quickly things go. To have things go really quickly, a semi-colon is added to summary(nri,1:2)=[nri toc] so the interim results are not printed out.

4.10.5 Solved Code

```
clear all
close all
commandwindow
clc

rows_per_M=10000.*[1:5];   % the rows_per_M will be 10,000,
20,000, ..., 50,000;
final_row_numbers_per_M=length(rows_per_M); % or 5 in this instance
columns_per_M=4;
columns_per_summary=2;
max_randi=10;
criterion_sum=5;
summary(1:final_row_numbers_per_M,1:columns_per_summary)=NaN;
for nri=1:final_row_numbers_per_M
    tic
    M=randi(max_randi,rows_per_M(nri),columns_per_M);
    good_M=[];
    good_rows=find(M(:,3)+M(:,4)>=criterion_sum);
    good_M=M(good_rows,:);
    M;
    good_M;
```

76 Contingencies

```
    size_of_M=size(M);
    size_of_good_M=size(good_M);
    summary(nri,1:2)=[nri toc];
end   % for nri=1:size(n_rows,2)
summary
```

4.10.6 Solved Output

```
summary =
            1      0.038059
            2       0.01457
            3      0.012594
            4      0.020581
            5      0.040441
```

5 Plotting

One of the students who took the class in which this book was developed said something amusing when I asked, on the first day of class, why the students were taking the class. The student answered with a big smile: "To make really *boss* graphs."

You can indeed make *boss* graphs with MATLAB. One of MATLAB's most celebrated features is its ability to generate beautiful, professional plots and other graphics. However, some practice is needed to take full advantage of MATLAB's graphic capabilities. As with the other topics covered in this book, there are endless opportunities to err. But as with these other domains, you can choose to celebrate rather than rue your mistakes (i.e., learn from your foul-ups). The plots you generate should never seem like plots against you!

5.1 Defining Terms for Plotting

5.1.1 Unsolved Problem Comment

You try to plot y as a function of x, showing the data as letter o's connected with lines. Everything looks fine, but on closer inspection, you see a problem.

5.1.2 Unsolved Problem Code

```
clear all
close all
commandwindow
clc

figure(1)
x=[0:20];
k=2;
y=k*x;
plot(x,'o-')
```

78 *Plotting*

5.1.3 Unsolved Problem Output

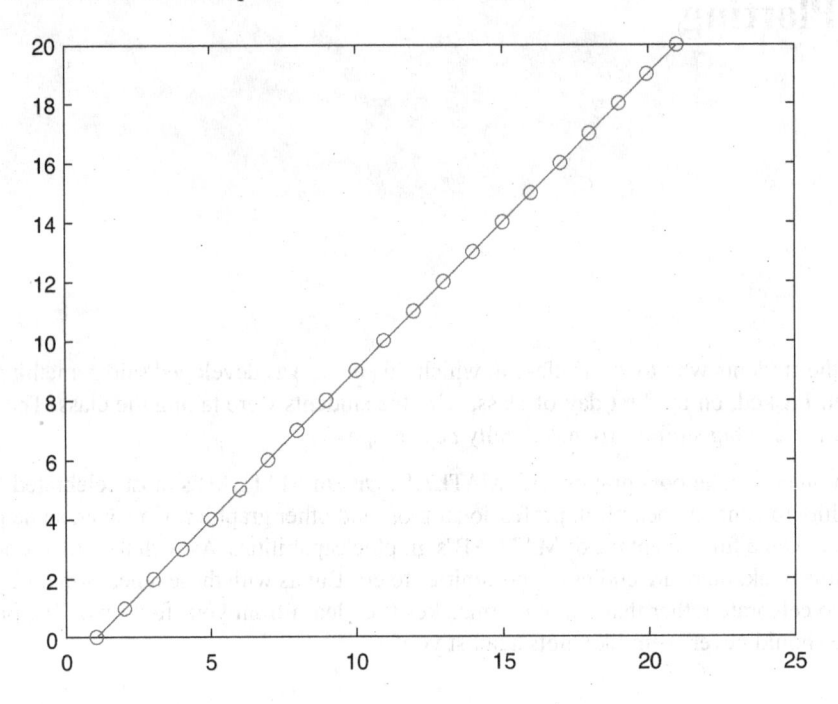

Figure 5.1

5.1.4 Solved Problem Comment

The graph that was created didn't actually show y as a function of x. The reason that y was omitted from the plot command. The syntax for plotting y as a function of x is plot(x, y). If you just say plot(x), MATLAB plots x against the indices for x. That is why in figure(1), 0 was plotted against 1 (the index of x = 0), 1 was plotted against 2 (the index of x = 1), and so on. In the corrected version of the program, y is explicitly plotted as a function of x. That said, the mistake that was made above can be turned to your advantage: If you want to plot a variable against its indices, you can do so by applying the plot command to the variable alone.

5.1.5 Solved Problem Code

```
clear all
close all
commandwindow
clc

figure(2)
x=[0:20];
k=2;
y=k*x;
plot(x,y,'o-')
```

5.1.6 Solved Problem Output

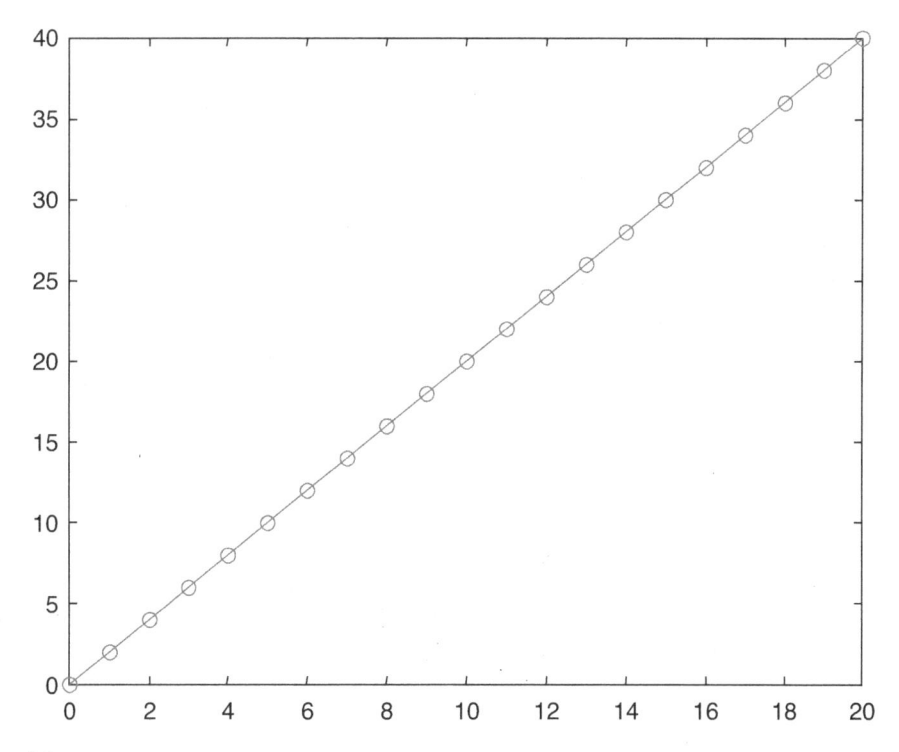

Figure 5.2

5.2 Showing Multiple Curves

5.2.1 Unsolved Problem Comment

In this program you try to plot y as a proportion of x with two different coefficients. You want to see two curves, but just one curve appears.

5.2.2 Unsolved Problem Code

```
clear all
close all
commandwindow
clc

figure(3)
x=[0:20];
k=[1 3];
for ki=1:size(k,2)
    y=k(ki)*x;
    plot(x,y,'o-')
end
```

80 Plotting

5.2.3 Unsolved Problem Output

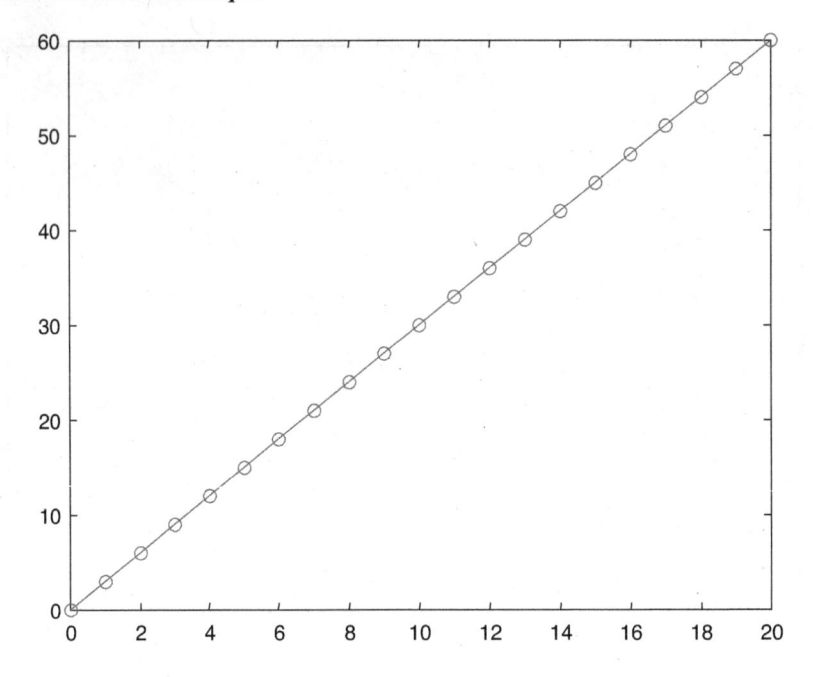

Figure 5.3

5.2.4 Solved Problem Comment

The problem is that the `hold on` command was not given. Without `hold on`, MATLAB's default is `hold off`, in which case the only plot that is kept is the last one. Use `hold on` to get multiple curves when the plot command is used more than once within a figure window. Use `hold off` if you *don't* want the previous plot command to stick (another example of learning from a mistake). To learn more, type the words 'help hold' in the command window. The command to show the command window is the single word `commandwindow`, as seen in the start of every program you have encountered so far in this book. The command to show the current figure, if it doesn't appear and is desired, is `shg`.

5.2.5 Solved Problem Code

```
clear all
close all
commandwindow
clc

figure(4)
hold on
x=[0:20];
k=[1 3];
for ki=1:size(k,2)
    y=k(ki)*x;
    plot(x,y,'o-')
end
```

5.2.6 Solved Problem Output

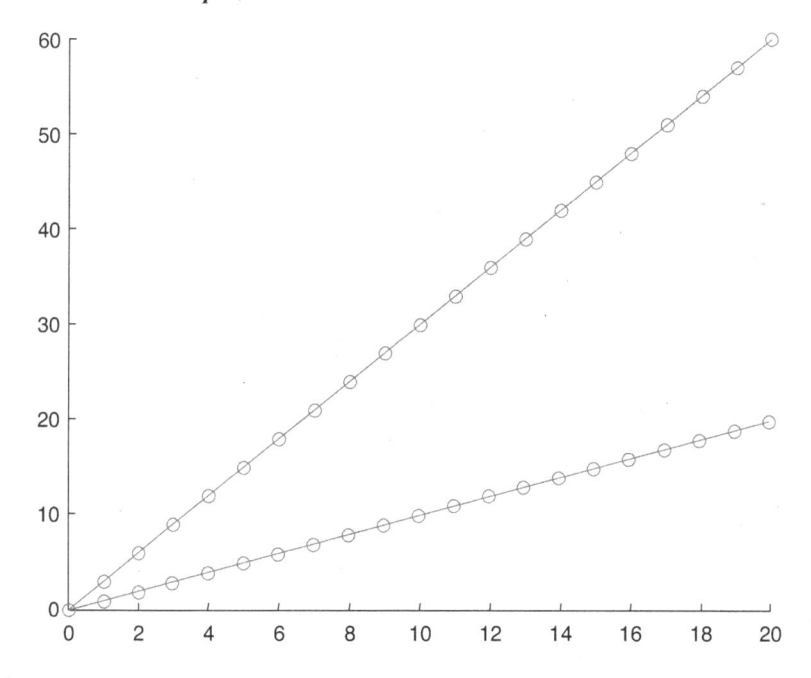

Figure 5.4

5.3 Controlling Colors, Point Shapes, Graph Limits, and Standard Error Bars

5.3.1 Unsolved Problem Comment

In this program the goal is to plot three points from three conditions of an experiment. Each point is a mean value on the y axis as well as the corresponding mean value on the x axis for the subjects who contributed the data in that condition. What's a bit unusual about this graph is that the x value is a dependent measure per subject, just as the y value is. Typically, x is the independent variable with values fixed by the experimental design.

Because there is some variability in the subjects' x values and y values, you want to include standard error bars along the x-axis and y-axis. This is done while including other things to make the graph look professional. These are included here to give you ideas for your own programs.

The graph as a whole looks good, but there is a problem. The lines between the points sit *on top* of the points rather than *behind* the points. This is a relatively minor problem, of course, but it would be nice to fix it.

Here are other things that were done to set up the graph. One was to specify the limits of the x-axis, culminating in the command `xlim([xlim_bottom xlim_top])`. Another was to specify the limits of the y axis, culminating in the command `ylim([ylim_bottom ylim_top])`.

Some steps were also taken to specify the markersize for the dots. As seen here, 'markersize' is an argument for the plot command, and so is 'markerfacecolor,' which in this case was assigned 'g' for green. That same color could be achieved with [0 1 0], where the three values refer to the proportional strength of red (0 in this case), green (1 in this case), and blue (0 in this case). To remember this red-green-blue order, think of RGB. If you want, think of a phrase that might help you remember it, such as Roy G. Biv, a fictional character whose only reason for being was to provide the acronym for helping people remember the color order red, green, blue.

Regarding the errorbar, the errorbar command requires three arguments and allows some optional arguments as well, as can be found by typing help errorbar in the command window. The required arguments are the horizontal position of the error bar center, the vertical position of the error bar center, and the length of the error bar. The optional argument used here is 'horizontal'. If this optional argument is not provided, MATLAB goes with its default, which is 'vertical.'

It took me a while to figure this out. The way I did was to think, "Gee, there must be a way to have horizontal error bars in MATLAB." Thinking that, I typed 'help error bar' in the command window, and voilà! There it was!

The broader lesson is that whenever you think there might be more functionality to a function than first meets the eye, get help about the function by typing 'help' or 'doc' followed by the function name. Often, your wish will come true.

Something else that was done here to control the figure was to specify the values that correspond to the tick marks on the x-axis. This was done by recognizing that the vector of those values is one property of gca, the current axes.

The entire graph is surrounded by a box, which I happen to like for aesthetic reasons. To add the surrounding box, the necessary command is box on. The command axis square also makes the graph look nice, at least in my judgment.

Despite all these preparations, the graph doesn't look quite as pretty or professional as one would like because the error bars sit on top of the points. It would be nice to correct this to show uninterrupted points with error bars extending out from behind or beneath them.

5.3.2   Unsolved Problem Code

```
clear all
close all
commandwindow
clc

x_means=[.1:.1:.4];
x_standard_errors=x_means/10;
y_means=[1:4];
y_standard_errors= y_means./10;
figure(5)
hold on

% Define the limits of the x axis and y axis.
kx=.1;
ky=.1;
xlim_bottom=[min(x_means-x_standard_errors)];
xlim_top=[max(x_means+x_standard_errors)];
xlim_top=xlim_top + (xlim_top-xlim_bottom)*kx;
xlim_bottom=xlim_bottom -(xlim_top-xlim_bottom)*kx;
ylim_bottom=[min(y_means-y_standard_errors)];
ylim_top=[max(y_means+y_standard_errors)];
```

```
ylim_top=ylim_top + (ylim_top-ylim_bottom)*ky;
ylim_bottom=ylim_bottom -(ylim_top-ylim_bottom)*ky;

xlim([xlim_bottom xlim_top]);
ylim([ylim_bottom ylim_top]);

% Define markersize, ms, computationally rather than by hand
kms=750;
ms=kms*min([x_standard_errors y_standard_errors]);

% Make the graph
plot(x_means,y_means,'ko','markerfacecolor','g','markersize',ms)

errorbar(x_means,y_means,y_standard_errors,'k')
errorbar(x_means,y_means,x_standard_errors,'k','horizontal')

set(gca,'xtick',x_means);
set(gca,'ytick',y_means);
box on
axis square
```

5.3.3 Unsolved Problem Output

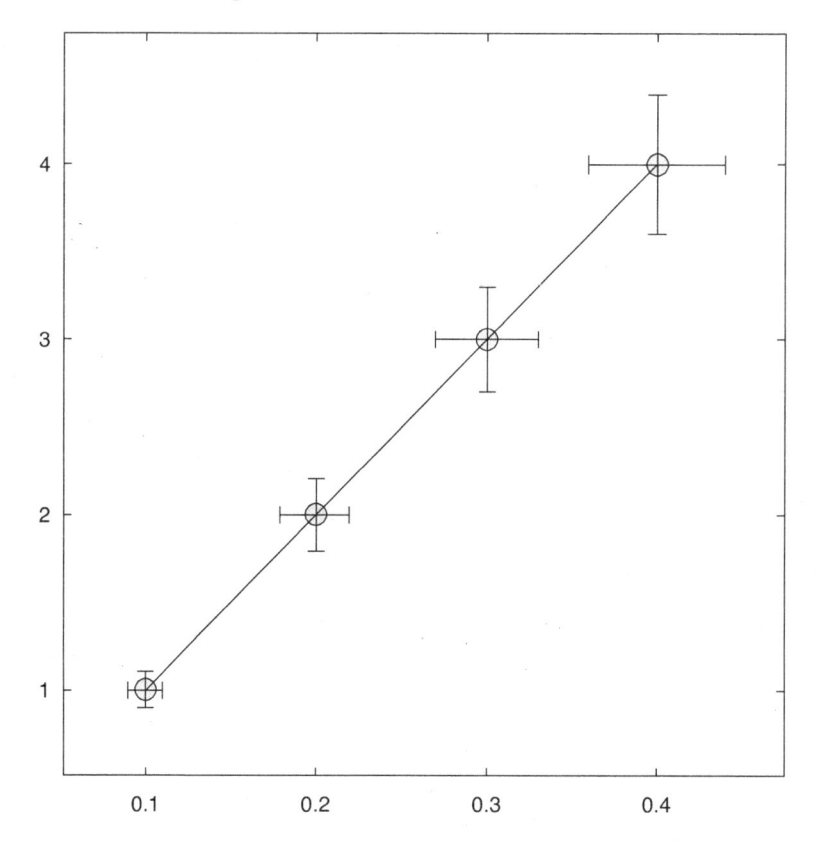

Figure 5.5

84 Plotting

5.3.4 Solved Problem Comment

Despite the sophistication of computer graphics, sometimes there is no harm in thinking about the simple order in which images and parts of images are applied. Much as an artist makes a collage by putting images on top of other images, that simple procedure can apply to creating images in MATLAB.

The mistake (or suboptimality) in the last figure was that the dots showing the mean values were laid down before the lines connecting the mean values were applied. Simply switching the order solves the problem.

Another lesson, implied by all the setup steps referred to above, is to use the 'help' command to look for options that you think MATLAB might provide and that you think you might be able to control or modify. Whenever MATLAB comes up with something on its own, it's actually using some built-in values that you can probably control yourself. If you do some digging, you can usually figure out how to gain that control.

5.3.5 Solved Problem Code

```
clear all
close all
commandwindow
clc

x_means=[.1:.1:.4];
x_standard_errors=x_means/10;
y_means=[1:4];
y_standard_errors= y_means./10;

figure(6)
hold on
errorbar(x_means,y_means,y_standard_errors,'k')
errorbar(x_means,y_means,x_standard_errors,'k','horizontal')

% Define the limits of the x axis, xlim, and  the limits of the y axis, ylim.
kx=.1;
ky=.1;
xlim_bottom=[min(x_means-x_standard_errors)];
xlim_top=[max(x_means+x_standard_errors)];
xlim_top=xlim_top + (xlim_top-xlim_bottom)*kx;
xlim_bottom=xlim_bottom -(xlim_top-xlim_bottom)*kx;

ylim_bottom=[min(y_means-y_standard_errors)];
ylim_top=[max(y_means+y_standard_errors)];
ylim_top=ylim_top + (ylim_top-ylim_bottom)*ky;
ylim_bottom=ylim_bottom -(ylim_top-ylim_bottom)*ky;

xlim([xlim_bottom xlim_top]);
ylim([ylim_bottom ylim_top]);

% Define markersize. ms, computationally rather than by hand
kms=750;
ms=kms*min([x_standard_errors y_standard_errors]);
```

```
% Make the graph
plot(x_means,y_means,'ko','markerfacecolor','g','markersize',ms)
set(gca,'xtick',x_means);
set(gca,'ytick',y_means);
box on
axis square
```

5.3.6 Solved Problem Output

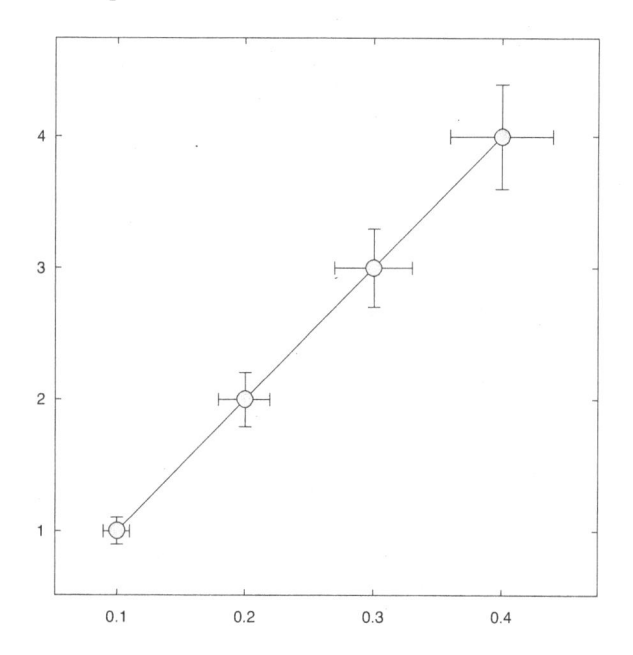

Figure 5.6

5.4 Adding Power Function Curves, Legends, and Labels for x- and y-Axes

5.4.1 Unsolved Problem Comment

The next program is concerned with the graph of x raised to different powers. The graph is meant to show x raised to the −.5 power and x raised to the −1 power. Remember that raising a non-negative value, x, to a negative power, -alpha, is the same as dividing by x to the alpha power. For example, if x equals 2 and alpha equals 3, then $x^{-alpha} = 2^{-3} = 1/(2^3) = 1/8$. The larger the value of x, the smaller the ratio. Similarly, the larger the value of alpha, the more steeply the downward gradient drops in the plot of $y=x^{-alpha}$.

In this program, that bit of math is applied to salaries in two companies, A and B. You are interested, down the road (in the next program), in relating job satisfaction to salary. When you first plot the graph, it doesn't look like what you expect. The numbers along the y-axis are crazy. So either the power function doesn't behave as advertised in mathematics for the past several centuries or there's a bug in the program.

Try to understand the bug, but also try to spend some time taking advantage of the graph-related code shown here so you can explore the effects of other parameter values on the power function.

86 *Plotting*

Of course, you can also explore other functions besides the power function. One of the great advantages of working with MATLAB is that it provides a convenient medium to explore and learn mathematics via the graphing capabilities that MATLAB affords.

A side remark is that this program creates a legend. Leading up to creation of a legend, when you issue the plot command, you can optionally give it, in this case, the command 'displayname', 'Company A'. The first term, 'displayname', is the fixed term for the property being specified. The string 'Company A' is just the particular displayname in this instance. You could just as well have said 'My Favorite Company, Which Sells My Favorite Product, Which My Kid Brother Sells'.

The command legend('show','location','northeast') creates the legend at the designated location in the graph. In the code that follows, legend('show','location','northeast') is followed by these two lines of code (uncommented when they appear):

```
get(legend)
set(legend,'FontSize',legend_font_size,'color','w') %[1 1 1]*1
```

These commands get all the properties of legend. Once you see what they are, you can set a property, such as the legend's 'Fontsize' (which here is set to legend_font_size) and 'color' (which here is set to 'w' or white, which is the same as [1 1 1]*1). The matrix [1 1 1] means that the proportion of red is 1, the proportion of green is 1, and the proportion of blue is 1. The color white is all three colors at their maximum value of 1. The color black is all three colors at the minimum value of 0. The reason to include *1 is just to convey that you can modulate the overall brightness to generate many shades of gray.

This program (and its successful successor) is also the first to use xticklabel and yticklabel. These are strings. The labels on xticks and yticks don't have to be the same as the actual values for the xticks and yticks. However, if the number of terms in the label strings don't match the number of terms in their corresponding xticks or yticks, you can be in for a weird surprise along the y-axis, as seen here.

This program is also the first in this set to use labels for the x-axis and y-axis. Hopefully, you'll find the xlabel and ylabel commands straightforward.

In case you didn't read every word of the foregoing comment, the error here concerns the numerical values along the y-axis. They are crazy!

5.4.2 Unsolved Problem Code

```
clear all
close all
commandwindow
clc

figure(7)
hold on
xlim_offset=0;
ms=14; % markersize
x=[1:101];
alpha=[-.5 -1];
max_salary=10;
```

```
legend_font_size=12;
for ai=1:size(alpha,2)
    y=max_salary*x.^alpha(ai);
    if ai==1
        plot(x,y,'b.-','markersize', ms, 'displayname','Company A');
    else
        plot(x,y,'r.-','markersize', ms, 'displayname','Company B');
    end
end
xlim([min(x)-xlim_offset max(x)+xlim_offset])
legend('show','location','northeast')
get(legend)
set(legend,'FontSize',legend_font_size,'color','w') %[1 1 1]*1
set(gca,'xtick',[1:10:101])
set(gca,'xticklabel',[1:10:101])
set(gca,'ytick',[0:10])
set(gca,'yticklabel',[0:25:100])
xlabel('Income Rank')
ylabel('Salary (thousands of dollars)')
```

5.4.3 Unsolved Problem Output

```
        AutoUpdate: 'on'
      BeingDeleted: 'off'
               Box: 'on'
         BusyAction: 'queue'
      ButtonDownFcn: @bdowncb
           Children: [0×0 GraphicsPlaceholder]
              Color: [1 1 1]
          CreateFcn: ''
          DeleteFcn: ''
          EdgeColor: [0.15 0.15 0.15]
          FontAngle: 'normal'
           FontName: 'Helvetica'
           FontSize: 9
         FontWeight: 'normal'
   HandleVisibility: 'on'
            HitTest: 'on'
        Interpreter: 'tex'
      Interruptible: 'off'
         ItemHitFcn: @defaultItemHitCallback
          LineWidth: 0.5
           Location: 'northeast'
        Orientation: 'vertical'
             Parent: [1×1 Figure]
       PickableParts: 'visible'
           Position: [0.67798 0.80992 0.20321 0.083095]
           Selected: 'off'
   SelectionHighlight: 'on'
             String: {'Company A'   'Company B'}
```

88 Plotting

```
            Tag: 'legend'
      TextColor: [0 0 0]
          Title: [1×1 Text]
           Type: 'legend'
  UIContextMenu: [1×1 ContextMenu]
          Units: 'normalized'
       UserData: []
        Visible: 'on'
```

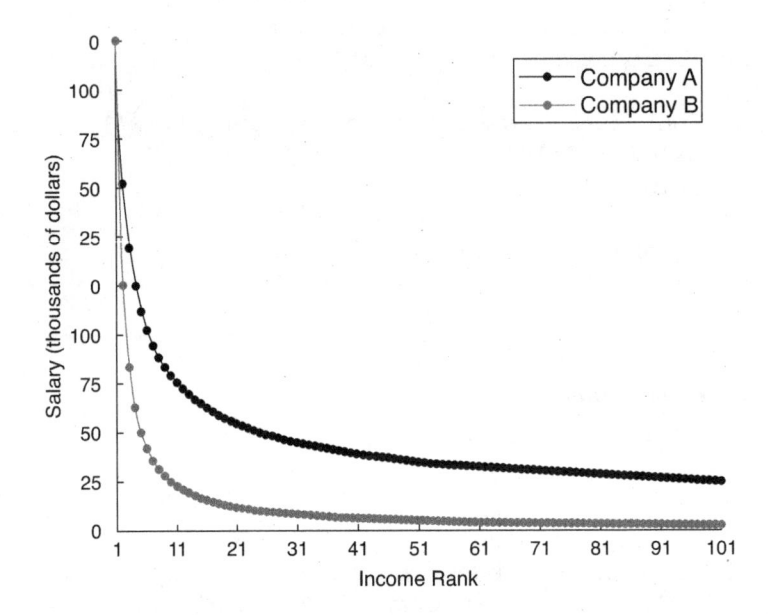

Figure 5.7

5.4.4 Solved Problem Comment

The numbers along the y-axis were crazy because of the line of code `set(gca,'ytick', [0:10])`. This line of code was bad because there were fewer ytick values than yticklabels. The number of values of `ytick` must set the stage correctly for `yticklabel` (and similarly for the values of `xtick` and `xticklabel`). There need to be as many `ytick` values as `yticklabel` values, and similarly for `xtick` and `xticklabel` values. That requirement wasn't met before. It is now.

5.4.5 Solved Problem Code

```
clear all
close all
commandwindow
clc

figure(8)
hold on
xlim_offset=0;
ms=14; % markersize
```

Plotting 89

```
x=[1:101];
alpha=[-.5 -1];
max_salary=10;
legend_font_size=12;

for ai=1:size(alpha,2)
    y=max_salary*x.^alpha(ai);
    if ai==1
        plot(x,y,'b.-','markersize', ms, 'displayname','Company A');
    else
        plot(x,y,'r.-','markersize', ms, 'displayname','Company B');
    end
end
xlim([min(x)-xlim_offset max(x)+xlim_offset])
legend('show','location','northeast')
get(legend)
set(legend,'FontSize',legend_font_size,'color','w') %[1 1 1]*1
set(gca,'xtick',[1:10:101])
set(gca,'xticklabel',[1:10:101])

% BAD CODE from before, which was bad because there were fewer ytick values
% than yticklabels.
% set(gca,'ytick',[0:10])
% GOOD CODE FOLLOWS
set(gca,'ytick',[0:2.5:10])

set(gca,'yticklabel',[0:25:100])
xlabel('Income Rank')
ylabel('Salary (thousands of dollars)')
```

5.4.6 Solved Problem Output

```
AutoUpdate: 'on'
      BeingDeleted: 'off'
               Box: 'on'
         BusyAction: 'queue'
       ButtonDownFcn: @bdowncb
           Children: [0×0 GraphicsPlaceholder]
              Color: [1 1 1]
           CreateFcn: ''
           DeleteFcn: ''
          EdgeColor: [0.15 0.15 0.15]
          FontAngle: 'normal'
           FontName: 'Helvetica'
           FontSize: 9
         FontWeight: 'normal'
    HandleVisibility: 'on'
            HitTest: 'on'
        Interpreter: 'tex'
```

```
           Interruptible: 'off'
              ItemHitFcn: @defaultItemHitCallback
               LineWidth: 0.5
                Location: 'northeast'
             Orientation: 'vertical'
                  Parent: [1×1 Figure]
           PickableParts: 'visible'
                Position: [0.67798 0.80992 0.20321 0.083095]
                Selected: 'off'
      SelectionHighlight: 'on'
                  String: {'Company A'   'Company B'}
                     Tag: 'legend'
               TextColor: [0 0 0]
                   Title: [1×1 Text]
                    Type: 'legend'
           UIContextMenu: [1×1 ContextMenu]
                   Units: 'normalized'
                UserData: []
                 Visible: 'on'
```

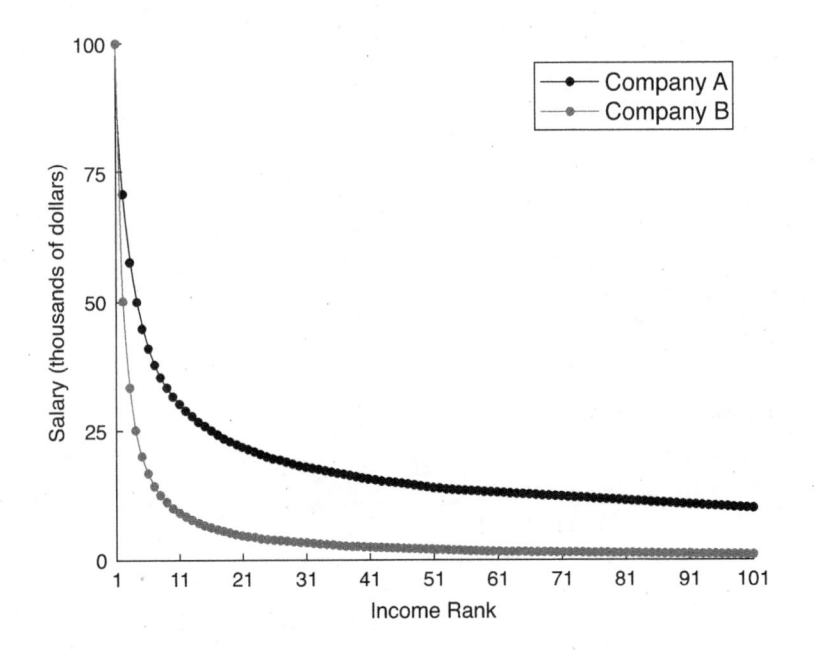

Figure 5.8

5.5 Creating Subplots

5.5.1 Unsolved Problem Comment

The fifth problem concerns subplots. These let you have more than one graph in a figure window. Here you generate subplots within a matrix of four subplots occupying 2 rows and 2 columns. The `subplot` function takes three arguments: the number of rows of subplots; the number of columns of subplots; and the number of the particular subplot being plotted at the time. The number of subplots cannot exceed the number of rows times the number of columns. In the program that follows, a problem arises because of how the subplot command is given.

Anticipating the graphics in the third plot, namely (2,2,3), we'll use red rings instead of red dots. It turns out that markersize looks different for dots ('.') and for shapes like rings ('o'), squares ('s'), apex-up triangles ('^') and apex-down triangles ('v'). The latter shapes (i.e., 's', '^', and 'v') are not used in this program. The difference in markersize is addressed here in the line of code that says `ring_markersize=round(dot_markersize*rds);`

A side remark, not evident in the code below, is that if the legends do not appear exactly where you like them, you can click on them and drag them to where you want them in the figure window.

Also, to save the figure for publication or display, I recommend that you save the figure as a .tif file. You can save the figure under the File tab of the figure window, or use the `saveas` command, as done here.

5.5.2 Unsolved Problem Code

```
clear all
close all
commandwindow
clc

figure(9)
legend_font_size=9;

subplot(2,2,1)
hold on
box on
xlim_offset=0;
dot_markersize=14;
rds=.3;
ring_markersize=round(dot_markersize*rds); % can't have
decimals, so round
x=[1:101];
alpha=[-.5 -1];
max_salary=10;
fs=8;
for ai=1:size(alpha,2)
    sy(ai,x)=max_salary*x.^alpha(ai);
    if ai==1
        plot(x,sy(ai,:),'b.-','markersize',dot_markersize, ...
            'displayname','Company A');
    else
        plot(x,sy(ai,:),'ro-','markersize',ring_markersize, ...
            'markerfacecolor','w','displayname','Company B');
    end
end
legend('show','location','north')
get(legend)
set(legend,'FontSize',legend_font_size,'color','w') %[1 1 1]*1
xlabel('Income Rank')
ylabel('Salary (thousands of dollars)')
set(gca,'xtick',[1:10:101])
set(gca,'xticklabel',[1:10:100])
```

92 Plotting

```
set(gca,'ytick',[0:2.5:10])
set(gca,'yticklabel',[0:25:100])
xlim([min(x)-xlim_offset max(x)+xlim_offset])

subplot(2,2,2)
hold on
box on
xlim_offset=0;
ms=14; % markersize
x=[1:101];
fc=[.2 .4];
max_salary=10;
fs=12;
for fci=1:size(fc,2)
    fy(fci,x)=fc(fci)*log(x);
    if fci==1
        plot(x,fy(fci,:),'b.-','markersize',dot_markersize,...
            'displayname','Company A');
    else
        plot(x,fy(fci,:),'ro-','markersize',ring_markersize, ...
            'markerfacecolor','w','displayname','Company B');
    end
end
legend('show','location','southeast')
get(legend)
set(legend,'FontSize',legend_font_size,'color','w') %[1 1 1]*1
xlabel('Income Rank')
ylabel('Friendship')
set(gca,'xtick',[1:10:101])
set(gca,'xticklabel',[1:10:101])
xlim([min(x)-xlim_offset max(x)+xlim_offset])

subplot(3:4)
hold on
box on
plot(sy(1,:),fy(1,:), 'ro',...
    'markersize',ring_markersize,'markerfacecolor','w')
plot(sy(2,:),fy(2,:),'b.-',sy(1,:),fy(1,:),'k-');
set(gca,'xtick',[0:2.5:10])
set(gca,'xticklabel',[0:25:100])
xlabel('Salary (thousands of dollars)')
ylabel('Friendship')
saveas(figure(10),'Fig_Salaries.tif')
```

5.5.3 Unsolved Problem Output

```
      AutoUpdate: 'on'
     BeingDeleted: 'off'
             Box: 'on'
       BusyAction: 'queue'
```

```
         ButtonDownFcn: @bdowncb
              Children: [0×0 GraphicsPlaceholder]
                 Color: [1 1 1]
             CreateFcn: ''
             DeleteFcn: ''
             EdgeColor: [0.15 0.15 0.15]
             FontAngle: 'normal'
              FontName: 'Helvetica'
              FontSize: 9
            FontWeight: 'normal'
      HandleVisibility: 'on'
               HitTest: 'on'
           Interpreter: 'tex'
         Interruptible: 'off'
            ItemHitFcn: @defaultItemHitCallback
             LineWidth: 0.5
              Location: 'north'
           Orientation: 'vertical'
                Parent: [1×1 Figure]
         PickableParts: 'visible'
              Position: [0.19589 0.80992 0.20321 0.083095]
              Selected: 'off'
    SelectionHighlight: 'on'
                String: {'Company A'   'Company B'}
                   Tag: 'legend'
             TextColor: [0 0 0]
                 Title: [1×1 Text]
                  Type: 'legend'
         UIContextMenu: [1×1 ContextMenu]
                 Units: 'normalized'
              UserData: []
               Visible: 'on'
            AutoUpdate: 'on'
          BeingDeleted: 'off'
                   Box: 'on'
            BusyAction: 'queue'
         ButtonDownFcn: @bdowncb
              Children: [0×0 GraphicsPlaceholder]
                 Color: [1 1 1]
             CreateFcn: ''
             DeleteFcn: ''
             EdgeColor: [0.15 0.15 0.15]
             FontAngle: 'normal'
              FontName: 'Helvetica'
              FontSize: 9
            FontWeight: 'normal'
      HandleVisibility: 'on'
               HitTest: 'on'
           Interpreter: 'tex'
         Interruptible: 'off'
            ItemHitFcn: @defaultItemHitCallback
```

94 Plotting

```
       LineWidth: 0.5
        Location: 'southeast'
     Orientation: 'vertical'
          Parent: [1×1 Figure]
    PickableParts: 'visible'
        Position: [0.67798 0.61556 0.20321 0.083095]
        Selected: 'off'
SelectionHighlight: 'on'
          String: {'Company A'   'Company B'}
             Tag: 'legend'
       TextColor: [0 0 0]
           Title: [1×1 Text]
            Type: 'legend'
   UIContextMenu: [1×1 ContextMenu]
           Units: 'normalized'
        UserData: []
         Visible: 'on'
Operands to the || and && operators must be convertible to
logical scalar values.
Error in subplot (line 157)
         elseif isgraphics(arg) || isa(arg,'matlab.graphics.Graphics')
```

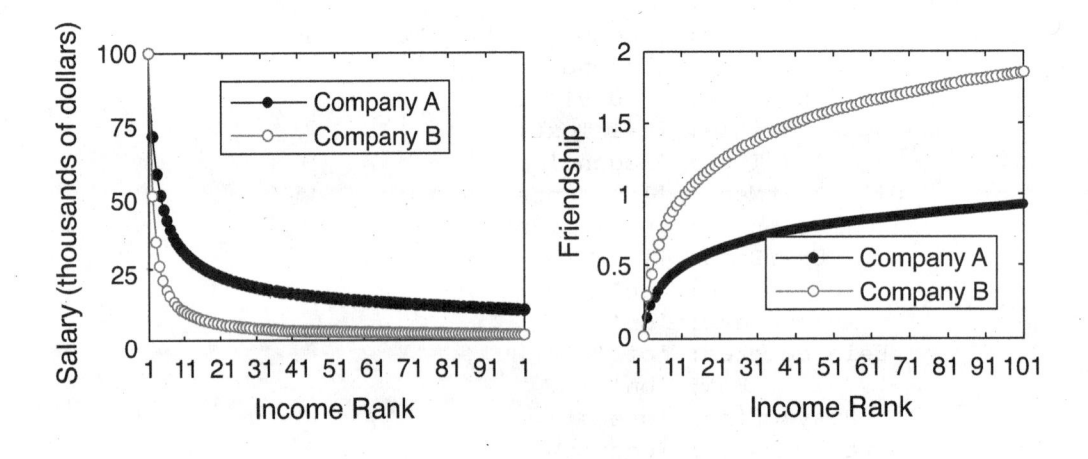

Figure 5.9

Plotting 95

5.5.4 Solved Problem Comment

The error was in the `subplot` command. Remember that the `subplot` function takes three arguments: the number of rows of subplots, the number of columns of subplots, and the number (or series of numbers) of the subplot (or subplots). In the unsolved version, the number of rows and the number of columns were omitted in `subplot(3:4)`. The problem is fixed here. The bottom row has two subplots in one. Subplots 3 and 4 are combined in a single array.

An important point to take note of is that the error is supposedly in line 157 of the subplot function provided by Mathworks. Actually, the error is *not* in the subplot function itself but in the way it is called. This often happens in MATLAB. An error in a program that calls a perfectly fine function provided by Mathworks triggers an error message that reads like there is a problem in the function from Mathworks itself. Be leery of supposed problems with Mathworks-provided functions. Chances are that you made a mistake in the way you called a function.

5.5.5 Solved Problem Code

```
clear all
close all
commandwindow
clc

figure(10)
legend_font_size=9;
subplot(2,2,1)
hold on
box on
xlim_offset=0;
dot_markersize=14;
rds=.3;
ring_markersize=round(dot_markersize*rds); % can't have
decimals, so round
x=[1:101];
alpha=[-.5 -1];
max_salary=10;
fs=8;
for ai=1:size(alpha,2)
    sy(ai,x)=max_salary*x.^alpha(ai);
    if ai==1
        plot(x,sy(ai,:),'b.-','markersize',dot_markersize,...
            'displayname','Company A');
    else
        plot(x,sy(ai,:),'ro-','markersize',ring_markersize,...
            'markerfacecolor','w','displayname','Company B');
    end
end
legend('show','location','north')
get(legend)
set(legend,'FontSize',legend_font_size,'color','w') %[1 1 1]*1
xlabel('Income Rank')
ylabel('Salary (thousands of dollars)')
set(gca,'xtick',[1:10:101])
```

96 Plotting

```
set(gca,'xticklabel',[1:10:100])
set(gca,'ytick',[0:2.5:10])
set(gca,'yticklabel',[0:25:100])
xlim([min(x)-xlim_offset max(x)+xlim_offset])

subplot(2,2,2)
hold on
box on
xlim_offset=0;
ms=14; % markersize
x=[1:101];
fc=[.2 .4];
max_salary=10;
fs=12;
for fci=1:size(fc,2)
    fy(fci,x)=fc(fci)*log(x);
    if fci==1
        plot(x,fy(fci,:),'b.-','markersize',dot_markersize,...
            'displayname','Company A');
    else
        plot(x,fy(fci,:),'ro-','markersize',ring_markersize,...
            'markerfacecolor','w','displayname','Company B');
    end
end
legend('show','location','southeast')
get(legend)
set(legend,'FontSize',legend_font_size,'color','w') %[1 1 1]*1
xlabel('Income Rank')
ylabel('Friendship')
set(gca,'xtick',[1:10:101])
set(gca,'xticklabel',[1:10:101])
xlim([min(x)-xlim_offset max(x)+xlim_offset])

subplot(2,2,3:4)
hold on
box on
plot(sy(1,:),fy(1,:), 'ro',...
    'markersize',ring_markersize,'markerfacecolor','w')
plot(sy(2,:),fy(2,:),'b.-',sy(1,:),fy(1,:),'k-');
set(gca,'xtick',[0:2.5:10])
set(gca,'xticklabel',[0:25:100])

xlabel('Salary (thousands of dollars)')
ylabel('Friendship')

saveas(figure(10),'Fig_Salaries.tif')
```

5.5.6 Solved Problem Output

```
AutoUpdate: 'on'
       BeingDeleted: 'off'
                Box: 'on'
```

```
            BusyAction: 'queue'
         ButtonDownFcn: @bdowncb
              Children: [0×0 GraphicsPlaceholder]
                 Color: [1 1 1]
             CreateFcn: ''
             DeleteFcn: ''
             EdgeColor: [0.15 0.15 0.15]
             FontAngle: 'normal'
              FontName: 'Helvetica'
              FontSize: 9
            FontWeight: 'normal'
      HandleVisibility: 'on'
               HitTest: 'on'
           Interpreter: 'tex'
         Interruptible: 'off'
            ItemHitFcn: @defaultItemHitCallback
             LineWidth: 0.5
              Location: 'north'
           Orientation: 'vertical'
                Parent: [1×1 Figure]
          PickableParts: 'visible'
              Position: [0.19589 0.80992 0.20321 0.083095]
              Selected: 'off'
     SelectionHighlight: 'on'
                String: {'Company A'    'Company B'}
                   Tag: 'legend'
             TextColor: [0 0 0]
                 Title: [1×1 Text]
                  Type: 'legend'
         UIContextMenu: [1×1 ContextMenu]
                 Units: 'normalized'
              UserData: []
               Visible: 'on'
            AutoUpdate: 'on'
          BeingDeleted: 'off'
                   Box: 'on'
            BusyAction: 'queue'
         ButtonDownFcn: @bdowncb
              Children: [0×0 GraphicsPlaceholder]
                 Color: [1 1 1]
             CreateFcn: ''
             DeleteFcn: ''
             EdgeColor: [0.15 0.15 0.15]
             FontAngle: 'normal'
              FontName: 'Helvetica'
              FontSize: 9
            FontWeight: 'normal'
      HandleVisibility: 'on'
               HitTest: 'on'
           Interpreter: 'tex'
         Interruptible: 'off'
```

```
           ItemHitFcn: @defaultItemHitCallback
            LineWidth: 0.5
             Location: 'southeast'
          Orientation: 'vertical'
               Parent: [1×1 Figure]
         PickableParts: 'visible'
             Position: [0.67798 0.61556 0.20321 0.083095]
             Selected: 'off'
     SelectionHighlight: 'on'
               String: {'Company A'    'Company B'}
                  Tag: 'legend'
            TextColor: [0 0 0]
                Title: [1×1 Text]
                 Type: 'legend'
         UIContextMenu: [1×1 ContextMenu]
                Units: 'normalized'
             UserData: []
              Visible: 'on'
```

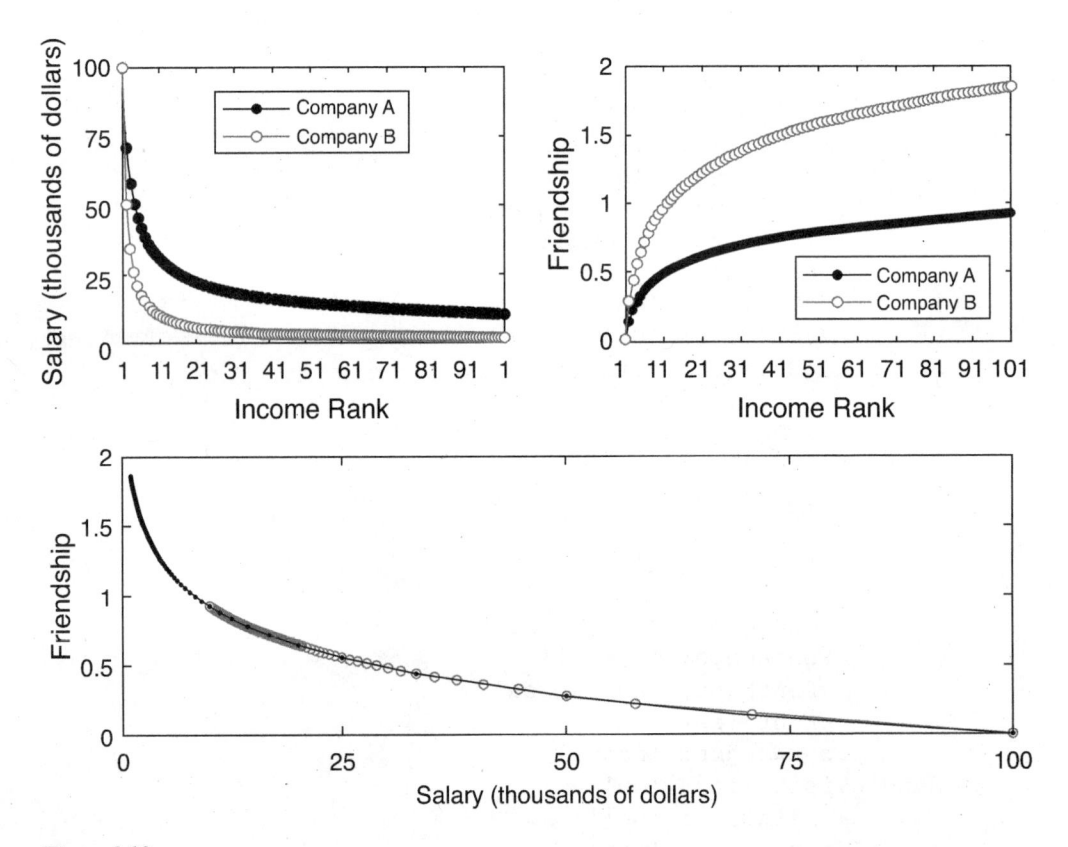

Figure 5.10

5.6 Adding Text, a Grid, and a Fitted Exponential Function

5.6.1 Unsolved Problem Comment

Consider perceptual similarity. According to Roger Shepard, the perceived similarity of one stimulus relative to a standard is a negative exponential function of the difference between the stimulus and standard. The program shown here is meant to illustrate this principle.[1]

The left subplot shows (fictional) data. The right subplot shows an attempt to fit an exponential function to those data. What is sought is a pair of lines, providing the best-fitting theoretical curves to the data, along with a report of the best-fitting parameter, a, for the negative exponential function and the proportion of variance, R^2, explained by the model.

The fit doesn't turn out sensibly. Three problems emerge. First, the best-fitting line is a flat line, which is wrong. Second, the best-fitting value of a is zero, which is wrong. Third, the proportion of variance explained is nothing like it should be.

The logic of the fitting procedure is as follows. It builds entirely on things that have been covered so far. The main idea is to iteratively vary two parameters to find the smallest sum of squared deviations between the observed and predicted values. Once the best values are found, they are used to show the best-fitting curve, but problems arise. Try to figure out why the results concerning the best-fitting curve are silly.

5.6.2 Unsolved Problem Code

```
clear all
close all
commandwindow
clc

figure(11)
hold on
x=[-10:.01:10];
a=.5;
y=exp(-a*abs(x));
plot(x,y,'k-')
sample_x=[-10:10];
stdr=.06;   % want something like .05
ms=5;
n_samples=8;
for sxi=1:size(sample_x,2)
    for nsi=1:n_samples
        sample_y(sxi,nsi)=exp(-a*abs(sample_x(sxi))) + stdr*randn;
    end
end
sample_y(sample_y>1)=1;   % id problem...
sample_y(sample_y<0)=0;   % id problem...
subplot(1,2,1)
plot(sample_x,sample_y,'o',...
```

---

[1] Shepard, R. N. (1987). Toward a universal law of generalization for psychological science. *Science*, 237, 1317–1323.

```
        'markerfacecolor',[1 .6 .6]*1,'markeredgecolor',[0 0 1]*1,
'markersize',ms)
box on
grid on
xlabel('Difference From Standard')
ylabel('Judged Similarity')
ylim([-.1 1.1])
set(gca,'ytick',[0:.2:1])

subplot(1,2,2)
hold on
for i=1:size(sample_x,2)
    errorbar(sample_x(i),mean(sample_y(i,:)),std(sample_y(i,:)),'k-')
end

% Fit exponential
a=[0:.01:1];
ssq=0;
best_ssq=inf;
for ai=1:size(a,2)
    for i=1:size(sample_y,1) % the rows corresponding to different differences from standard
        for j=1:size(sample_y,2) % the columns corresponding to different observations
            term_1=exp(-a(ai)*abs(sample_x(i)));
            term_2=sample_y(i,j);
            ssq=ssq+(term_1-term_2)^2;
        end
    end
    if ssq<best_ssq
        best_ssq=ssq;
        best_ai=ai;
    end
end
a(best_ai)
best_ai
best_ssq
raw_ssq=sum(sum(sample_y-mean(sample_y).^2))
r_square = 1-(best_ssq/raw_ssq)
best_y=exp(-a(best_ai)*abs(x));
plot(x,best_y,'k-')
plot(sample_x,mean(sample_y'),...
    'o','markerfacecolor',[1 .6 .6]*1,'markeredgecolor',[0 0 1]*1,
'markersize',ms)
box on
grid on
xlabel('Difference From Standard')
ylabel('Judged Similarity')
ylim([-.1 1.1])
set(gca,'ytick',[0:.2:1])
text_object=text(0,0,[' a = -.',...
```

Plotting 101

```
    num2str(100*a(best_ai)), newline, 'R^2 = .',num2str(100*r_square,2)],...
    'horizontalalignment','center','fontangle','ital','edgecolor','k')
get(text_object)
shg
```

5.6.3 Unsolved Problem Output

```
ans =
     0
best_ai =
     1
best_ssq =
    117.48
raw_ssq =
    27.144
r_square =
    -3.3282
text_object = 
  Text ( a = -.0, R^2 = .-3.3e+02) with properties:

                   String: {2×1 cell}
                 FontSize: 10
               FontWeight: 'normal'
                 FontName: 'Helvetica'
                    Color: [0 0 0]
      HorizontalAlignment: 'center'
                 Position: [0 0 0]
                    Units: 'data'
  Show all properties
          BackgroundColor: 'none'
             BeingDeleted: 'off'
               BusyAction: 'queue'
             ButtonDownFcn: ''
                 Children: [0×0 GraphicsPlaceholder]
                 Clipping: 'off'
                    Color: [0 0 0]
                CreateFcn: ''
                DeleteFcn: ''
                EdgeColor: [0 0 0]
                  Editing: 'off'
                   Extent: [-4.6482 -0.065965 9.2964 0.13193]
                FontAngle: 'italic'
                 FontName: 'Helvetica'
                 FontSize: 10
            FontSmoothing: 'on'
                FontUnits: 'points'
               FontWeight: 'normal'
         HandleVisibility: 'on'
                  HitTest: 'on'
      HorizontalAlignment: 'center'
              Interpreter: 'tex'
            Interruptible: 'on'
```

```
            LineStyle: '-'
            LineWidth: 0.5
               Margin: 3
               Parent: [1×1 Axes]
        PickableParts: 'visible'
             Position: [0 0 0]
             Rotation: 0
             Selected: 'off'
   SelectionHighlight: 'on'
               String: {2×1 cell}
                  Tag: ''
                 Type: 'text'
        UIContextMenu: [0×0 GraphicsPlaceholder]
                Units: 'data'
             UserData: []
     VerticalAlignment: 'middle'
              Visible: 'on'
```

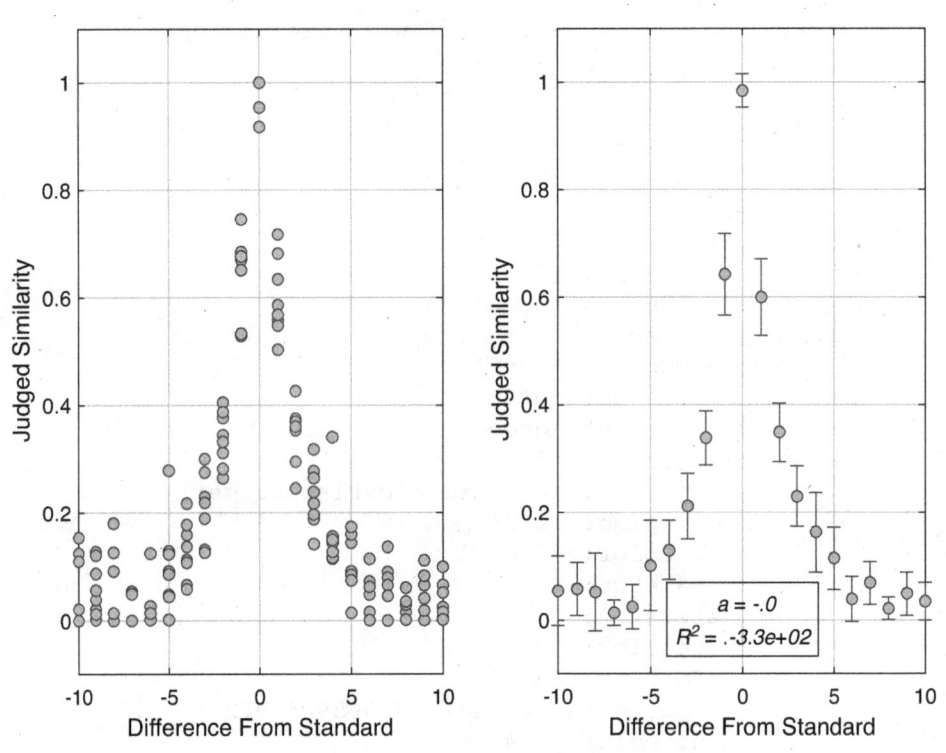

Figure 5.11

5.6.4 Solved Problem Comment

The problem was due to the placement of `ssq=0`. The assignment should be within the for loop where different parameter values (different possible values of a) are evaluated. That way, each time a new possible value of a is evaluated, ssq is reset to zero. That didn't happen in the previous version.

With that error solved, it's worth pointing to two new features of plots that are used here. One is `grid on`, which lets you see a grid. With `grid off`, there is no grid.

The other is `text`. This function has a slew of possible arguments, which you can learn about, as usual, with the `help` command or `doc` command. However, you can also use `get(text_object)`, where `text_object` is the name you created for the text object created with the `text` command. The name simply refers to the text object itself; you could just as easily have called it Pony_Express.

Actually, you don't need to assign text to a variable that serves as input to the `get` function. Instead, you can put the entire text command into `get`. However, creating new variables often helps makes things more readable. The variables named and set in the text command shown here were ones I learned about by using the `get` command.

5.6.5 Solved Problem Code

```
clear all
close all
commandwindow
clc

figure(12)
hold on
x=[-10:.01:10];
a=.5;
y=exp(-a*abs(x));
plot(x,y,'k-')
sample_x=[-10:10];
stdr=.06;   % want someting like .05
ms=5;
n_samples=8;
for sxi=1:size(sample_x,2)
    for nsi=1:n_samples
        sample_y(sxi,nsi)=exp(-a*abs(sample_x(sxi))) + stdr*randn;
    end
end
sample_y(sample_y>1)=1;   % id problem...
sample_y(sample_y<0)=0;   % id problem...
subplot(1,2,1)
plot(sample_x,sample_y,'o',...
    'markerfacecolor',[1 .6 .6]*1,'markeredgecolor',[0 0 1]*1,
'markersize',ms)
box on
grid on
xlabel('Difference From Standard')
ylabel('Judged Similarity')
ylim([-.1 1.1])
set(gca,'ytick',[0:.2:1])

subplot(1,2,2)
hold on
for i=1:size(sample_x,2)
    errorbar(sample_x(i),mean(sample_y(i,:)),std(sample_y(i,:)),'k-')
end
```

104 Plotting

```
% Fit exponential
a=[0:.01:1];
best_ssq=inf;
for ai=1:size(a,2)
    ssq=0;
    for i=1:size(sample_y,1) % the rows corresponding to different differences from standard
        for j=1:size(sample_y,2) % the columns corresponding to different observations
            term_1=exp(-a(ai)*abs(sample_x(i)));
            term_2=sample_y(i,j);
            ssq=ssq+(term_1-term_2)^2;
        end
    end
    if ssq<best_ssq
        best_ssq=ssq;
        best_ai=ai;
    end
end
a(best_ai)
best_ai
best_ssq
raw_ssq=sum(sum(sample_y-mean(sample_y).^2))
r_square = 1-(best_ssq/raw_ssq)
best_y=exp(-a(best_ai)*abs(x));
plot(x,best_y,'k-')
plot(sample_x,mean(sample_y'),'o',...
    'markerfacecolor',[1 .6 .6]*1,'markeredgecolor',[0 0 1]*1,...
    'markersize',ms)
box on
grid on
xlabel('Difference From Standard')
ylabel('Judged Similarity')
ylim([-.1 1.1])
set(gca,'ytick',[0:.2:1])
text_object=text(0,0,[' a = -.',...
    num2str(100*a(best_ai)), newline, 'R^2 = .',num2str(100*r_square,2)],...
    'horizontalalignment','center','fontangle','ital','edgecolor','k')
get(text_object)
shg
```

5.6.6 Solved Problem Output

```
ans =
        0.49
best_ai =
    50
best_ssq =
      0.42636
raw_ssq =
       26.776
```

```
r_square =
    0.98408
text_object =
  Text ( a = -.49, R^2 = .98) with properties:

                   String: {2×1 cell}
                 FontSize: 10
               FontWeight: 'normal'
                 FontName: 'Helvetica'
                    Color: [0 0 0]
      HorizontalAlignment: 'center'
                 Position: [0 0 0]
                    Units: 'data'

  Show all properties
          BackgroundColor: 'none'
             BeingDeleted: 'off'
                BusyAction: 'queue'
             ButtonDownFcn: ''
                 Children: [0×0 GraphicsPlaceholder]
                 Clipping: 'off'
                    Color: [0 0 0]
                CreateFcn: ''
                DeleteFcn: ''
                EdgeColor: [0 0 0]
                  Editing: 'off'
                   Extent: [-2.6439 -0.065965 5.2878 0.13193]
                FontAngle: 'italic'
                 FontName: 'Helvetica'
                 FontSize: 10
            FontSmoothing: 'on'
                FontUnits: 'points'
               FontWeight: 'normal'
         HandleVisibility: 'on'
                  HitTest: 'on'
      HorizontalAlignment: 'center'
              Interpreter: 'tex'
            Interruptible: 'on'
                LineStyle: '-'
                LineWidth: 0.5
                   Margin: 3
                   Parent: [1×1 Axes]
             PickableParts: 'visible'
                 Position: [0 0 0]
                 Rotation: 0
                 Selected: 'off'
        SelectionHighlight: 'on'
                   String: {2×1 cell}
                      Tag: ''
                     Type: 'text'
              UIContextMenu: [0×0 GraphicsPlaceholder]
                    Units: 'data'
                 UserData: []
         VerticalAlignment: 'middle'
                  Visible: 'on'
```

106   *Plotting*

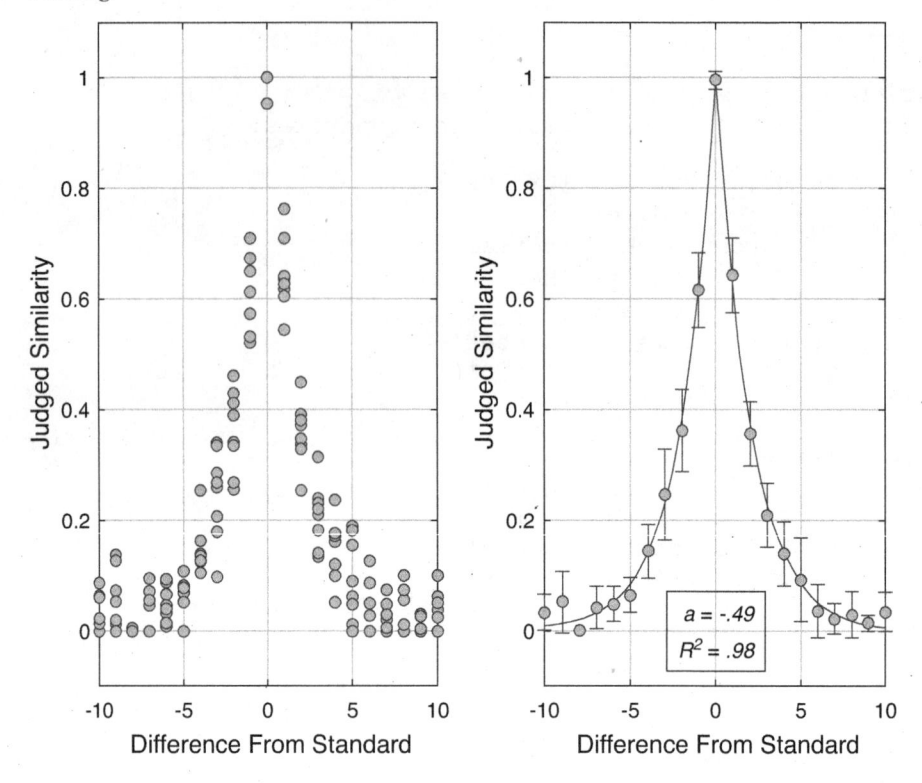

Figure 5.12

5.7   Adding Titles and Comparing Power Versus Exponential Functions

5.7.1   Unsolved Problem Comment

The preceding programs used a power function in the case of the salary data, and an exponential function in the case of perceptual similarity. What's the difference between these two functions, practically speaking?

Here the two functions are shown in the left and right subplots, respectively. An aim of the graphing is to show that plotting a power function in log-log coordinates yields a straight line, whereas plotting an exponential function does not. Also, for the first time in this set of programs, titles are used. A title is added to the top two subplots only. For some reason, no curves appear.

5.7.2   Unsolved Problem Code

```
clear all
close all
commandwindow
clc

figure(13)
x=[0:-.02:1];

% Exponential
y=exp(-2*x);
subplot(2,2,1)
```

```
plot(x,y,'ro-')
title('Exponential','fontweight','normal')
xlabel('x')
ylabel('y')
grid on

subplot(2,2,3)
plot(log(x),log(y),'ro-')
xlabel('log(x)')
ylabel('log(y)')
grid on

% Power
y=x.^-2;
subplot(2,2,2)
plot(x,y,'bo-')
title('Power','fontweight','normal')
xlabel('x')
ylabel('y')
grid on

subplot(2,2,4)
plot(log(x),log(y),'bo-')
xlabel('log(x)')
ylabel('log(y)')
grid on
```

5.7.3 Unsolved Problem Output

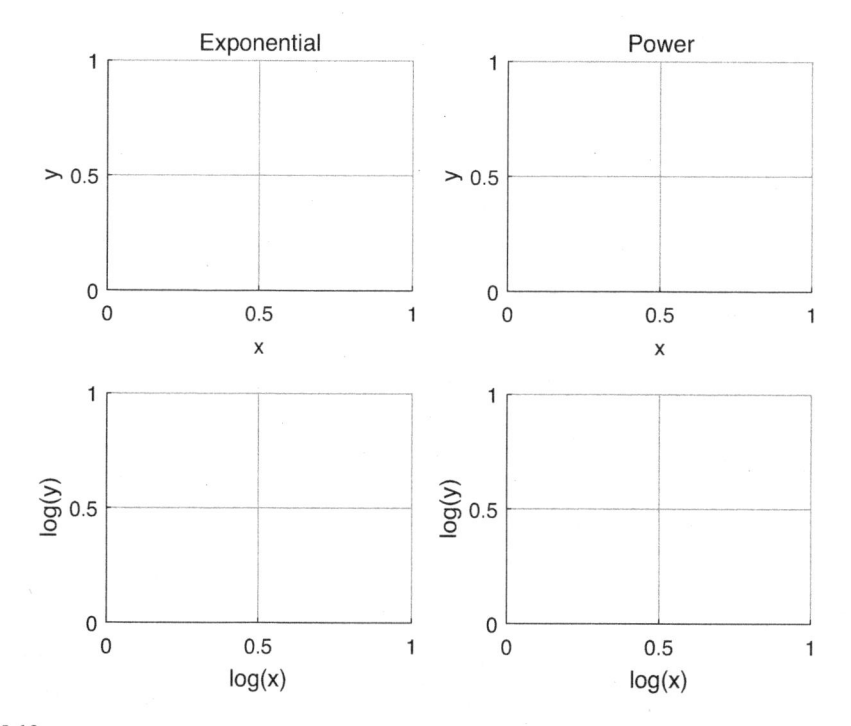

Figure 5.13

108 *Plotting*

5.7.4 Solved Problem Comment

The reason no curves appeared is that the following assignment was undefined: x=[0:-.02:1];. Unfortunately, MATLAB doesn't give an error message equivalent to saying "You can't go from a smaller number to a larger number in negative steps." That one minus sign caused the problem. The broader message is to be on the lookout for tiny, trivial typos that can cause things to fail.

5.7.5 Solved Problem Code

```
clear all
close all
commandwindow
clc

figure(14)
x=[0:.02:1];

% Exponential
y=exp(-2*x);
subplot(2,2,1)
plot(x,y,'ro-')
title('Exponential','fontweight','normal')
xlabel('x')
ylabel('y')
grid on

subplot(2,2,3)
plot(log(x),log(y),'ro-')
xlabel('log(x)')
ylabel('log(y)')
grid on

% Power
y=x.^-2;
subplot(2,2,2)
plot(x,y,'bo-')
title('Power','fontweight','normal')
xlabel('x')
ylabel('y')
grid on

subplot(2,2,4)
plot(log(x),log(y),'bo-')
xlabel('log(x)')
ylabel('log(y)')
grid on
```

5.7.6 Solved Problem Output

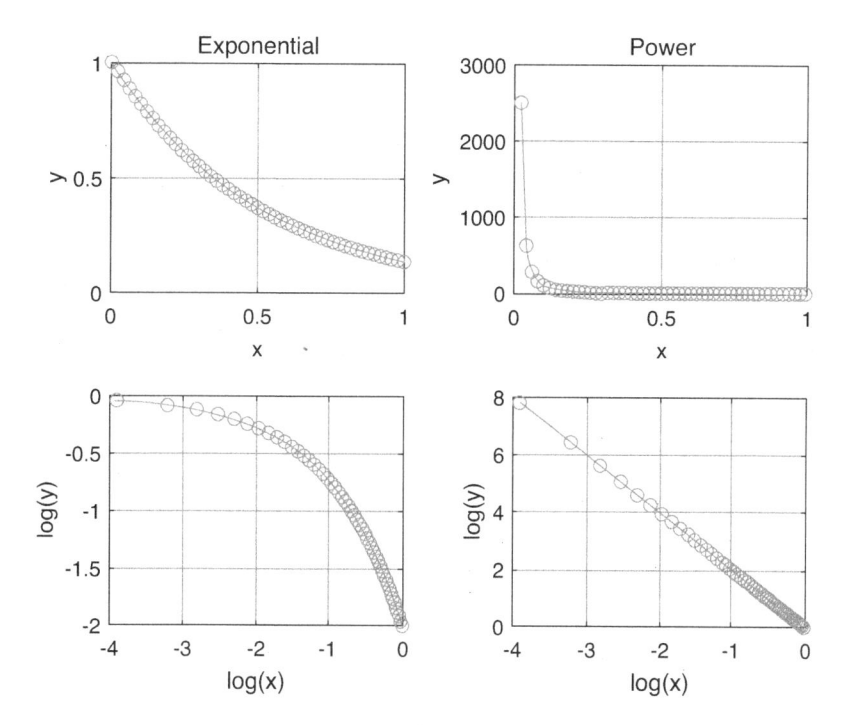

Figure 5.14

5.8 Creating Bar Graphs

5.8.1 Unsolved Problem Comment

This program uses bar graphs. The aim is to show normal distributions centered on different means and with different standard deviations. A further purpose is to show that the range is affected by the standard deviation but not by the mean, whereas the midpoint is affected by the mean but not by the standard deviation.

To make the graphs comparable, the lower bound of x and the upper bound of x are set to the smallest and largest values of all the normal distributions generated ahead of time. This is done by eye.

In this first version of the program, the text boxes for each subplot are messed up for some reason. Can you spot what the reason is?

5.8.2 Unsolved Problem Code

```
clear all
close all
commandwindow
```

110 Plotting

```
clc
figure(15)
n=10000;
n_bins=11;
mean=[-1 1];
standard_deviation=[.01 .5];
subplot_number=0;

% color combinations for the 4 bars. Each row is for a subplot. Each column
% is the proportion of red (column 1), green (column 2), and blue (column 3)
cmp=[
    .75 .50 .25;
    .50 .25 .75
    .25 .75 .50;
    .99 .50 .50];
xp=.67;
yp=.82;
fs=7;

for si=1:size(standard_deviation,2)   % I put this above the mean
loop so the small means would be on the left
    for mi=1:size(mean,2)
        clear R
        R=mean(mi) + standard_deviation(si).*randn(1,n);
        range(R)
        subplot_number=subplot_number+1;
        subplot(size(mean,2),size(standard_deviation,2),subplot_number)
        hist(R,n_bins)
        set(get(gca,'child'),'FaceColor',cmp(subplot_number,1:3));
        xlim_array=xlim;
        ylim_array=ylim;

        text(xlim_array(1)+xp*(xlim_array(2)-xlim_array(1)),...
            ylim_array(1)+yp*(ylim_array(2)-ylim_array(1)),...
            ['mean = ' (mean(mi)), newline, ...
            'std = ' (standard_deviation(mi)), newline, ...
            'range = ' (range(R))],'fontsize',fs,'edgecolor','k');

    end
end
```

5.8.3 Unsolved Problem Output

```
ans =
    0.084955
ans =
    0.076771
ans =
    3.7469
ans =
    3.7666
```

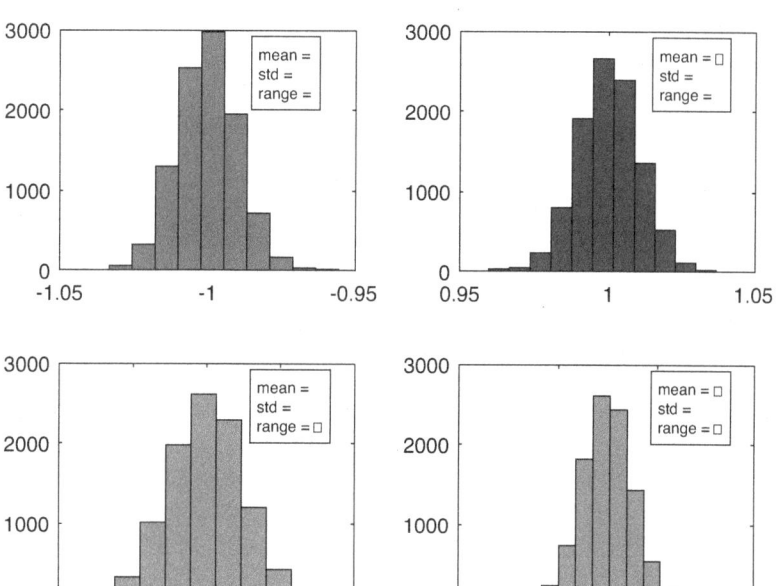

Figure 5.15

5.8.4 Solved Problem Comment

The numbers failed to appear in the text because `num2str` was missing. The `text` command applies to literal strings. The numbers needed to be converted to text strings, which is what `num2str` does.

5.8.5 Solved Problem Code

```
clear all
close all
commandwindow
clc

figure(16)
n=10000;
n_bins=11;
mean=[-1 1];
standard_deviation=[.01 .5];
subplot_number=0;

% color combinations for the 4 bars. Each row is for a subplot. Each column
% is the proportion of red (column 1), green (column 2), and blue (column 3)
cmp=[
    .75  .50  .25;
    .50  .25  .75
    .25  .75  .50;
    .99  .50  .50];
xp=.67;
yp=.82;
fs=7;
```

112 Plotting

```
for si=1:size(standard_deviation,2)
    for mi=1:size(mean,2)
        clear R
        R=mean(mi) + standard_deviation(si).*randn(1,n);
        range(R)
        subplot_number=subplot_number+1;
        subplot(size(mean,2),size(standard_deviation,2),subplot_number)
        hist(R,n_bins)
        set(get(gca,'child'),'FaceColor',cmp(subplot_number,1:3));
        xlim_array=xlim;
        ylim_array=ylim;

        text(xlim_array(1)+xp*(xlim_array(2)-xlim_array(1)),...
            ylim_array(1)+yp*(ylim_array(2)-ylim_array(1)),...
            ['mean = ' num2str(mean(mi)), newline, ...
            'std = ' num2str(standard_deviation(si)), newline, ...
            'range = ' num2str(range(R),2)],'fontsize',fs,'edgecolor','k');
    end
end
```

5.8.6 Solved Problem Output

```
 ans =
     0.085786
 ans =
     0.073254
 ans =
        3.5234
 ans =
        3.7412
```

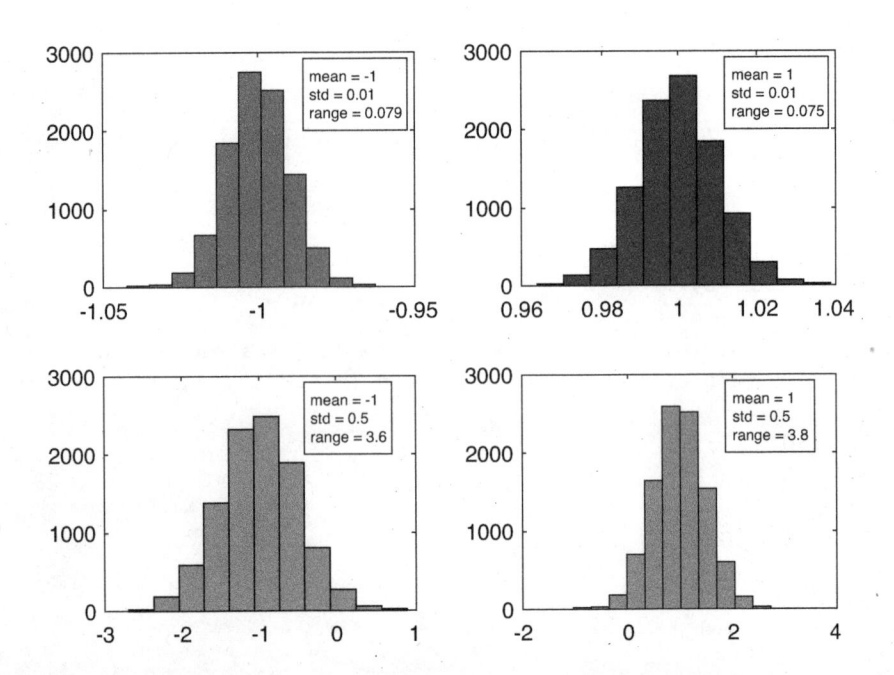

Figure 5.16

5.9 Controlling Bars for Bar Graphs and xtick Labels

5.9.1 Unsolved Problem Comment

Here bars are presented in pairs with different color schemes and with the xlabel being letters. The xlabel is a mess, however.

5.9.2 Unsolved Problem Code

```
clear all
close all
commandwindow
clc
figure(17)
n=8;
bar_shift=.1;
bar_width=.2;
rp=randperm(n)';
data= [rp n+1-rp]
sorted_data=sortrows(data,1);
hold on
bh_1=bar([1:n]-bar_shift,sorted_data(:,1),...
    'barwidth',bar_width,'displayname','Questionnaire 1')
set(bh_1,'FaceColor',[1 1 1]*.9);
bh_2=bar([1:n]+bar_shift,sorted_data(:,2),...
    'barwidth',bar_width,'displayname','Questionnaire 2');
set(bh_2,'FaceColor',[1 1 1]*.6);
set(gca,'xtick',[1:8])
set(gca,'xticklabel',['A','B','C','D','E','F','G','H'])
legend('show','location','north')
xlabel('Item')
ylabel('Number of Agreements')
```

5.9.3 Unsolved Output

```
data =
     1     8
     4     5
     6     3
     8     1
     5     4
     2     7
     7     2
     3     6
bh_1 =
  Bar (Questionnaire 1) with properties:

    BarLayout: 'grouped'
     BarWidth: 0.2
    FaceColor: 'flat'
    EdgeColor: [0 0 0]
    BaseValue: 0
        XData: [0.9 1.9 2.9 3.9 4.9 5.9 6.9 7.9]
        YData: [1 2 3 4 5 6 7 8]
```

114   Plotting

```
Show all properties
```

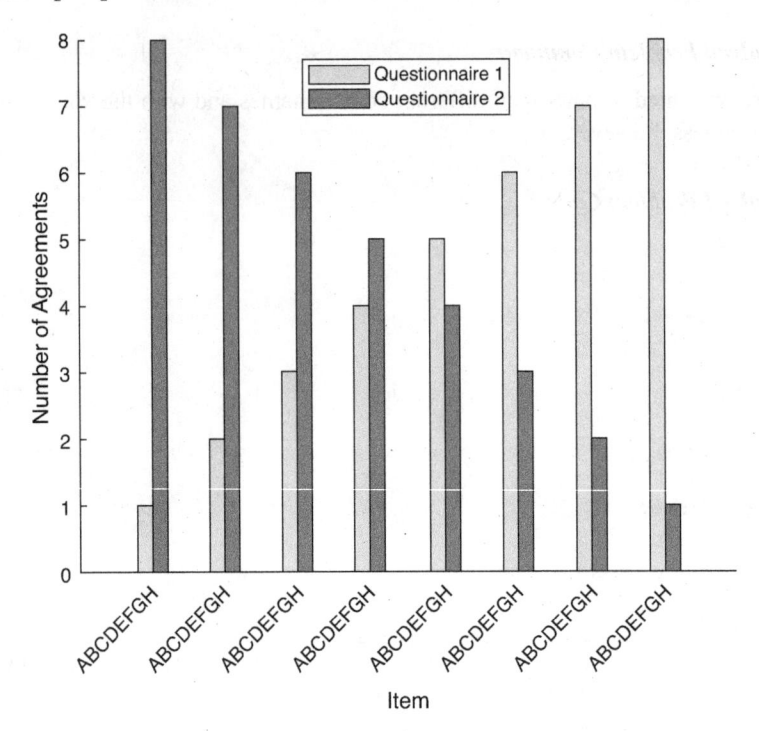

Figure 5.17

5.9.4 Solved Problem Comment

Strings with identical numbers of elements per string need to be separated with semi-colons if they go to `xticklabel` and `yticklabel`. Functionally, they need to occupy different rows of their respective matrices.

5.9.5 Solved Problem Code

```
clear all
close all
commandwindow
clc

figure(18)
n=8;
bar_shift=.1;
bar_width=.2;
rp=randperm(n)';
data= [rp n+1-rp]
sorted_data=sortrows(data,1);
hold on
bh_1=bar([1:n]-bar_shift,sorted_data(:,1),...
    'barwidth',bar_width,'displayname','Questionnaire 1')
set(bh_1,'FaceColor',[1 1 1]*.9)
bh_2=bar([1:n]+bar_shift,sorted_data(:,2),...
    'barwidth',bar_width,'displayname','Questionnaire 2');
```

```
set(bh_2,'FaceColor',[1 1 1]*.6)
set(gca,'xtick',[1:8])
set(gca,'xticklabel',['A';'B';'C';'D';'E';'F';'G';'H'])
legend('show','location','north')
xlabel('Item')
ylabel('Number of Agreements')
```

5.9.6 Solved Problem Output

```
data =
      6     3
      5     4
      3     6
      2     7
      1     8
      8     1
      7     2
      4     5
bh_1 =
  Bar (Questionnaire 1) with properties:

    BarLayout: 'grouped'
     BarWidth: 0.2
    FaceColor: 'flat'
    EdgeColor: [0 0 0]
    BaseValue: 0
        XData: [0.9 1.9 2.9 3.9 4.9 5.9 6.9 7.9]
        YData: [1 2 3 4 5 6 7 8]
  Show all properties
```

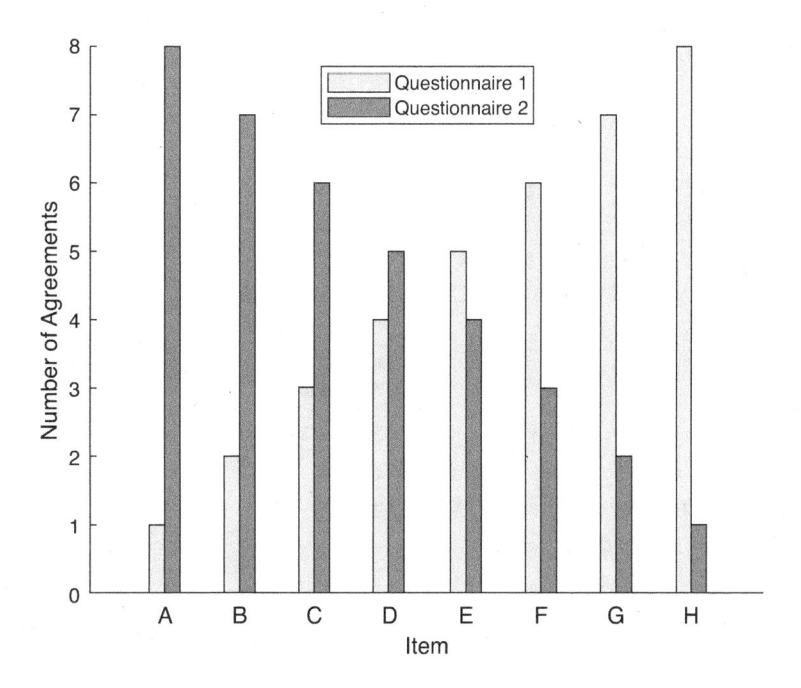

Figure 5.18

5.10 Thinking Clearly While "Bar Hopping"

5.10.1 Unsolved Problem Comment

You want to see a bar graph reflecting the probability that participants say "Yes" to a stimulus whose magnitude on some dimension exceeds the magnitude of a standard on that dimension. For example, subjects are shown a line length and are supposed to say "Yes" if the next line they see is longer than the standard, or "No" if the next line they see is not longer. You expect p("Yes") to grow with the size of the difference, but the graph you get doesn't look like that. Either your hypothesis and prediction are wrong, or there is a mistake in the code.

5.10.2 Unsolved Problem Code

```
clear all
close all
commandwindow
clc

figure(19)
ms=8; % markersize
hold on
stim=[-6:6];
n_stim=size(stim,2);
n_observations=500;
sdev=3;
for si=1:n_stim
    n_yeses(si)=0;
    for oi=1:n_observations
        if stim(si)+sdev*randn<stim(si)
            n_yeses(si)=n_yeses(si)+1;
        end
    end
end
n_yeses=n_yeses./n_observations;
bar(stim,n_yeses)
colormap([1 1 1]*.8)
for si=1:n_stim
    se_binomial=((n_yeses(si)*(1-n_yeses(si)))/n_observations).^.5;
    errorbar(stim(si),n_yeses(si),se_binomial,'k.-','markersize',ms)
end
xlim([min(stim)-1 max(stim)+1])
xLim=xlim;
ylim([0 1.05])
plot([xLim(1) xLim(2)],[.5 .5],'k--') % dashed line at chance
xlabel('Difference From Standard')
ylabel('p(''Yes'')')  % how to display quote marks
box on
```

5.10.3 Unsolved Output

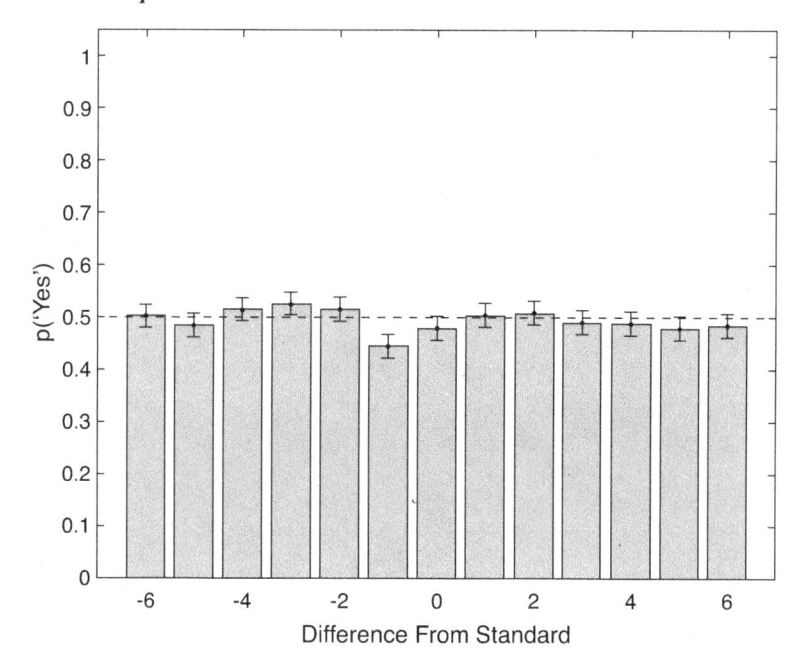

Figure 5.19

5.10.4 Solved Problem Comment

There was a bad line of code: `if stim(si)+sdev*randn<stim(si)`. This was simply a mistake of math or logic. The corrected line is `if sdev*randn<stim(si)`. The mistake was to add in the value of `stimulus(si)` to the random draw. The take-home message is to be as clear as possible in your thinking. The error in the last code example wasn't contrived by the author to show a possible mistake. It arose because I was confused at the moment. Feeling confused from time to time is normal, and you can often run code that you feel confused about and use the error feedback you get to help you see what's wrong (or right) about the code.

5.10.5 Solved Problem Code

```
clear all
close all
commandwindow
clc

figure(20)
ms=8; % markersize
hold on
stim=[-6:6];
n_stim=size(stim,2);
n_observations=500;
```

118 Plotting

```
sdev=3;
for si=1:n_stim
    n_yeses(si)=0;
    for oi=1:n_observations
        if sdev*randn<stim(si)
            n_yeses(si)=n_yeses(si)+1;
        end
    end
end
n_yeses=n_yeses./n_observations;
bar(stim,n_yeses)
colormap([1 1 1]*.8)
for si=1:n_stim
    se_binomial=((n_yeses(si)*(1-n_yeses(si)))/n_observations).^.5;
    errorbar(stim(si),n_yeses(si),se_binomial,'k-','markersize',ms)
end
xlim([min(stim)-1 max(stim)+1])
xLim=xlim;
ylim([0 1.05])
plot([xLim(1) xLim(2)],[.5 .5],'k--') % dashed line at chance
xlabel('Difference From Standard')
ylabel('p(''Yes'')')  % this is how to display quote marks
box on
```

5.10.6 Solved Problem Output

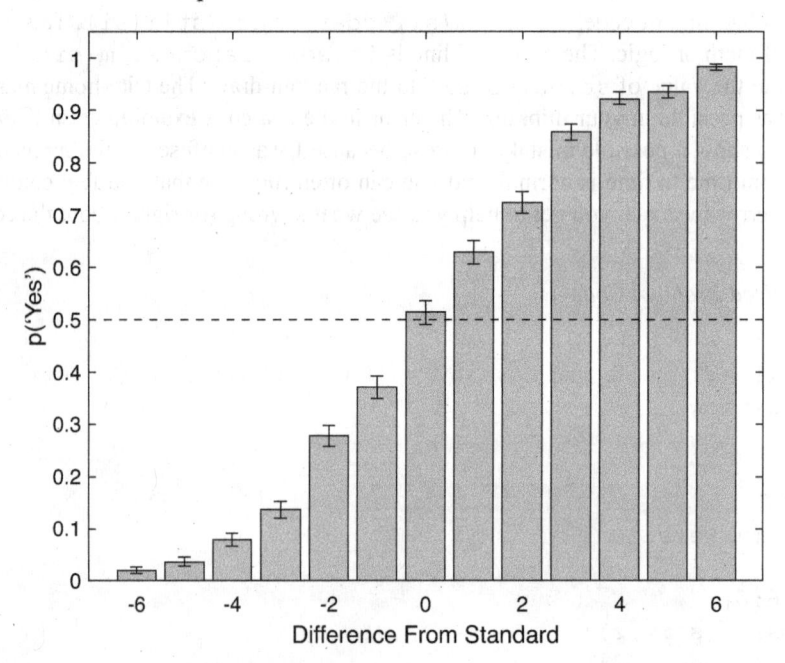

Figure 5.20

6 Input-Output

MATLAB is often used with other applications. For example, it is often used with Microsoft Excel to read in data and/or write data to Excel, especially for use by non-MATLAB users. MATLAB is also used to moderate interactions between users and the computer, as in running dialogs with users to gather information or in providing images for users to respond to by, for example, clicking points of interest. This chapter is concerned with such uses of MATLAB.

6.1 Writing to Excel

6.1.1 Unsolved Problem Comment

The aim of this program is to generate a matrix and export it to Excel. The program identifies the most typical student in a class of n_students and then assigns students to different training methods depending on whether they are below or not below the typical student's score. There is a problem with exporting the matrix to Excel, however. The error message makes it sound like there is an error in the `xlswrite` function because the line number referred to in the error message goes beyond the current section of this program. Did the programmers at Mathworks actually make a mistake in the code they wrote for `xlswrite`?

6.1.2 Unsolved Problem Code

```
clear all
close all
commandwindow
clc

mu=80;
sigma=5;
n_students=20;
min_diff_thusfar=100;
exceptional_score=9;
scores=mu + randn(n_students,1)*sigma;
scores(:,2)=abs(scores-mean(scores));
for k = 1:length(scores)
    difference = abs(scores(k)-mean(scores));
    if difference <  min_diff_thusfar
        min_diff_thusfar = difference;
        most_typical_student = k;
    end
```

120 *Input-Output*

```
end
most_typical_student
criterion=scores(most_typical_student)
for si=1:n_students
    if scores(si,1)<criterion
        training_method=1;
    else
        training_method=2;
    end
    scores_plus(si,:)=[scores(si,1:2) training_method];
end
% add 0 for unexceptional score or 1 for exceptional score to column 4
for si=1:n_students
    if scores(si,2)<exceptional_score
        outlier=0;
    else
        outlier=1;
    end
    scores_plus(si,4)=outlier;
end
sorted_scores_plus=sortrows(scores_plus,3);
scores_plus_plus=[[1:size(scores_plus,1)]' sorted_scores_plus]
xlswrite(scores_plus_plus,'Student_Scores.xls')
```

6.1.3 Unsolved Problem Output

```
most_typical_student =
     1
criterion =
       74.027
scores_plus_plus =
            1        71.986         7.7463          1          0
            2        72.812         6.9212          1          0
            3        74.027         5.7062          2          0
            4        79.996         0.26286         2          0
            5        77.726         2.0069          2          0
            6        77.79          1.9427          2          0
            7        80.768         1.0355          2          0
            8        80.541         0.80782         2          0
            9        82.402         2.6691          2          0
           10        76.039         3.6937          2          0
           11        86.296         6.5628          2          0
           12        79.645         0.087741        2          0
           13        77.375         2.3574          2          0
           14        84.276         4.5436          2          0
           15        84.944         5.2116          2          0
           16        76.342         3.3911          2          0
           17        77.709         2.024           2          0
           18        87.905         8.1722          2          0
           19        80.34          0.607           2          0
           20        85.737         6.0046          2          0
```

```
Error using xlswrite (line 172)
File name must be a character vector.
```

6.1.4 Solved Problem Comment

The problem was that the order of arguments in xlswrite should be the filename followed by the name of the exported data, not the reverse.

6.1.5 Solved Problem Code

```
clear all
close all
commandwindow
clc

mu=80;
sigma=5;
n_students=20;
min_diff_thusfar=100;
exceptional_score=9;
scores=mu + randn(n_students,1)*sigma;
scores(:,2)=abs(scores-mean(scores));

for k = 1:length(scores)
    difference = abs(scores(k)-mean(scores));
    if difference <  min_diff_thusfar
        min_diff_thusfar = difference;
        most_typical_student = k;
    end
end
most_typical_student
criterion=scores(most_typical_student)
for si=1:n_students
    if scores(si,1)<criterion
        training_method=1;
    else
        training_method=2;
    end
    scores_plus(si,:)=[scores(si,1:2) training_method];
end
% add 0 for unexceptional score or 1 for exceptional score to column 4
for si=1:n_students
    if scores(si,2)<exceptional_score
        outlier=0;
    else
        outlier=1;
    end
    scores_plus(si,4)=outlier;
end
sorted_scores_plus=sortrows(scores_plus,3);
scores_plus_plus=[[1:size(scores_plus,1)]' sorted_scores_plus]

xlswrite('Student_Scores.xls',scores_plus_plus)
```

6.1.6 Solved Problem Output

```
most_typical_student =
     1
criterion =
    79.162
scores_plus_plus =
         1        77.783        2.5941        1        0
         2        78.256        2.1212        1        0
         3        75.822        4.5549        1        0
         4        73.484        6.8927        1        0
         5        78.985        1.3924        1        0
         6        73.527        6.8502        1        0
         7        78.091        2.286         1        0
         8        77.047        3.33          1        0
         9        73.163        7.2143        1        0
        10        79.162        1.2151        2        0
        11        85.193        4.8157        2        0
        12        85.191        4.8144        2        0
        13        79.488        0.88913       2        0
        14        87.762        7.3845        2        0
        15        83.315        2.9382        2        0
        16        80.96         0.58267       2        0
        17        80.239        0.13769       2        0
        18        89.986        9.6087        2        1
        19        83.871        3.4937        2        0
        20        86.217        5.8399        2        0
```

6.2 Writing to Excel With Column Headers Using the array2table Function

6.2.1 Unsolved and Solved Problem Comment

The aim of this program is to write a table with column headings and then export the table to Excel. (The same problem will be tackled in a different way in Problem 6.6.) The program uses the function `array2table`, which makes it possible to add column headers. There is an error, however, which is evident in the Excel spreadsheet that is produced (not shown here). Each individual letter of `col_header` occupies its own column.

The problem with the column heading format can be solved by using a construct that has not been formally introduced yet, but is introduced here to address this problem (and will be covered in more detail in the next chapter). The solution is to replace straight brackets with curly braces. Curly braces let you use cells, which allow for different numbers of elements in analogous positions, unlike straight brackets which do not. This makes it possible to have column headings (literal strings) that have different numbers of elements per string. The unsolved version is shown here along with the solved version just to save space.

6.2.2 Unsolved and Solved Problem Code

```
clear all
close all
```

```
commandwindow
clc

mu=80;
sigma=5;
n_students=20;
min_diff_thusfar=100;
scores=mu + randn(n_students,1)*sigma;
scores(:,2)=abs(scores-mean(scores));
for k = 1:length(scores)
    difference = abs(scores(k)-mean(scores));
    if difference <  min_diff_thusfar
        min_diff_thusfar = difference;
        most_typical_student = k;
    end
end
most_typical_student
criterion=scores(most_typical_student)
for si=1:n_students
    if scores(si,1)<criterion
        training_method=1;
    else
        training_method=2;
    end
    scores_plus(si,:)=[scores(si,1:2) training_method];
end
for si=1:n_students %creates outlier column tracking if absdifference > 9
    if scores(si,2)<9
        outlier=0;
    else
        outlier=1;
    end
    scores_plus(si,4)=outlier;
end
sorted_scores_plus=sortrows(scores_plus,3);
scores_plus_plus=[[1:size(scores_plus,1)]' sorted_scores_plus]
scores_plus_plus_table = ...
    array2table(scores_plus_plus,...
    'VariableNames',{'student','score',...
    'abs_difference','training_group','outlier'})
xlswrite('David_Table_Without_Col_Heads.xlsx',scores_plus_plus)

% Include row names and column names in another excel spreadsheet
% Bad code (commented)
col_header=['student','scores','abs_difference','training_group','outlier'];
% Good code (uncommented)
%
col_header={'student','scores','abs_difference','training_group','outlier'};
xlswrite('David_Table_With_Col_Heads.xls',...
    col_header,'Sheet1','A1');   %Write column header
```

124 Input-Output

```
xlswrite('David_Table_With_Col_Heads.xls',...
    scores_plus_plus,'Sheet1','A2'); %Write data
```

6.2.3 Solved Problem Output

```
most_typical_student =
     8
criterion =
     79.547
scores_plus_plus =
         1       70.53      8.8374        1        0
         2       76.054     3.3136        1        0
         3       74.639     4.7282        1        0
         4       73.769     5.5981        1        0
         5       72.383     6.9838        1        0
         6       77.387     1.9802        1        0
         7       76.591     2.7762        1        0
         8       75.559     3.808         1        0
         9       80.044     0.6767        2        0
        10       82.815     3.4478        2        0
        11       82.007     2.6402        2        0
        12       86.874     7.5064        2        0
        13       79.547     0.17948       2        0
        14       79.926     0.559         2        0
        15       83.595     4.2282        2        0
        16       83.218     3.8511        2        0
        17       88.015     8.6476        2        0
        18       81.717     2.3495        2        0
        19       80.857     1.4897        2        0
        20       81.817     2.45          2        0
scores_plus_plus_table =
  20×5 table
```

student	score	abs_difference	training_group	outlier
1	70.53	8.8374	1	0
2	76.054	3.3136	1	0
3	74.639	4.7282	1	0
4	73.769	5.5981	1	0
5	72.383	6.9838	1	0
6	77.387	1.9802	1	0
7	76.591	2.7762	1	0
8	75.559	3.808	1	0
9	80.044	0.6767	2	0
10	82.815	3.4478	2	0
11	82.007	2.6402	2	0
12	86.874	7.5064	2	0
13	79.547	0.17948	2	0
14	79.926	0.559	2	0
15	83.595	4.2282	2	0

16	83.218	3.8511	2	0
17	88.015	8.6476	2	0
18	81.717	2.3495	2	0
19	80.857	1.4897	2	0
20	81.817	2.45	2	0

6.3 Writing Out and Reading Back in a .dlm file

6.3.1 Unsolved Problem Comment

MATLAB allows for several formats for writing out and reading in data. I have found that .dlm files are easiest to use, and I recommend their use.

The aim of this program is to write out a file in .dlm format and then read it back in to check that it survived the export-import process. The data that are read back in should match the data written out. The data file in this case is trivial because the point being made doesn't really depend on the size of the data file. The test yields a positive result, but is the test informative? Could it possibly yield a negative result?

6.3.2 Unsolved Problem Code

```
clear all
close all
commandwindow
clc

S=[1 2 3 4]
dlmwrite('Data_For_dlm_Check',S)
old_S=S;
dlmread('Data_For_dlm_Check')
new_S=S;
equality_of_old_S_and_new_S=isequal(old_S,new_S)
```

6.3.3 Unsolved Problem Output

```
S =
     1     2     3     4
ans =
     1     2     3     4
equality_of_old_S_and_new_S =
  logical
   1
```

6.3.4 Solved Problem Comment

The test could not have failed because of a simple logic error. The identical array, S, was assigned to old_S and new_S, so old_S and new_S *had* to be the same no matter what happened with dlmwrite or dlmread. The problem is fixed here by assigning the originally written data to old_S and by assigning the newly read data to new_S.

126   Input-Output

6.3.5 Solved Problem Code

```
clear all
close all
commandwindow
clc

S=[1 2 3 4]
dlmwrite('Data_For_dlm_Check',S)
old_S=S;
new_S=dlmread('Data_For_dlm_Check')
equality_of_old_S_and_new_S=isequal(old_S,new_S)
```

6.3.6 Solved Problem Output

```
S =
     1     2     3     4
new_S =
     1     2     3     4
equality_of_old_S_and_new_S =
  logical
   1
```

6.4 Avoiding Overwriting Existing Files

6.4.1 Unsolved Problem Comment

It is often important to avoid overwriting files. Suppose, for example, that data reach you from subjects at different locations. There is imperfect communication between or among the labs at those locations. You may already have data from some subjects and don't want to overwrite any subject's data with data from someone else. You want to assign a unique subject number to each of the subjects tested, and since subject number is arbitrary for this particular study, such a numbering scheme is acceptable.

Here fictional data are generated in two runs. The first output file was assigned to subject 1, so the second output file should be assigned to subject 2. The program doesn't work, however. It generates just one file, for subject 1.

6.4.2 Unsolved Problem Code

```
clear all
close all
commandwindow
clc

for run_through=1:2
% generate fictional data for this subject whose filename number is uncertain
    n_data=20;
    clear data
    RT=1000+randn(n_data,1)*50;
    Heart_Rate=80+randn(n_data,1)*10;
    data=[RT Heart_Rate]
```

```
    % now assign a fresh subject number to this subject
    possible_si=0;
    new_subject=false;
    while new_subject==false
        possible_si=possible_si+1;
        if ~exist(['data_for_subject',num2str(possible_si),'.csv'])
            si=possible_si
            new_subject=true;
            subject_col(1:n_data,1)=si;
            data=[subject_col data];
            csvwrite(['data_for_subject_',num2str(si),'.csv'],data)
        end
    end
end % for run_through=1:2
```

6.4.3 Unsolved Problem Output

```
data =
        1013.2         86.885
        955.32          58.12
        992.16         74.813
        1039.5         94.198
        968.98         87.793
        1022.5         76.345
        941.15         69.551
        1043.6         80.237
        941.78         71.962
        957.91         73.342
         927.3         77.119
        1062.8          76.25
        1047.8         79.866
        1008.3         85.482
        1045.9         90.831
        992.58         84.959
        1009.1         83.258
        1043.9         82.385
        914.04         60.548
        1016.9         77.064
si =
     1
data =
        1065.7         93.513
        1071.8         89.445
        991.77         76.996
         911.2         78.503
          1014          84.67
        985.35         86.996
        959.64         87.722
        911.72         83.484
```

128 Input-Output

```
        950.2        87.666
        951.66       79.193
        929.72       86.899
        908.11       63.391
        994.68       84.895
       1017.4        56.479
       1069.2        98.763
       1060.9        85.91
       1082.2        87.259
        998.99       75.082
       1021.8        68.172
        943.39       66.941
si =
     1
```

6.4.4 Solved Problem Comment

The mistake was a low-level clerical error which, truth be told, I made inadvertently and took quite a bit of time to spot. There was an underscore in one mention of the file name but not in the other. No matter how advanced or seemingly advanced your objectives in programming may be, low-level clerical errors can still dog you.

6.4.5 Solved Problem Code

```
clear all
close all
commandwindow
clc

for run_through=1:2
% generate fictional data for this subject whose filename number is uncertain
    n_data=20;
    clear data
    RT=1000+randn(n_data,1)*50;
    Heart_Rate=80+randn(n_data,1)*10;
    data=[RT Heart_Rate]

    % now assign a fresh subject number to this subject
    possible_si=0;
    new_subject=false;
    while new_subject==false
        possible_si=possible_si+1;
        if ~exist(['data_for_subject_',num2str(possible_si),'.csv'])
            si=possible_si
            new_subject=true;
            subject_col(1:n_data,1)=si;
            data=[subject_col data];
            csvwrite(['data_for_subject_',num2str(si),'.csv'],data)
```

```
        end
    end
end % for run_through=1:2
```

6.4.6 Solved Problem Output

```
data =
        1039.9          70.071
        940.27          73.149
        1093.4          64.842
        906.41          74.236
        1045.4          78.955
        1042.2          79.075
        996.68          88.526
        1089.9          92.241
        1130.5          87.835
        1023.5          69.12
        914.24          82.688
        940.98          67.015
        942.83          78.826
        1074.9          83.215
        964.56          83.828
        872.36          83.418
        1036.6          84.077
        973.94          76.974
         963.8          78.421
        997.26          73.688
si =
     2
data =
        962.54          82.976
        999.06          84.497
        952.17          79.347
          1021          86.296
        989.61          75.962
          1016          62.631
         956.3          75.317
        1019.6          78.937
        972.08          69.762
        975.46          83.445
        965.81          78.188
        986.08          94.452
        981.41          69.469
        1064.9          59.867
        1017.8          82.273
        963.95         100.71
        967.84          82.962
        1086.5          95.736
        969.37          73.766
          1023          95.553
```

130   Input-Output

```
si =
     3
```

6.5   Formatting Data Printouts

6.5.1   Unsolved Problem Comment

It is often important to format data printouts. Here the aim is to create pseudo-data and print them out to check the formatting before saving the data to a text file. A problem arises, however. The printed data aren't readable because they go on and on "forever" in one line. A less glaring problem, but one that's there nonetheless and needs to be addressed, is that in the unformatted data the decimal points (if they exist) don't line up.

6.5.2   Unsolved Problem Code

```
clear all
close all
commandwindow
clc

n_subjects=20;
clear data
for si=1:n_subjects
    subject_id=-inf;
    while (subject_id<1000) | (subject_id>9999)
        subject_id=randi(10000);
    end
    RT=1000+randn*50;
    Heart_Rate=80+randn*10;
    data(si,1:4)=[si subject_id RT Heart_Rate];
end
disp('Unformatted data')
data
disp('')

disp('Formatted data')
fprintf('\n');
for row=1:size(data,1)
    fprintf('%4d',data(row,1));
    fprintf('%12d',data(row,2));
    fprintf('%12.2f',data(row,3:4));
end
```

6.5.3   Unsolved Problem Output

```
Unformatted data
data =
           1        1202      1030.8      79.305
           2        6764      957.55      69.015
           3        8670      1041.9      85.867
```

4	1187	927.62	77.114
5	8285	956.44	84.923
6	4740	1030.4	67.584
7	2702	981.25	83.974
8	1074	1004.9	95.262
9	5424	1114.2	80.664
10	4432	952.21	73.3
11	8172	1041.5	93.207
12	3394	1076	87.752
13	8657	968.22	82.123
14	4277	967.51	73.365
15	6094	974.88	73.573
16	9533	1053.5	86.682
17	6234	1033.5	85.936
18	1309	1060	65.049
19	9842	989.94	91.596
20	8392	1009.7	69.738

Formatted data

```
   1      1202    1030.78      79.31     2     6764     957.55
69.01    3       8670    1041.92      85.87     4     1187     927.62
77.11    5       8285     956.44      84.92     6     4740    1030.39
67.58    7       2702     981.25      83.97     8     1074    1004.85
95.26    9       5424    1114.18      80.66    10     4432     952.21
73.30   11       8172    1041.49      93.21    12     3394    1075.97
87.75   13       8657     968.22      82.12    14     4277     967.51
73.37   15       6094     974.88      73.57    16     9533    1053.54
86.68   17       6234    1033.55      85.94    18     1309    1059.96
65.05   19       9842     989.94      91.60    20     8392    1009.70
69.74>>
```

6.5.4 Solved Problem Comment

No command was given to insert line returns. Having line returns in one's mind does not get the computer to insert them. Returns are now generated.

6.5.5 Solved Problem Code

```
clear all
close all
commandwindow
clc

n_subjects=20;
clear data
for si=1:n_subjects
    subject_id=-inf;
    while (subject_id<1000) | (subject_id>9999)
        subject_id=randi(10000);
    end
```

132 Input-Output

```
        RT=1000+randn*50;
        Heart_Rate=80+randn*10;
        data(si,1:4)=[si subject_id RT Heart_Rate];
end
disp('Unformatted data')
data
disp('')

disp('Formatted data')
fprintf('\n');
for row=1:size(data,1)
    fprintf('%4d',data(row,1));
    fprintf('%12d',data(row,2));
    fprintf('%12.2f',data(row,3:4));
    fprintf('\n');
end

% save formatted data to a text file after first opening (creating) and
% being sure to close the file after data have been written to it
fid = fopen('david_week_5_formatted_data.txt','wt');
for row=1:size(data,1)
    fprintf(fid,'%4d',data(row,1));
    fprintf(fid,'%12d',data(row,2));
    fprintf(fid, '%12.2f',data(row,3:4));
    % Good code added
    fprintf('\n');   % insert a line return

end
fclose(fid);
```

6.5.6 Solved Problem Output

```
Unformatted data
data =
             1        1444         962.3        62.384
             2        6272        957.14        89.009
             3        2656        1026.6        81.616
             4        2477        1021.7        75.353
             5        6165        1002.2        55.825
             6        1266        1005.2        74.325
             7        5000        970.14        96.431
             8        2354        986.33        65.317
             9        8319        1015.9        89.525
            10        4438          1014        88.269
            11        5712        969.47        79.923
            12        9471        1077.5        68.644
            13        5217        921.15        84.665
            14        7712         925.5        66.365
            15        4731        989.04        69.592
            16        4551          1036        81.296
```

```
               17          9471         1023.7        65.677
               18          1308         973.66        85.607
               19          7578         940.91        77.724
               20          8975         900.21        73.193
Formatted data

                1          1444         962.30        62.38
                2          6272         957.14        89.01
                3          2656        1026.61        81.62
                4          2477        1021.73        75.35
                5          6165        1002.16        55.82
                6          1266        1005.23        74.33
                7          5000         970.14        96.43
                8          2354         986.33        65.32
                9          8319        1015.87        89.52
               10          4438        1013.99        88.27
               11          5712         969.47        79.92
               12          9471        1077.51        68.64
               13          5217         921.15        84.66
               14          7712         925.50        66.37
               15          4731         989.04        69.59
               16          4551        1036.00        81.30
               17          9471        1023.70        65.68
               18          1308         973.66        85.61
               19          7578         940.91        77.72
               20          8975         900.21        73.19
```

6.6 Creating Formatted Data and Headers for Excel

6.6.1 Unsolved Problem Comment

In an earlier program (Program 6.2), the `array2table` function was used to create column headers for an Excel spreadsheet. Here another approach is taken. This approach just uses standard data formatting.

The aim of the program is to assign letter grades to students based on their scores. The student numbers and letter grades are to be printed out and saved to an Excel file. The first row, generated before the student loop is begun, has the column headings.

In this demonstration program, the scores are random integers. The cutoff score for each grade is listed explicitly to help the instructor make sure s/he is assigning letter grades correctly. This is an instance where more compact code might be possible, but helping the user feel secure may be just as important or even more so. (Chapter 1 spoke about the acceptability of less than super-streamlined code.)

Oddly, the program sometimes fails. MATLAB sometimes gives an error message to the effect that the variable called letter is undefined. Whether it does depends on the random integers that are generated.

6.6.2 Unsolved Problem Code

```
clear all
close all
```

134 *Input-Output*

```
commandwindow
clc

n_students=20;
max_grade=100;

score(1:n_students,1:2)=[[1:n_students]' randi(max_grade,n_students,1)]
disp(' ')
fid_xls=fopen('Grades.xls','w');
fprintf('%s \t %s \n', 'Student_ID', 'Letter_Grade');
fprintf(fid_xls,'%s \t %s \n', 'Student_ID', 'Letter_Grade');

for i=1:size(score,1)

    if score(i,2) >= 64
        letter='D-';
    end
    if score(i,2) >= 67
        letter='D';
    end
    if score(i,2) >= 70
        letter='D+';
    end
    if score(i,2) >= 73
        letter='C-';
    end
    if score(i,2) >= 76
        letter='C';
    end
    if score(i,2) >= 79
        letter='C+';
    end
    if score(i,2) >= 82
        letter='B-';
    end
    if score(i,2) >= 85
        letter='B';
    end
    if score(i,2) >= 88
        letter='B+';
    end
    if score(i,2) >= 91
        letter='A-';
    end
    if score(i,2) >= 94
        letter='A';
    end
    if score(i,2) >= 97
        letter='A+';
    end
```

```
        fprintf('%d \t %s \n', score(i,1), letter)
        fprintf(fid_xls,'%d \t %s \n', score(i,1),letter);

end
fclose(fid_xls);
```

6.6.3 Unsolved Problem Output

```
score =
       1    49
       2    71
       3    55
       4    37
       5    95
       6    80
       7    91
       8    21
       9    29
      10    13
      11    40
      12    97
      13     4
      14    45
      15    51
      16    69
      17    21
      18     8
      19    97
      20    13

Student_ID   Letter_Grade
Undefined function or variable 'letter'.
```

6.6.4 Solved Problem Comment

The problem occurred because if a student's score was less than 64, no letter was given. Starting every student with the default letter of 'F' solves this problem.

6.6.5 Solved Problem Code

```
clear all
close all
commandwindow
clc

n_students=20;
max_grade=100;

score(1:n_students,1:2)=[[1:n_students]' randi(max_grade,n_students,1)]
disp(' ')
```

136 Input-Output

```
fid_xls=fopen('Grades.xls','w');
fprintf('%s \t %s \n', 'Student_ID', 'Letter_Grade');
fprintf(fid_xls,'%s \t %s \n', 'Student_ID', 'Letter_Grade');

for i=1:size(score,1)
    letter='F';

    if score(i,2) >= 64
        letter='D-';
    end
    if score(i,2) >= 67
        letter='D';
    end
    if score(i,2) >= 70
        letter='D+';
    end
    if score(i,2) >= 73
        letter='C-';
    end
    if score(i,2) >= 76
        letter='C';
    end
    if score(i,2) >= 79
        letter='C+';
    end
    if score(i,2) >= 82
        letter='B-';
    end
    if score(i,2) >= 85
        letter='B';
    end
    if score(i,2) >= 88
        letter='B+';
    end
    if score(i,2) >= 91
        letter='A-';
    end
    if score(i,2) >= 94
        letter='A';
    end
    if score(i,2) >= 97
        letter='A+';
    end

    fprintf('%d \t %s \n', score(i,1), letter)
    fprintf(fid_xls,'%d \t %s \n', score(i,1),letter);

end
fclose(fid_xls);
```

6.6.6 Solved Problem Output

```
score =
     1    36
     2    84
     3    59
     4    55
     5    92
     6    29
     7    76
     8    76
     9    39
    10    57
    11     8
    12     6
    13    54
    14    78
    15    94
    16    13
    17    57
    18    47
    19     2
    20    34

Student_ID Letter_Grade
1  F
2  B-
3  F
4  F
5  A-
6  F
7  C
8  C
9  F
10 F
11 F
12 F
13 F
14 C
15 A
16 F
17 F
18 F
19 F
20 F
```

6.7 Interacting With Users Via the input Function

6.7.1 Unsolved Problem Comment

This program is written to have people interact with a computer via MATLAB's input function. There is a problem, however. If users just hit the Enter key, the message that comes back is nonsensical.

138   *Input-Output*

6.7.2   Unsolved Problem Code

```
clear all
close all
commandwindow
clc

name = input('What is your name? ', 's');
sprintf('Hello, %s, I will try to help you.', name)
```

6.7.3   Unsolved Problem Output

```
What is your name?
ans =
    'Hello, , I will try to help you.'
```

6.7.4   Solved Problem Comment

The problem is solved by requiring an actual character, not just the Enter key.

6.7.5   Solved Problem Code

```
clear all
close all
commandwindow
clc

name_gotten=false;
while name_gotten==false
    name = input('What is your name? ', 's');
    if ~isempty(name)
        sprintf('Hello, %s, I will try to help you.', name)
        name_gotten=true;
    else
        sprintf('Oops, be sure to type something, and not just hit the Enter key.')
    end
end
```

6.7.6   Solved Problem Output

```
What is your name?
ans =
    'Oops, be sure to type something, and not just hit the Enter key.'
What is your name? David
ans =
    'Hello, David, I will try to help you.'
```

6.8 Looking for Particular Inputs

6.8.1 Unsolved Problem Comment

This program interacts with users in a more extended way. It uses \n to insert a line break and checks that the input from the user is acceptable. The only acceptable inputs are letters, either lowercase or uppercase. To avoid typing every lowercase and every uppercase letter in the acceptable class (not an impossible task but a laborious one), it helps to create the variable `lower_case_letter_doubles`, to which `double(['a' 'z'])` is assigned. Similarly, it is helpful to create the variable `upper_case_letter_doubles` to which `double(['A' 'Z'])` is assigned.

There is a problem, however. When a typical text-based name is typed in and the computer is supposed to greet the user with that name, it spits out numbers, as shown here when the name that is typed happens to be Al (short for Alan, which is chosen for this example because it has just two letters, capital A and lower-case "el"). The computer replies, 'Hello, 65, I will try to help you now.'

6.8.2 Unsolved Problem Code

```
clear all
close all
commandwindow
clc

% list numerical equivalents of the lower-case letters from 'a' through 'z'
double(['a' 'z'])
% list numerical equivalents of the upper-case letters from 'A' through 'Z'
double(['A' 'Z'])
lower_case_letter_doubles=double(char([97:122]))
upper_case_letter_doubles=double(char([65:90]))
both_case_letter_doubles=[lower_case_letter_doubles
upper_case_letter_doubles];

% initiate and carry out the conversation
conversation_OK=false; % initialized to false but can become true
need_to_scold=false; % initialized to false but can become true
while conversation_OK==false
    clc
    if need_to_scold==true
        disp(['Sorry but that''s not in my lexicon.'])
    end
    name = input(['What is your name?\n' ...
        'Please don''t put in characters other than letters or you''ll confuse me! '], 's');

    if ~isempty(name)    % Don't accept Enter key alone
        % Check if name is letters.
        OK_string=true;
```

140 *Input-Output*

```
            for i=1:length(name)
                OK_letter(i)=false;
                for j=1:length(both_case_letter_doubles)
                    if double(name(i))==both_case_letter_doubles(j)
                        OK_letter(i)=true;
                    end
                end
                if OK_letter(i)==false
                    OK_string=false;
                    break
                end
            end
            if OK_string==true
                conversation_OK=true;
                sprintf('Hello, %d, I will try to help you now.', name)
            else
                need_to_scold=true;
            end
        end % while conversation_OK==false
end
```

6.8.3 Unsolved Problem Output

```
What is your name?
Please don't put in characters other than letters or you'll
confuse me! Al
ans =
    'Hello, 65, I will try to help you now.Hello, 108, I will try
to help you now.'
```

6.8.4 Solved Problem Comment

There was one bad line, or one line with one bad character. The bad line was `sprintf('Hello, %d, I will try to help you now. ', name)`. Changing `%d` to `%s` solves the problem because `%s` tells MATLAB to display a string (literal text). By contrast, `%d` tells MATLAB to display integers—in this case, the integers corresponding to the letters corresponding to the letters in the name.

6.8.5 Solved Problem Code

```
clear all
close all
commandwindow
clc

name_gotten=false;
while name_gotten==false
    name = input('What is your name? ', 's');
    if ~isempty(name)
        sprintf('Hello, %s, I will try to help you.', name)
```

```
            name_gotten=true;
        else
            sprintf('Oops, be sure to type something, and not just
hit the Enter key.')
        end
    end
end
```

6.8.6 Solved Problem Output

```
What is your name?
Please don't put in characters other than letters or you'll confuse me! Al
ans =
    'Hello, Al, I will try to help you now.'
```

6.9 Checking Users' Email Addresses

6.9.1 Unsolved Problem Comment

This is a program to collect and check emails. The user is prompted to enter an email address. The idea is to have the user input the email twice, being unable to see the first entry while entering the second. A reminder is given to include the @ sign. The problem with this version of the program is that even if the user does enter the @ sign, the program keeps asking for it. You can finally break out using Ctrl-c.

6.9.2 Unsolved Problem Code

```
clear all
close all
commandwindow
clc
emails_match=false;
while emails_match == false
    characters_bad=true;
    while characters_bad==true
        email=...
            input(...
            ['Please enter your email. Make sure it has an @ sign. '],...
            's');
        if ~contains(email,'@')
            disp(['Oops, I''m' ' not seeing a @'])
        end
    end % while characters_bad==true
    clc
    characters_bad=true;
    while characters_bad==true
        email_2=...
            input(...
            ['Please confirm your email by re-entering it.' ...
            'Again make sure it has an @ sign. '],'s');
```

142 *Input-Output*

```
            if ~contains(email,'@')
                disp(['Oops, I''m' ' not seeing a @'])
            end
        end % while characters_bad==true
        clc
        if email == email_2
            disp (['Thank you, your email has been entered.']);
            emails_match=true;
        else
            disp(['Your confirmation did not match.'...
                'Please enter your email address again.']);
        end
end
```

6.9.3 Unsolved Problem Output

```
Please enter your email. Make sure it has an @ sign. david.rosenbaum@ucr.edu
Please enter your email. Make sure it has an @ sign. david.rosenbaum@ucr.edu
Please enter your email. Make sure it has an @ sign.
```

6.9.4 Solved Problem Comment

The problem arose because the Boolean variable `characters_bad` remained true even if @ was entered. So this was just a logic error, not an error pertaining to input-output requirements per se. The output that is shown below is the last line that appeared in the command window because the screen was cleared after every email entry.

6.9.5 Solved Problem Code

```
clear all
close all
commandwindow
clc

emails_match=false;
while emails_match == false
    characters_bad=true;
    while characters_bad==true
        email=input ([...
            'Please enter your email. Make sure it has an @ sign. '],'s');
        if ~contains(email,'@')
            disp(['Oops, I''m' ' not seeing a @'])
        else characters_bad=false;    % leave out for error!!!
        end
    end % while characters_bad==true
    clc

    characters_bad=true;
    while characters_bad==true
        email_2=input(...
```

```
            ['Please confirm your email by re-entering it.'...
            'Again make sure it has an @ sign. '],'s');
        if ~contains(email_2,'@')
            disp(['Oops, I''m' ' not seeing a @'])
        else characters_bad=false;    % leave out for error!!!
        end
    end % while characters_bad==true
    clc
    if email == email_2
        disp (['Thank you, your email has been entered.']);
        emails_match=true;
    else
        disp (['Your confirmation did not match.'...
            'Please enter your email address again.']);
    end
end
```

6.9.6 Solved Problem Output

```
Thank you, your email has been entered.
```

6.10 Clicking on Figures and Saving Figures

6.10.1 Problem Comment (Solved Only)

This program shows dots in a circle. Participants are supposed to click on the one dot whose diameter differs from all the others. The position of the target dot is uncertain. The other independent variable, besides the position of the target dot, is how different the target dot's size is from the size of the other distractor dots.

This code is provided to offer an example of a fairly elaborate program for stimulus presentation and data collection. Although mistakes were made along the way, none was sufficiently novel or instructive to warrant showing it.

Images of the displays and clicked positions are saved as .tif files. Just one of the display images is shown here.

6.10.2 Problem Code (Solved Only)

```
clear all
close all
commandwindow
clc

n_stim=8; % number of stimuli arrayed around an imaginary circle
max_angle=((n_stim-1)/n_stim)*(2*pi); % the largest angle out from the center
of the imaginary circle where the stim with the largest number appears
stim_angle=linspace(0,max_angle,n_stim); % the possible angles
out from the center of the imaginary circle
stim_dist=1; % distance of each dot from the center
x_center=0; % the x value of the center
```

```
y_center=0; % the y value of the center
ms=14;   % markersize
stim_radius=.15; % the default radius of each dot

fill_angles=linspace(0,2*pi,360); % angles needed to fill each dot
with a [red green blue] combination
n_trials=4;  % number of trials

min_scp = .5; % minimum size change proportion of the target
stim relative to distractors
max_scp = 1.5; % minimum size change proportion of the target
stim relative to distractors

data=[];  % initialize data
for trial=1:n_trials
    odd_stim=randperm(n_stim,1);  % which stim will be the odd one
    scp = min_scp+rand*(max_scp-min_scp);

    % set figure number and fill the screen with the figure.
    % the values for 'OuterPosition' were gotten by clicking on the
    % "blowup" icon when the figure was shown to make it as big as
    % possible, and then the author used get(gcf) to find the position
values.
    set(figure(trial),...
        'units','normalized', 'OuterPosition',[-0.005 0.10389 1.01 0.905])
    hold on
    axis square
    axis off
    xlim([-stim_dist-1 stim_dist+1])
    ylim([-stim_dist-1 stim_dist+1])
    xL=xlim; % need this for filling the screen; can't use xlim directly
    yL=ylim; % need this for filling the screen; can't use ylim directly
    for si=1:n_stim
        if si==odd_stim
            temp_stim_radius=stim_radius*scp;
        else
            temp_stim_radius=stim_radius;
        end
        acceptable_distance(si)=temp_stim_radius;
        fill...
            (x_center+stim_dist*cos(stim_angle(si))+...
            temp_stim_radius*cos(fill_angles),...
            y_center+stim_dist*sin(stim_angle(si))+...
            temp_stim_radius*sin(fill_angles),...
            [1 1 1]*.5);
    end %for si=1:n_stim

    % collect response click
    a_target_has_been_clicked=false;
    while a_target_has_been_clicked==false
```

```
            [x_click y_click]=ginput(1);  % have user click on target
showing crosshairs
        for si=1:n_stim

            if (abs(x_click-(x_center+stim_dist*cos(stim_angle(si)))) < ...
                    acceptable_distance(si)) && ...
                    (abs(y_click-(y_center+stim_dist*sin(stim_angle(si)))) <
...
                    acceptable_distance(si))

                a_target_has_been_clicked=true;
                clicked_stim=si;
                if clicked_stim == odd_stim
                    text(x_center,y_center,...
                        'Correct','horizontalalignment','center')
                    accuracy=1;
                else
                    text(x_center,y_center,...
                        'Incorrect','horizontalalignment','center')
                    accuracy=0;
                end
                data=[data; ...
                    trial si clicked_stim odd_stim scp ...
                    accuracy x_click  x_center+stim_dist*cos(stim_angle(si))
...
                    y_click  y_center+stim_dist*sin(stim_angle(si)) ...
                    ]
                break

            end
        end % for si=1:n_stim
    end %  while a_target_has_been_clicked==false
    plot(x_click,y_click,'k+','markersize',40)
    saveas(gcf,['figure_',num2str(trial),'.tif'])
    pause(1)  % pause for 1 second
    % clear the figure window; then have it fill computer screen again
    set(figure(trial),'units','normalized',...
    'OuterPosition',[-0.005 0.10389 1.01 0.905])

end %  for trial=1:n_trials
data

% end of block feedback
set(figure(trial+1),'units','normalized',...
    'OuterPosition',[-0.005 0.10389 1.01 0.905])
hold on
axis square
axis off
xlim([-stim_dist-1 stim_dist+1])
ylim([-stim_dist-1 stim_dist+1])
```

146 *Input-Output*

```
xL=xlim;  % need this for filling screen
yL=ylim;  % need this for filling screen
text(x_center,y_center,['Total correct trials out of ' ...
    num2str(n_trials) ' =  ' num2str(sum(data(:,5))),...
    newline,'Hit enter when done'], ...
    'horizontalalignment','center')
saveas(gcf,['end_of_block,.tif'])
```

6.10.3 Problem Output (Solved Only)

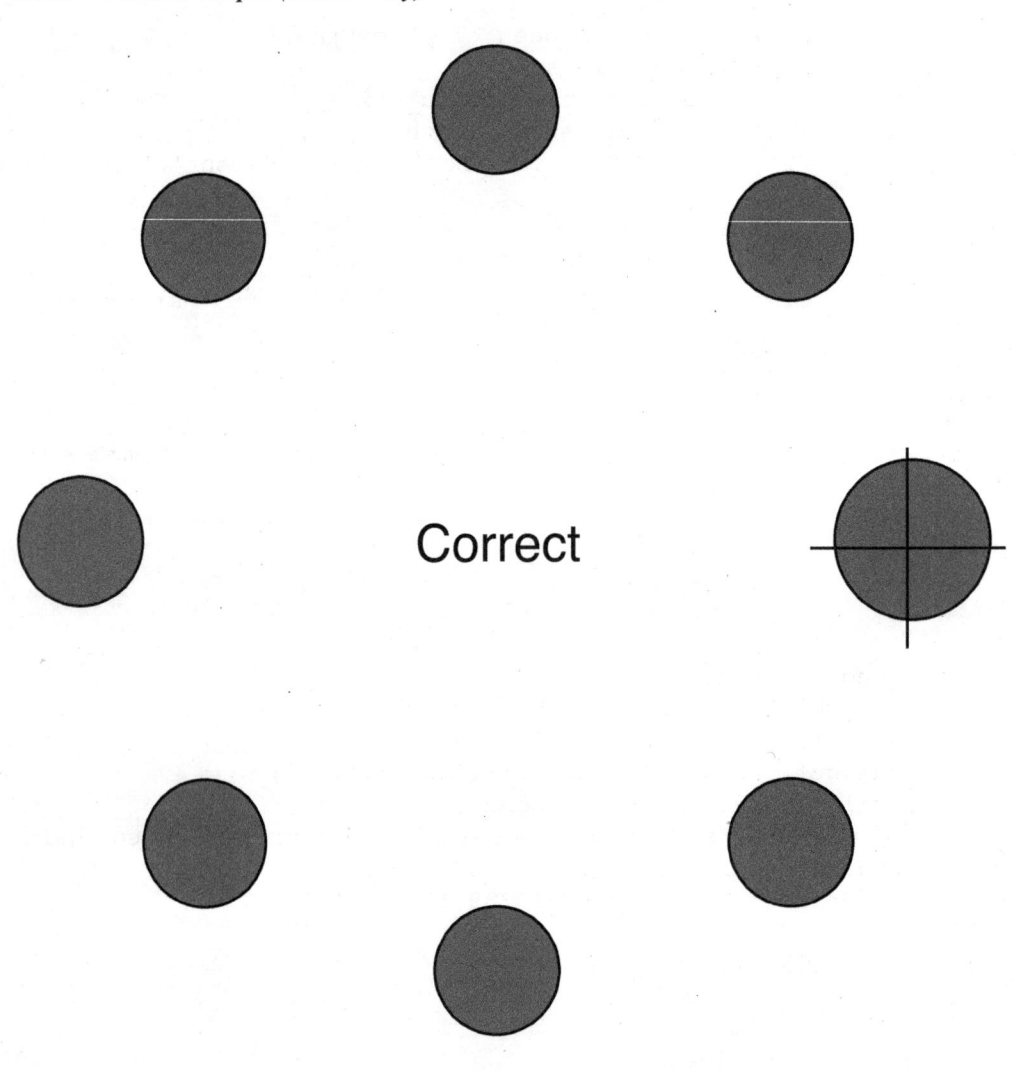

Figure 6.1

7 Data Types

MATLAB uses a variety of data types, including the following, which were obtained by typing `help class` in the command line:

```
double           -- Double precision floating point number array
                    (this is the traditional MATLAB matrix or array)
single           -- Single precision floating point number array
logical          -- Logical array
char             -- Character array
cell             -- Cell array
struct           -- Structure array
function_handle  -- Function Handle
int8             -- 8-bit signed integer array
uint8            -- 8-bit unsigned integer array
int16            -- 16-bit signed integer array
uint16           -- 16-bit unsigned integer array
int32            -- 32-bit signed integer array
uint32           -- 32-bit unsigned integer array
int64            -- 64-bit signed integer array
uint64           -- 64-bit unsigned integer array
<class_name>     -- MATLAB class name for MATLAB objects
<java_class>     -- Java class name for java objects
```

By default, numbers are of type `double`, but they can be "demoted" (requiring half as much storage space) to single precision, as in this one-line program, which is followed by the output that ensues:

```
x=1, class(x), x=single(x), class(x)
x =
     1
ans =
    'double'
x =
  single
     1
ans =
    'single'
```

148 *Data Types*

Arrays of type `logical` are Boolean and can take just two values: 1 for "true" or 0 for "false." You have encountered Boolean values in this book. You have also encountered literal strings (characters surrounded with single quote marks), which are of type `char`.

This chapter will focus on two other data types: cells (`cell` in the listing above) and structures (`struc` in the listing above).

Cells have advantages over matrices, and structures have advantages over cells. Cells allow for different numbers of elements in different rows, whereas matrices do not. Cells also allow for different types of data within them, whereas matrices do not. A cell variable, which is identified as such because it is surrounded by curly braces, { }, can have data of type double *and* data of type char, for example. By contrast, a matrix, which is identified as such because it is surrounded by square brackets, [ ], can have data of only one type: double or char, for example.

Structures have advantages over cells (and matrices). The structure is the most versatile data type for our purposes. A structure can have fields of different kinds and numbers. One way to think of a structure is as a hierarchy of fields. A given field can be conceived of as a variable, represented, say, by a matrix of size 1 × 1. It in turn is a member of a larger set of variables, which can in turn be a member of a larger set, and so on. So if your office number is 1135, for example, that office number may be within a building called Psychology, and that building may be within a university called UC Riverside, which may be in a university system called UC (the University of California system). Your office (or my office at the time of this writing) could then be written UC(6).Building(12).Office(1135) provided UCR is the sixth UC campus, Psychology is the 12th building on the UCR campus, and so on. A great feature of structures is that if a given branch of the hierarchy, such as a building, has one sort of element such as one or more offices, that doesn't mean all buildings must have that same number of offices. It's not even necessary that all buildings have offices. A building associated with Agriculture might have pig pens. A building associated with Psychology probably wouldn't, though you should see what my office looks like sometimes!

7.1 Using Cells to Concatenate Double and Char Variables

7.1.1 Unsolved Problem Comment

Suppose you want to concatenate variables of two different types: numbers of type double and a string of type char. You might want to do this to add the word 'Apple' to the end of the listing for values 1, 2, 3, in columns 1, 2, and 3, respectively.

When you try to do this, the result isn't what you want. MATLAB turns the numbers (of type double) into 'garbage' characters. The command `whos` reveals that Matrix, which you intended to consist of numbers (of type double) and a word (of type string), has been transformed into one type, char.

7.1.2 Unsolved Problem Code

```
clear all
close all
commandwindow
clc

numbers=[1:3]
word='Apple'
Matrix=[numbers,word]
```

```
disp(' ')
whos
```

7.1.3 Unsolved Problem Output

```
numbers =
     1     2     3
word =
    'Apple'
Matrix =
    '_____Apple'

  Name           Size             Bytes  Class     Attributes

  Matrix         1x8                 16  char
  numbers        1x3                 24  double
  word           1x5                 10  char
```

7.1.4 Solved Problem Comment

The problem arose because a matrix, which is delimited by straight brackets, cannot have different data types within it, such as double and char. By contrast, a cell, which is surrounded by curly braces, *can* have different data types. Knowing this, you use curly braces. The whos command reveals that the new variable, called Cell, is indeed of that type.

7.1.5 Solved Problem Code

```
clear all
close all
commandwindow
clc

numbers=[1:3]
Matrix=[numbers, 'Apple']
Cell={numbers,'Apple'}
whos
```

7.1.6 Solved Problem Output

```
numbers =
     1     2     3
Matrix =
    '_____Apple'
Cell =
  1×2 cell array
    [1×3 double]    'Apple'
  Name           Size             Bytes  Class     Attributes

  Cell           1x2                258  cell
  Matrix         1x8                 16  char
  numbers        1x3                 24  double
```

150 Data Types

7.2 Seeing Cell Contents

7.2.1 Unsolved Problem Comment

In the last program, when you issued the `whos` command, you got

```
Cell =
    1×2 cell array
    [1×3 double]    'Apple'
```

However, you didn't get to see the contents of Cell. You attempt to do so here, but the result isn't very satisfying. You don't get an error message, but you also don't see numbers for the first part of Cell. You decide to explore this issue further by creating a cell with 2 rows, attempting to see the second number in the first row. The command you issue for this purpose yields an error message.

7.2.2 Unsolved Problem Code

```
clear all
close all
commandwindow
clc

clear all
close all
commandwindow
clc

numbers=[1:3]
Matrix=[numbers, 'Apple']
Cell={numbers,'Apple'}
Cell_With_2_Rows={numbers;'Apple'}
who
Cell{1,:}
Cell_With_2_Rows{1,2}
```

7.2.3 Unsolved Problem Output

```
numbers =
     1    2    3
Matrix =
    '_____Apple'
Cell =
  1×2 cell array
    [1×3 double]    'Apple'
Cell_With_2_Rows =
  2×1 cell array
    [1×3 double]
    'Apple'

Your variables are:
Cell              Cell_With_2_Rows  Matrix              numbers
```

```
ans =
     1     2     3
ans =
    'Apple'
Index exceeds matrix dimensions.
```

7.2.4 Solved Problem Comment

The problem is solved with a mix of curly braces and parentheses.

7.2.5 Solved Problem Code

```
clear all
close all
commandwindow
clc

numbers=[1:3]
Matrix=[numbers, 'Apple']
Cell={numbers,'Apple'}
Cell_With_2_Rows={numbers;'Apple'}
who
Cell{1,:}

Cell_With_2_Rows{1}     % what are the values of row 1 all columns?
Cell_With_2_Rows{1}(2)  % what is value of row 1, column 2?
Cell_With_2_Rows{2}     % what are the values of row 2, all columns?
Cell_With_2_Rows{2}(2)  % what is value of row 2, column 2?
```

7.2.6 Solved Problem Output

```
numbers =
     1     2     3
Matrix =
    '                   Apple'
Cell =
  1×2 cell array
    [1×3 double]    'Apple'
Cell_With_2_Rows =
  2×1 cell array
    [1×3 double]
    'Apple'

Your variables are:

Cell              Cell_With_2_Rows   Matrix            numbers
ans =
     1     2     3
ans =
    'Apple'
ans =
     1     2     3
ans =
     2
```

152 *Data Types*

```
ans =
    'Apple'
ans =
    'p'
```

7.3 Using Cells to Allow for Tick Labels With Different Numbers of Characters

7.3.1 Unsolved Problem Comment

You want to have the words 'Near' and 'Far' as xticklabels for a bar graph, but when you do this the program crashes.

7.3.2 Unsolved Problem Code

```
clear all
close all
commandwindow
clc

bar([0 1],[1 2]);
colormap([1 1 1]*.85)
set(gca,'xtick',[0 1],'xticklabel',['Near'; 'Far']),
xlim([-.5 1.5])
```

7.3.3 Unsolved Problem Output

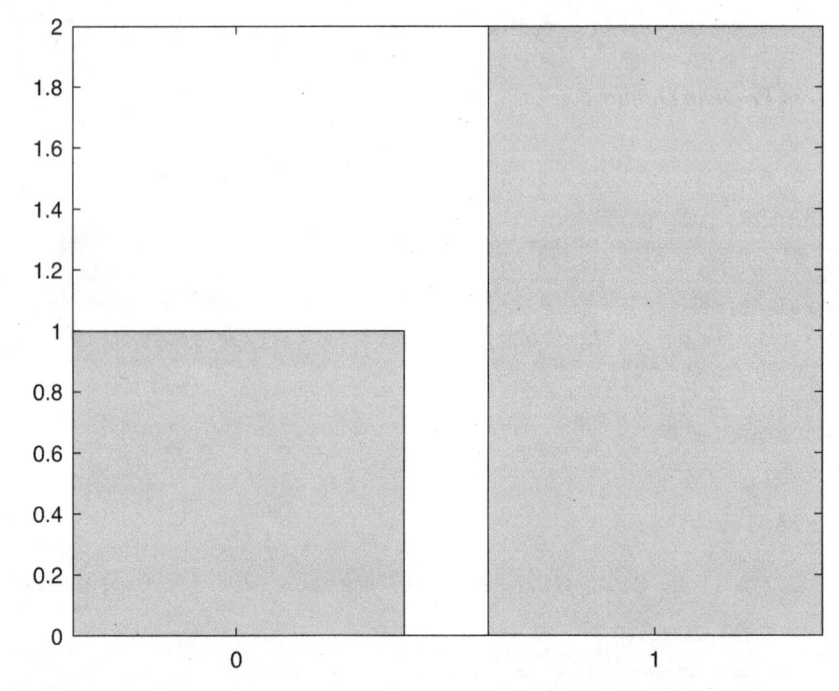

Figure 7.1

```
Dimensions of matrices being concatenated are not consistent.
```

7.3.4 Solved Problem Comment

The words 'Near' and 'Far' have different numbers of letters. 'Near' has four letters. 'Far' has three. If you surround 'Near'; 'Far' with brackets, you tell MATLAB to treat the list as a matrix with 2 rows, the first row with 4 columns, and the second row with 3 columns. But a matrix cannot have different numbers of columns in different rows. Cells save the day here. Replacing the square brackets with curly braces solves the problem.

7.3.5 Solved Problem Code

```
clear all
close all
commandwindow
clc

bar([0 1],[1 2]);
colormap([1 1 1]*.85)
set(gca,'xtick',[0 1],'xticklabel',{'Near'; 'Far'}),
xlim([-.5 1.5])
```

7.3.6 Solved Problem Output

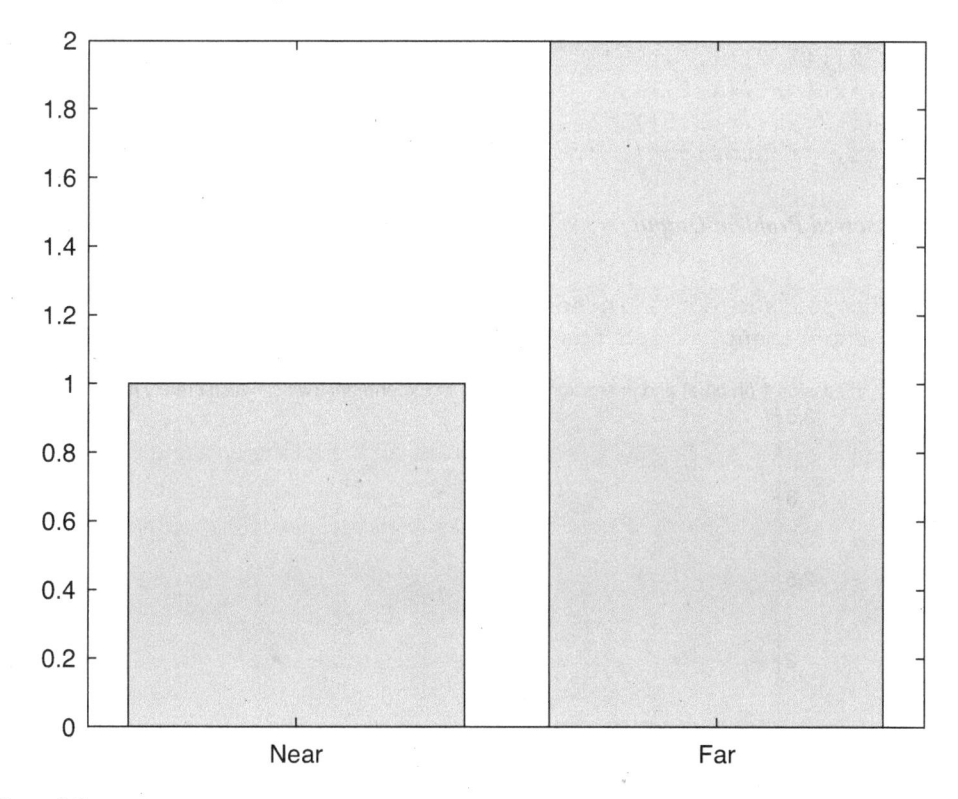

Figure 7.2

7.4 Using Cells to Allow for Figure Titles With Different Numbers of Characters per Row

7.4.1 Unsolved Problem Comment

You'd like to put a return in the title of a figure, but when you try to do so, a problem arises.

7.4.2 Unsolved Problem Code

```
clear all
close all
commandwindow
clc

subject=1;
string_1=['Data for subject ', num2str(subject), ' in session 1 (in blue)'];
string_2=[' and in session 2 (in red) in Experiment 3'];
string_3=['which wasn''t really my favorite experiment.'];

str=[string_1, string_2, string_3]

title(str, 'fontweight', 'normal');   % this turns off bold
figure(1)
hold on
plot([1 2],[1 2],'.b--')
plot([1 2],[1 2]+1,'.r--')
set(gca,'xtick',[1 2])
axis([.75 2.25 .5 3.5])
title(str, 'fontweight', 'normal');
```

7.4.3 Unsolved Problem Output

```
str =
    'Data for subject 1 in session 1 (in blue) and in session 2 (in red) in Experiment 3which wasn't really my favorite experiment.'
```

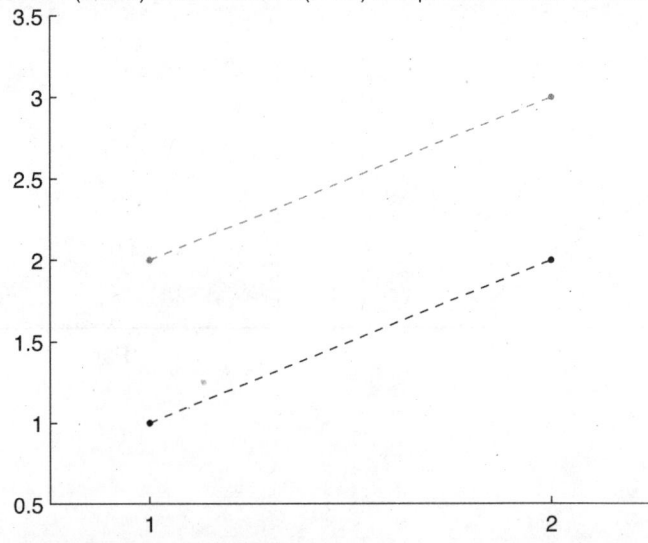

Figure 7.3

7.4.4 Solved Problem Comment

Cells save the day again. Semi-colons were needed when string_1, string_2, and string_3 were assigned to str, but because of the different lengths of the strings, they needed to be surrounded by curly braces (for a cell) rather than by straight brackets (for a matrix).

7.4.5 Solved Problem Code

```
clear all
close all
commandwindow
clc

subject=1;
string_1=['Data for subject ', num2str(subject), ' in session 1 (in blue)'];
string_2=['and in session 2 (in red) in Experiment 3,'];
string_3=['which wasn''t really my favorite experiment.'];

str={string_1; string_2; string_3}

title(str, 'fontweight', 'normal');   % this turns off bold
figure(1)
hold on
plot([1 2],[1 2],'.b--')
plot([1 2],[1 2]+1,'.r--')
set(gca,'xtick',[1 2])
axis([.75 2.25 .5 3.5])
title(str, 'fontweight', 'normal');
```

7.4.6 Solved Problem Output

```
str =
  3×1 cell array
    'Data for subject 1 in session 1 (in blue)'
    'and in session 2 (in red) in Experiment 3,'
    'which wasn't really my favorite experiment.'
```

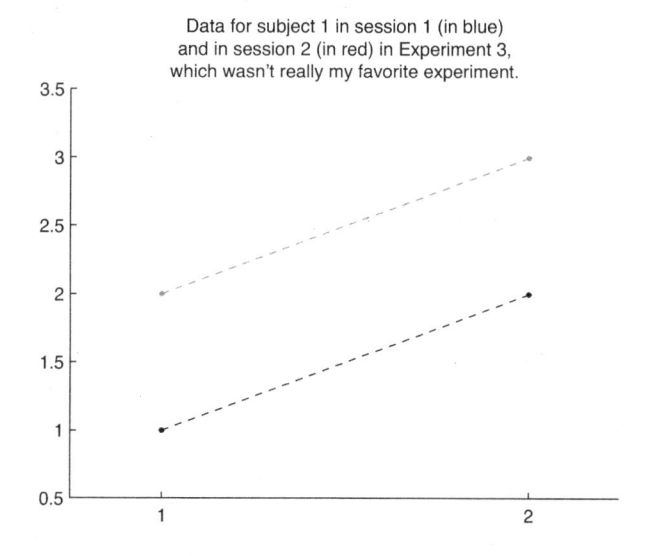

Figure 7.4

156 Data Types

7.5 Assigning Values to Cell Positions

7.5.1 Unsolved Problem Comment

The goal here is to put particular values in particular cell positions. The code doesn't work and yields an error message.

7.5.2 Unsolved Problem Code

```
clear all
close all
commandwindow
clc

c = {[ 1 2 3]
     [4 5 6 7]
     ['rats mice'] [' voles']
     [1 3]}
c_second_row = c{2}
c_second_row_middle_numbers = c{2}(2:3)
c_third_row = c{3}
c_third_row_second_character = c{3}(2)
c_fourth_row = c{4}
c_fifth_row_back_to_front = c{5} (end:-1:1)
whos
```

7.5.3 Unsolved Problem Output

```
Dimensions of matrices being concatenated are not consistent.
```

7.5.4 Solved Problem Comment

A semi-colon was missing or, equivalently, ['voles'] could have been put on a new line after ['rats mice'].

7.5.5 Solved Problem Code

```
clear all
close all
commandwindow
clc
c = {[ 1 2 3]
     [4 5 6 7]
     ['rats mice']; [' voles']
     [1 3]}
c_second_row = c{2}
c_second_row_middle_numbers = c{2}(2:3)
c_third_row = c{3}
c_third_row_second_character = c{3}(2)
c_fourth_row = c{4}
```

```
c_fifth_row_back_to_front = c{5} (end:-1:1)
whos
```

7.5.6 Solved Problem Output

```
c =
  5×1 cell array
    [1×3 double]
    [1×4 double]
    'rats mice'
    ' voles'
    [1×2 double]
c_second_row =
     4     5     6     7
c_second_row_middle_numbers =
     5     6
c_third_row =
    'rats mice'
c_third_row_second_character =
    'a'
c_fourth_row =
    ' voles'
c_fifth_row_back_to_front =
     3     1
  Name                              Size            Bytes  Class    Attributes

  c                                 5x1               662  cell
  c_fifth_row_back_to_front         1x2                16  double
  c_fourth_row                      1x6                12  char
  c_second_row                      1x4                32  double
  c_second_row_middle_numbers       1x2                16  double
  c_third_row                       1x9                18  char
  c_third_row_second_character      1x1                 2  char
```

7.6 Putting Structure Elements Into a Matrix

7.6.1 Unsolved Problem Comment

Create a structure and then put the structure elements into a matrix. The first attempt fails.

7.6.2 Unsolved Problem Code

```
clear all
close all
commandwindow
clc

n=3;
P=[1:n]
for i=1:n
```

158 Data Types

```
        i
        a(i).x=P(i)      % notice that you don't see the value when it prints
        disp(a(i).x)     % but disp shows it
end

Q=[];

for i=1:3
     Q=[Q a(i.x)];
     endS
     Q
     isequal(P,Q)
     Q=[Q a(i.x)];
end
```

7.6.3 Unsolved Problem Output

```
P =
     1     2     3
i =
     1
a =
  struct with fields:

     x: 1
     1
i =
     2
a =
  1×2 struct array with fields:
     x
     2
i =
     3
a =
  1×3 struct array with fields:
     x
     3
Struct contents reference from a non-struct array object
```

7.6.4 Solved Problem Comment

The syntax for the value added to Q was wrong. Here the syntax is fixed, so field x for the ith value of a is concatenated to Q.

7.6.5 Solved Problem Code

```
clear all
close all
commandwindow
clc
```

```
n=3;
P=[1:n]
for i=1:n
    i
    a(i).x=P(i);  % because you don't see the value even without
the ; it is included now
    disp(a(i).x)  % but disp shows the value
end
Q=[];
for i=1:3
    Q=[Q a(i).x];
end
Q
isequal(P,Q)
```

7.6.6 Solved Problem Output

```
P =
     1     2     3
i =
     1
     1
i =
     2
     2
i =
     3
     3
Q =
     1     2     3
ans =
  logical
   1
```

7.7 Creating a Deeply Nested (Three-Tiered) Structure

7.7.1 Unsolved Problem Comment

The aim here is to create a more deeply nested (three-tiered) structure than the one created in the last problem and to create an analogous matrix whose first three values per row are the indexes for the three tiers of the structure. Notice that you can call for values more easily with the structure format than with the matrix format. This is one of the most useful features of structures. A problem arises, nonetheless.

7.7.2 Unsolved Problem Code

```
clear all
close all
commandwindow
clc
```

160 Data Types

```
n=3;
M=[];
for ai=1:n
    for bi=1:n
        for ci=1:n
            a(ai).b(bi).c(ci).terminal_value(i)=ai+bi+ci
            temp_print=a(ai).b(bi).c(ci).terminal_value
            M=[M;ai bi ci temp_print]
        end
    end
end
```

7.7.3 Unsolved Problem Output

```
Subscript indices must either be real positive integers or logicals.
```

7.7.4 Solved Problem Comment

The error was adding an undefined index to terminal_value. MATLAB didn't know what i was. Actually, since the number of terminal values per combination of a, b, and c is always just 1, you could also omit (i) to the left of the equal sign in `a(ai).b(bi).c(ci). terminal_value(i)=ai+bi+ci`.

7.7.5 Solved Problem Code

```
clear all
close all
commandwindow
clc

n=3;
M=[];
for ai=1:n
    for bi=1:n
        for ci=1:n
            i=1;
            a(ai).b(bi).c(ci).terminal_value(i)=ai+bi+ci
            % this works too: a(ai).b(bi).c(ci).
            terminal_value=ai+bi+ci
            temp_print=a(ai).b(bi).c(ci).terminal_value
            M=[M;ai bi ci temp_print]
        end
    end
end
```

7.7.6 Solved Problem Output

```
a = 
  struct with fields:

    b: [1×1 struct]
temp_print =
     3
```

```
M =
     1     1     1     3
a =
  struct with fields:

    b: [1×1 struct]
temp_print =
     4
M =
     1     1     1     3
     1     1     2     4
a =
  struct with fields:

    b: [1×1 struct]
temp_print =
     5
M =
     1     1     1     3
     1     1     2     4
     1     1     3     5
a =
  struct with fields:

    b: [1×2 struct]
temp_print =
     4
M =
     1     1     1     3
     1     1     2     4
     1     1     3     5
     1     2     1     4
a =
  struct with fields:

    b: [1×2 struct]
temp_print =
     5
M =
     1     1     1     3
     1     1     2     4
     1     1     3     5
     1     2     1     4
     1     2     2     5
a =
  struct with fields:

    b: [1×2 struct]
temp_print =
     6
M =
     1     1     1     3
     1     1     2     4
```

162   Data Types

```
         1       1       3       5
         1       2       1       4
         1       2       2       5
         1       2       3       6
a =
  struct with fields:

    b: [1×3 struct]
temp_print =
    5
M =
         1       1       1       3
         1       1       2       4
         1       1       3       5
         1       2       1       4
         1       2       2       5
         1       2       3       6
         1       3       1       5
a =
  struct with fields:

    b: [1×3 struct]
temp_print =
    6
M =
         1       1       1       3
         1       1       2       4
         1       1       3       5
         1       2       1       4
         1       2       2       5
         1       2       3       6
         1       3       1       5
         1       3       2       6
a =
  struct with fields:

    b: [1×3 struct]
temp_print =
    7
M =
         1       1       1       3
         1       1       2       4
         1       1       3       5
         1       2       1       4
         1       2       2       5
         1       2       3       6
         1       3       1       5
         1       3       2       6
         1       3       3       7
a =
  1×2 struct array with fields:
    b
```

```
temp_print =
     4
M =
     1     1     1     3
     1     1     2     4
     1     1     3     5
     1     2     1     4
     1     2     2     5
     1     2     3     6
     1     3     1     5
     1     3     2     6
     1     3     3     7
     2     1     1     4
a =
  1×2 struct array with fields:
    b
temp_print =
     5
M =
     1     1     1     3
     1     1     2     4
     1     1     3     5
     1     2     1     4
     1     2     2     5
     1     2     3     6
     1     3     1     5
     1     3     2     6
     1     3     3     7
     2     1     1     4
     2     1     2     5
a =
  1×2 struct array with fields:
    b
temp_print =
     6
M =
     1     1     1     3
     1     1     2     4
     1     1     3     5
     1     2     1     4
     1     2     2     5
     1     2     3     6
     1     3     1     5
     1     3     2     6
     1     3     3     7
     2     1     1     4
     2     1     2     5
     2     1     3     6
a =
  1×2 struct array with fields:
    b
```

164 Data Types

```
temp_print =
     5
M =
     1     1     1     3
     1     1     2     4
     1     1     3     5
     1     2     1     4
     1     2     2     5
     1     2     3     6
     1     3     1     5
     1     3     2     6
     1     3     3     7
     2     1     1     4
     2     1     2     5
     2     1     3     6
     2     2     1     5
a =
  1×2 struct array with fields:
    b
temp_print =
     6
M =
     1     1     1     3
     1     1     2     4
     1     1     3     5
     1     2     1     4
     1     2     2     5
     1     2     3     6
     1     3     1     5
     1     3     2     6
     1     3     3     7
     2     1     1     4
     2     1     2     5
     2     1     3     6
     2     2     1     5
     2     2     2     6
a =
  1×2 struct array with fields:
    b
temp_print =
     7
M =
     1     1     1     3
     1     1     2     4
     1     1     3     5
     1     2     1     4
     1     2     2     5
     1     2     3     6
     1     3     1     5
     1     3     2     6
     1     3     3     7
```

```
           2     1     1     4
           2     1     2     5
           2     1     3     6
           2     2     1     5
           2     2     2     6
           2     2     3     7
a =
  1×2 struct array with fields:
    b
temp_print =
     6
M =
           1     1     1     3
           1     1     2     4
           1     1     3     5
           1     2     1     4
           1     2     2     5
           1     2     3     6
           1     3     1     5
           1     3     2     6
           1     3     3     7
           2     1     1     4
           2     1     2     5
           2     1     3     6
           2     2     1     5
           2     2     2     6
           2     2     3     7
           2     3     1     6
a =
  1×2 struct array with fields:
    b
temp_print =
     7
M =
           1     1     1     3
           1     1     2     4
           1     1     3     5
           1     2     1     4
           1     2     2     5
           1     2     3     6
           1     3     1     5
           1     3     2     6
           1     3     3     7
           2     1     1     4
           2     1     2     5
           2     1     3     6
           2     2     1     5
           2     2     2     6
           2     2     3     7
           2     3     1     6
           2     3     2     7
```

166 *Data Types*

```
a =
  1×2 struct array with fields:
    b
temp_print =
     8
M =
     1     1     1     3
     1     1     2     4
     1     1     3     5
     1     2     1     4
     1     2     2     5
     1     2     3     6
     1     3     1     5
     1     3     2     6
     1     3     3     7
     2     1     1     4
     2     1     2     5
     2     1     3     6
     2     2     1     5
     2     2     2     6
     2     2     3     7
     2     3     1     6
     2     3     2     7
     2     3     3     8
a =
  1×3 struct array with fields:
    b
temp_print =
     5
M =
     1     1     1     3
     1     1     2     4
     1     1     3     5
     1     2     1     4
     1     2     2     5
     1     2     3     6
     1     3     1     5
     1     3     2     6
     1     3     3     7
     2     1     1     4
     2     1     2     5
     2     1     3     6
     2     2     1     5
     2     2     2     6
     2     2     3     7
     2     3     1     6
     2     3     2     7
     2     3     3     8
     3     1     1     5
a =
  1×3 struct array with fields:
```

```
        b
temp_print =
        6
M =
        1        1        1        3
        1        1        2        4
        1        1        3        5
        1        2        1        4
        1        2        2        5
        1        2        3        6
        1        3        1        5
        1        3        2        6
        1        3        3        7
        2        1        1        4
        2        1        2        5
        2        1        3        6
        2        2        1        5
        2        2        2        6
        2        2        3        7
        2        3        1        6
        2        3        2        7
        2        3        3        8
        3        1        1        5
        3        1        2        6
a =
  1×3 struct array with fields:
    b
temp_print =
        7
M =
        1        1        1        3
        1        1        2        4
        1        1        3        5
        1        2        1        4
        1        2        2        5
        1        2        3        6
        1        3        1        5
        1        3        2        6
        1        3        3        7
        2        1        1        4
        2        1        2        5
        2        1        3        6
        2        2        1        5
        2        2        2        6
        2        2        3        7
        2        3        1        6
        2        3        2        7
        2        3        3        8
        3        1        1        5
        3        1        2        6
        3        1        3        7
```

168 *Data Types*

```
a =
  1×3 struct array with fields:
    b
temp_print =
     6
M =
     1     1     1     3
     1     1     2     4
     1     1     3     5
     1     2     1     4
     1     2     2     5
     1     2     3     6
     1     3     1     5
     1     3     2     6
     1     3     3     7
     2     1     1     4
     2     1     2     5
     2     1     3     6
     2     2     1     5
     2     2     2     6
     2     2     3     7
     2     3     1     6
     2     3     2     7
     2     3     3     8
     3     1     1     5
     3     1     2     6
     3     1     3     7
     3     2     1     6
a =
  1×3 struct array with fields:
    b
temp_print =
     7
M =
     1     1     1     3
     1     1     2     4
     1     1     3     5
     1     2     1     4
     1     2     2     5
     1     2     3     6
     1     3     1     5
     1     3     2     6
     1     3     3     7
     2     1     1     4
     2     1     2     5
     2     1     3     6
     2     2     1     5
     2     2     2     6
     2     2     3     7
     2     3     1     6
```

```
           2         3         2         7
           2         3         3         8
           3         1         1         5
           3         1         2         6
           3         1         3         7
           3         2         1         6
           3         2         2         7
a =
  1×3 struct array with fields:
    b
temp_print =
     8
M =
           1         1         1         3
           1         1         2         4
           1         1         3         5
           1         2         1         4
           1         2         2         5
           1         2         3         6
           1         3         1         5
           1         3         2         6
           1         3         3         7
           2         1         1         4
           2         1         2         5
           2         1         3         6
           2         2         1         5
           2         2         2         6
           2         2         3         7
           2         3         1         6
           2         3         2         7
           2         3         3         8
           3         1         1         5
           3         1         2         6
           3         1         3         7
           3         2         1         6
           3         2         2         7
           3         2         3         8
a =
  1×3 struct array with fields:
    b
temp_print =
     7
M =
           1         1         1         3
           1         1         2         4
           1         1         3         5
           1         2         1         4
           1         2         2         5
           1         2         3         6
           1         3         1         5
```

```
           1       3       2       6
           1       3       3       7
           2       1       1       4
           2       1       2       5
           2       1       3       6
           2       2       1       5
           2       2       2       6
           2       2       3       7
           2       3       1       6
           2       3       2       7
           2       3       3       8
           3       1       1       5
           3       1       2       6
           3       1       3       7
           3       2       1       6
           3       2       2       7
           3       2       3       8
           3       3       1       7
a =
  1×3 struct array with fields:
    b
temp_print =
     8
M =
           1       1       1       3
           1       1       2       4
           1       1       3       5
           1       2       1       4
           1       2       2       5
           1       2       3       6
           1       3       1       5
           1       3       2       6
           1       3       3       7
           2       1       1       4
           2       1       2       5
           2       1       3       6
           2       2       1       5
           2       2       2       6
           2       2       3       7
           2       3       1       6
           2       3       2       7
           2       3       3       8
           3       1       1       5
           3       1       2       6
           3       1       3       7
           3       2       1       6
           3       2       2       7
           3       2       3       8
           3       3       1       7
           3       3       2       8
a =
  1×3 struct array with fields:
    b
```

```
temp_print =
     9
M =
     1     1     1     3
     1     1     2     4
     1     1     3     5
     1     2     1     4
     1     2     2     5
     1     2     3     6
     1     3     1     5
     1     3     2     6
     1     3     3     7
     2     1     1     4
     2     1     2     5
     2     1     3     6
     2     2     1     5
     2     2     2     6
     2     2     3     7
     2     3     1     6
     2     3     2     7
     2     3     3     8
     3     1     1     5
     3     1     2     6
     3     1     3     7
     3     2     1     6
     3     2     2     7
     3     2     3     8
     3     3     1     7
     3     3     2     8
     3     3     3     9
```

7.8 Printing Structure Contents

7.8.1 Unsolved Problem Comment

You want to print out the contents of a structure whose contents are (from lowest level up to highest level) the room number, r; the building, b; the campus, c; and the university, u. Attempting to print out room numbers by leaving off semi-colons doesn't prove as informative as you would like.

7.8.2 Unsolved Problem Code

```
clear all
close all
commandwindow
clc

u(1).c(1).b(1).r(1)=1135
u(1).c(1).b(1).r(2)=1135
u(2).c(1).b(1).r(1)=2134
u(2).c(1).b(1).r(2)=2136
```

172 Data Types

7.8.3 Unsolved Problem Output

```
u =
  struct with fields:
    c: [1×1 struct]
u =
  struct with fields:
    c: [1×1 struct]
u =
  1×2 struct array with fields:
    c
u =
  1×2 struct array with fields:
    c
```

7.8.4 Solved Problem Comment

The `disp` command provides a convenient way to see structure contents.

7.8.5 Solved Problem Code

```
clear all
close all
commandwindow
clc

n_u=2;
n_c=1;
n_b=1;
n_r=2;

u(1).c(1).b(1).r(1)=1135;
u(1).c(1).b(1).r(2)=1135;
u(2).c(1).b(1).r(1)=2134;
u(2).c(1).b(1).r(2)=2136;

disp(' ')
disp('Data for university ui, campus ci, building bi, and room ri')
for ui=1:n_u
    for ci=1:n_c
        for bi=1:n_b
            for ri=1:n_r
                disp([ ui ci bi ri u(ui).c(ci).b(bi).r(ri)])
            end
        end
    end
end
```

7.8.6 Solved Problem Output

```
Data for university ui, campus ci, building bi, and room ri
```

Data Types 173

1	1	1	1	1135
1	1	1	2	1135
2	1	1	1	2134
2	1	1	2	2136

7.9 Using a Structure to Graph a Deeply Nested Structure With Different Kinds of Fields

7.9.1 Unsolved Problem Comment

Use a structure to graph a deeply nested structure with different kinds of fields, in this case to explore a possible model of happiness in communication. According to the model, happiness grows with the congruence between a speaker's desires to communicate messages and the recipient's desire to receive those messages. Here you look at two situations: an unhappy marriage and a happy marriage. The graph doesn't turn out as expected. The goal was to show full messages at different points in the graphs, but single letters appear.

7.9.2 Unsolved Problem Code

```
clear all
close all
commandwindow
clc

% Fill the screen with the figure window
set(gcf, 'Position', get(0, 'Screensize'));
% Another way to fill the screen with the figure window
% figure('units','normalized','outerposition',[0 0 1 1])

for situation=1:2
    subplot(1,2,situation)
    axis([0 1 0 1])
    hold on
    box on
    grid on
    xlabel('Speaker''s Desire to Say')
    ylabel('Recipient''s Desire to Hear')

    n_messages=3;
    ms=12; % markersize
    fs=12; % fontsize
    text_shift=.01;

    switch situation

        case 1 % Happy marriage

            speaker(1).recipient(2).message(1).content =['You''re beautiful']
            speaker(1).recipient(2).message(1).speaker_desire_to_say=.9
            speaker(1).recipient(2).message(1).recipient_desire_to_hear =.9

            speaker(1).recipient(2).message(2).content =['You''re smart']
            speaker(1).recipient(2).message(2).speaker_desire_to_say =.6
            speaker(1).recipient(2).message(2).recipient_desire_to_hear =.6
```

174 Data Types

```
            speaker(1).recipient(2).message(3).content = ...
                ['Your cooking''s so so.']
            speaker(1).recipient(2).message(3).speaker_desire_to_say =.2
            speaker(1).recipient(2).message(3).recipient_desire_to_hear =.2

            title('Happy Marriage','fontweight','normal')

        case 2 % Unhappy marriage

            speaker(1).recipient(2).message(1).content =['You''re beautiful']
            speaker(1).recipient(2).message(1).speaker_desire_to_say=.1
            speaker(1).recipient(2).message(1).recipient_desire_to_hear =.9

            speaker(1).recipient(2).message(2).content =['You''re smart']
            speaker(1).recipient(2).message(2).content
            speaker(1).recipient(2).message(2).speaker_desire_to_say =.4
            speaker(1).recipient(2).message(2).recipient_desire_to_hear =.6

            speaker(1).recipient(2).message(3).content = ...
                ['Your cooking''s so so.']
            speaker(1).recipient(2).message(3).content
            speaker(1).recipient(2).message(3).speaker_desire_to_say =.8
            speaker(1).recipient(2).message(3).recipient_desire_to_hear =.2

            title('Unhappy Marriage','fontweight','normal')
    end

    for si=1
        for ri=2
            for mi=1:n_messages
                [si ri mi]
                x=speaker(si).recipient(ri).message(mi).speaker_desire_to_say
                y= ...
                speaker(si).recipient(ri).message(mi).recipient_desire_to_hear
                phrase=speaker(si).recipient(ri).message(mi).content
                plot([0 1],[0 1],'k-')
                plot(x,y,'k.','markersize',ms)
                text(x+text_shift,y,phrase,...
                    'horizontalalignment','left','fontsize',fs)
            end
        end
    end
end  % for situation=1:2
```

7.9.3 Unsolved Problem Output

```
speaker =
  struct with fields:

    recipient: [1×2 struct]
speaker =
  struct with fields:

    recipient: [1×2 struct]
```

```
speaker =
  struct with fields:

    recipient: [1×2 struct]
speaker =
  struct with fields:

    recipient: [1×2 struct]
speaker =
  struct with fields:

    recipient: [1×2 struct]
speaker =
  struct with fields:

    recipient: [1×2 struct]
speaker =
  struct with fields:

    recipient: [1×2 struct]
speaker =
  struct with fields:

    recipient: [1×2 struct]
speaker =
  struct with fields:

    recipient: [1×2 struct]
ans =
     1     2     1
x =
         0.9
y =
         0.9
phrase =
    'Y'
ans =
     1     2     2
x =
         0.6
y =
         0.6
phrase =
    'o'
ans =
     1     2     3
x =
         0.2
y =
         0.2
phrase =
    'u'
speaker =
  struct with fields:
```

176 *Data Types*

```
        recipient: [1×2 struct]
speaker =
  struct with fields:

        recipient: [1×2 struct]
speaker =
  struct with fields:

        recipient: [1×2 struct]
speaker =
  struct with fields:

        recipient: [1×2 struct]
ans =
    'You're smart'
speaker =
  struct with fields:

        recipient: [1×2 struct]
speaker =
  struct with fields:

        recipient: [1×2 struct]
speaker =
  struct with fields:

        recipient: [1×2 struct]
ans =
    'Your cooking's so so.'
speaker =
  struct with fields:

        recipient: [1×2 struct]
speaker =
  struct with fields:

        recipient: [1×2 struct]
ans =
     1     2     1
x =
          0.1
y =
          0.9
phrase =
    'Y'
ans =
     1     2     2
x =
          0.4
y =
          0.6
phrase =
    'o'
```

```
ans =
     1     2     3
x =
     0.8
y =
     0.2
phrase =
    'u'
```

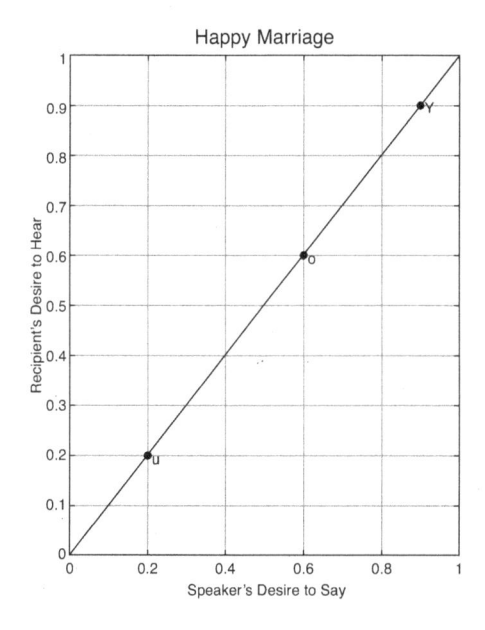

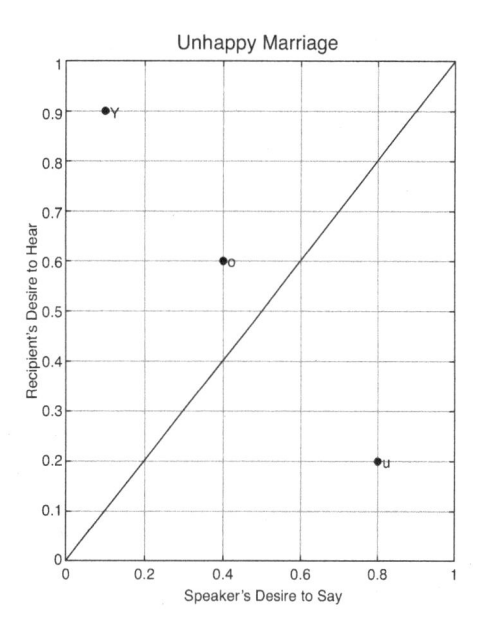

Figure 7.5

7.9.4 Solved Problem Comment

There was no need to provide an index for content in `phrase=speaker(si).recipient(ri).message(mi).content(mi)`. Doing so only caused problems. Note that it's not the case that a terminal field can't or shouldn't have an index or range of indices. It can, but if no index is needed, there is no harm in omitting it.

7.9.5 Solved Problem Code

```
clear all
close all
commandwindow
clc

% Fill the screen with the figure window
set(gcf, 'Position', get(0, 'Screensize'));
% Another way to fill the screen with the figure window
% figure('units','normalized','outerposition',[0 0 1 1])

for situation=1:2
    subplot(1,2,situation)
    axis([0 1 0 1])
    hold on
```

178 *Data Types*

```
box on
grid on
xlabel('Speaker''s Desire to Say')
ylabel('Recipient''s Desire to Hear')

n_messages=3;
ms=12; % markersize
fs=12; % fontsize
text_shift=.01;

switch situation

    case 1 % Happy marriage

        speaker(1).recipient(2).message(1).content =['You''re beautiful']
        speaker(1).recipient(2).message(1).speaker_desire_to_say=.9
        speaker(1).recipient(2).message(1).recipient_desire_to_hear =.9

        speaker(1).recipient(2).message(2).content =['You''re smart']
        speaker(1).recipient(2).message(2).speaker_desire_to_say =.6
        speaker(1).recipient(2).message(2).recipient_desire_to_hear =.6
        speaker(1).recipient(2).message(3).content = ...
            ['Your cooking''s so so.']
        speaker(1).recipient(2).message(3).speaker_desire_to_say =.2
        speaker(1).recipient(2).message(3).recipient_desire_to_hear =.2

        title('Happy Marriage','fontweight','normal')

    case 2 % Unhappy marriage

        speaker(1).recipient(2).message(1).content =['You''re beautiful']
        speaker(1).recipient(2).message(1).speaker_desire_to_say=.1
        speaker(1).recipient(2).message(1).recipient_desire_to_hear =.9

        speaker(1).recipient(2).message(2).content =['You''re smart']
        speaker(1).recipient(2).message(2).content
        speaker(1).recipient(2).message(2).speaker_desire_to_say =.4
        speaker(1).recipient(2).message(2).recipient_desire_to_hear =.6
        speaker(1).recipient(2).message(3).content = ...
            ['Your cooking''s so so.']
        speaker(1).recipient(2).message(3).content
        speaker(1).recipient(2).message(3).speaker_desire_to_say =.8
        speaker(1).recipient(2).message(3).recipient_desire_to_hear =.2

        title('Unhappy Marriage','fontweight','normal')
end

for si=1
    for ri=2
        for mi=1:n_messages
            [si ri mi]
```

```
                x=speaker(si).recipient(ri).message(mi).speaker_desire_to_say
                      y= ...
            speaker(si).recipient(ri).message(mi).recipient_desire_to_hear
                phrase=speaker(si).recipient(ri).message(mi).content
                plot([0 1],[0 1],'k-')
                plot(x,y,'k.','markersize',ms)
                text(x+text_shift,y,phrase,...
                    'horizontalalignment','left','fontsize',fs)
            end
        end
    end
end  % for situation=1:2
```

7.9.6 Solved Problem Output

```
speaker =
  struct with fields:

    recipient: [1×2 struct]
speaker =
  struct with fields:

    recipient: [1×2 struct]
speaker =
  struct with fields:

    recipient: [1×2 struct]
speaker =
  struct with fields:

    recipient: [1×2 struct]
speaker =
  struct with fields:

    recipient: [1×2 struct]
speaker =
  struct with fields:

    recipient: [1×2 struct]
speaker =
  struct with fields:

    recipient: [1×2 struct]
speaker =
  struct with fields:

    recipient: [1×2 struct]
speaker =
  struct with fields:

    recipient: [1×2 struct]
ans =
     1     2     1
x =
```

```
            0.9
y =
            0.9
phrase =
    'You're beautiful'
ans =
     1     2     2
x =
            0.6
y =
            0.6
phrase =
    'You're smart'
ans =
     1     2     3
x =
            0.2
y =
            0.2
phrase =
    'Your cooking's so so.'
speaker =
  struct with fields:

    recipient: [1×2 struct]
speaker =
  struct with fields:

    recipient: [1×2 struct]
speaker =
  struct with fields:

    recipient: [1×2 struct]
speaker =
  struct with fields:

    recipient: [1×2 struct]
ans =
    'You're smart'
speaker =
  struct with fields:

    recipient: [1×2 struct]
speaker =
  struct with fields:

    recipient: [1×2 struct]
speaker =
  struct with fields:

    recipient: [1×2 struct]
ans =
    'Your cooking's so so.'
```

```
speaker =
  struct with fields:

    recipient: [1×2 struct]
speaker =
  struct with fields:

    recipient: [1×2 struct]
ans =
     1     2     1
x =
        0.1
y =
        0.9
phrase =
    'You're beautiful'
ans =
     1     2     2
x =
        0.4
y =
        0.6
phrase =
    'You're smart'
ans =
     1     2     3
x =
        0.8
y =
        0.2
phrase =
    'Your cooking's so so.'
```

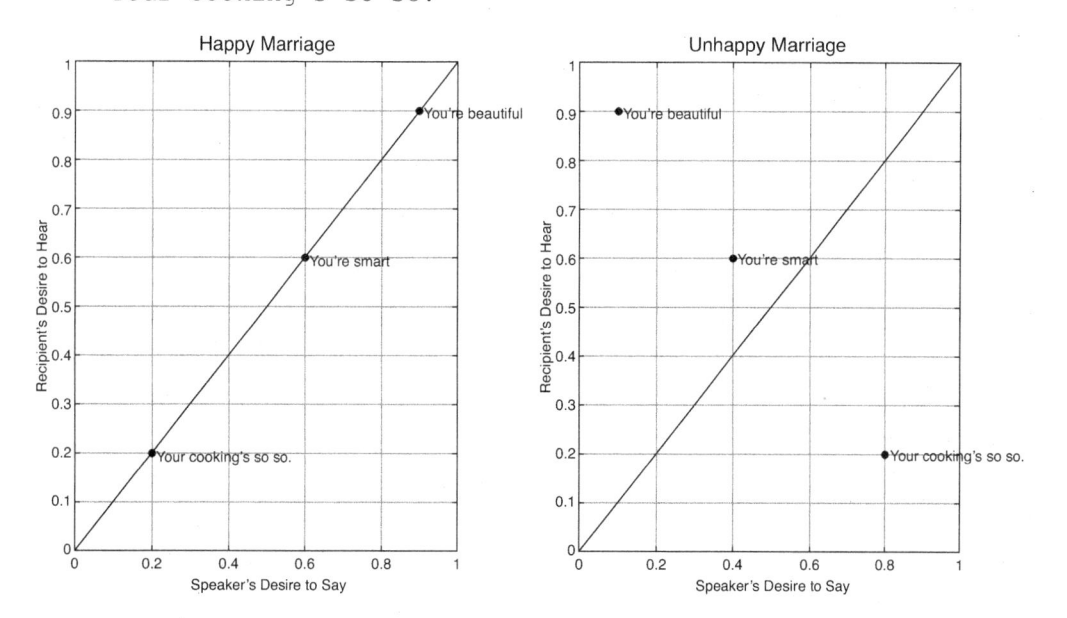

Figure 7.6

182 Data Types

7.10 Using Fit, Understanding Its Fields

7.10.1 Unsolved Problem Comment

MATLAB's fit function returns values in a format that is fully usable when you understand structures and fields. This particular program, which uses MATLAB's fit function, doesn't work as hoped, however.

7.10.2 Unsolved Problem Code

```
clear all
close all
commandwindow
clc

standard_dev=2;
k1=.1;
k2=.1;
k3=10;
x=1:20;
y=k3 + k2*x + k1*x.^2
y=y+(randn(1,20)*standard_dev);
% plot(x,y,'.')
hold on
scatter(x,y,'bo','filled')
flm = fitlm(x,y,'quadratic')
[f g h] = fit(x',y','poly2')
y_hat=f(p3) + f(p2)*x + f(p1)*x.^2;
plot(x,y_hat,'r--')
```

7.10.3 Unsolved Problem Output

```
y =
  Columns 1 through 8
        10.2           10.6          11.2           12            13
14.2         15.6          17.2
  Columns 9 through 16
          19             21          23.2          25.6          28.2
31           34           37.2
  Columns 17 through 20
        40.6          44.2            48            52
flm =
Linear regression model:
    y ~ 1 + x1 + x1^2

Estimated Coefficients:
                   Estimate         SE           tStat         pValue
                   _____      _____      _____      _____

    (Intercept)     11.564        0.86581        13.356       1.9233e-10
    x1             -0.15494       0.18989       -0.81596        0.42581
    x1^2            0.1101       0.0087831       12.536       5.1431e-10
```

```
Number of observations: 20, Error degrees of freedom: 17
Root Mean Squared Error: 1.16
R-squared: 0.993,  Adjusted R-Squared 0.992
F-statistic vs. constant model: 1.22e+03, p-value = 4.34e-19
f =
    Linear model Poly2:
    f(x) = p1*x^2 + p2*x + p3
    Coefficients (with 95% confidence bounds):
      p1 =      0.1101  (0.09157, 0.1286)
      p2 =     -0.1549  (-0.5556, 0.2457)
      p3 =       11.56  (9.737, 13.39)
g =
  struct with fields:

          sse: 23.024
      rsquare: 0.99309
          dfe: 17
    adjrsquare: 0.99227
         rmse: 1.1638
h =
  struct with fields:

        numobs: 20
      numparam: 3
     residuals: [20×1 double]
      Jacobian: [20×3 double]
      exitflag: 1
     algorithm: 'QR factorization and solve'
    iterations: 1

Undefined function or variable 'p3'.
```

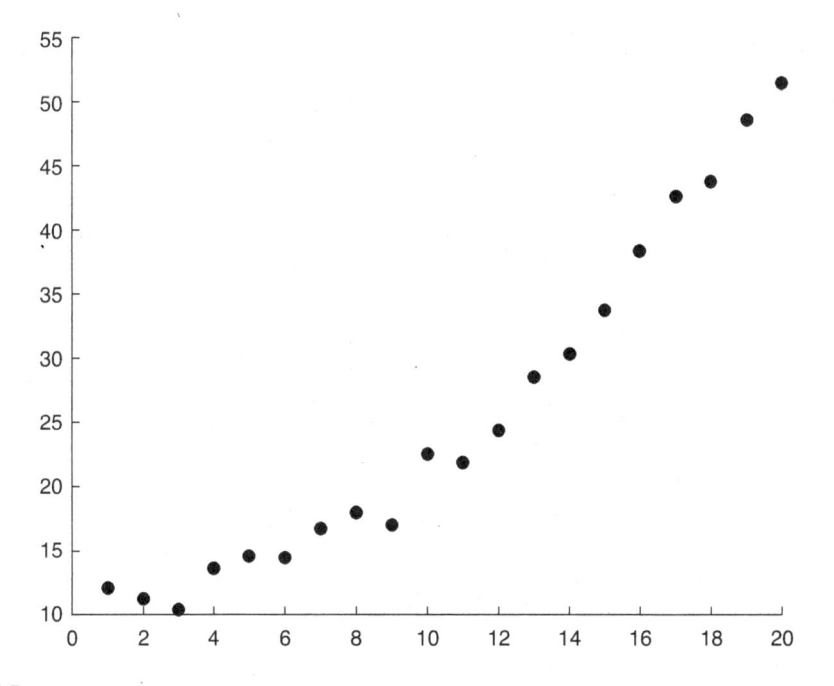

Figure 7.7

7.10.4 Solved Problem Comment

The program didn't put up the best-fitting curve because of an inappropriate way of referring to the fields of the structures that the fit function returned. Here the fields are referred to more effectively (in the y_hat ... line).

7.10.5 Solved Problem Code

```
clear all
close all
commandwindow
clc

standard_dev=2;
k1=.1;
k2=.1;
k3=10;
x=1:20;
y=k3 + k2*x + k1*x.^2
y=y+(randn(1,20)*standard_dev);
% plot(x,y,'.')
hold on
scatter(x,y,'bo','filled')
flm = fitlm(x,y,'quadratic')
[f g h] = fit(x',y','poly2')
y_hat=f.p3 + f.p2*x + f.p1*x.^2;
plot(x,y_hat,'r--')
```

7.10.6 Solved Problem Output

```
y =
  Columns 1 through 8
        10.2          10.6         11.2          12           13
14.2         15.6          17.2
  Columns 9 through 16
              19            21         23.2         25.6         28.2
31           34           37.2
  Columns 17 through 20
        40.6         44.2          48           52
flm =
Linear regression model:
    y ~ 1 + x1 + x1^2

Estimated Coefficients:
                   Estimate         SE         tStat       pValue
                   _____      _____     _____    _____

    (Intercept)     11.217        1.3332       8.4131     1.8268e-07
    x1             -0.22695       0.2924      -0.77617    0.44831
    x1^2            0.11974       0.013525     8.8537     8.9385e-08

Number of observations: 20, Error degrees of freedom: 17
Root Mean Squared Error: 1.79
```

```
R-squared: 0.986,   Adjusted R-Squared 0.984
F-statistic vs. constant model: 581, p-value = 2.24e-16
f =
     Linear model Poly2:
     f(x) = p1*x^2 + p2*x + p3
     Coefficients (with 95% confidence bounds):
       p1 =       0.1197  (0.09121, 0.1483)
       p2 =      -0.2269  (-0.8439, 0.39)
       p3 =        11.22  (8.404, 14.03)
g =
  struct with fields:

            sse: 54.593
        rsquare: 0.98558
            dfe: 17
      adjrsquare: 0.98389
           rmse: 1.792
h =
  struct with fields:

         numobs: 20
       numparam: 3
      residuals: [20×1 double]
       Jacobian: [20×3 double]
       exitflag: 1
      algorithm: 'QR factorization and solve'
     iterations: 1
```

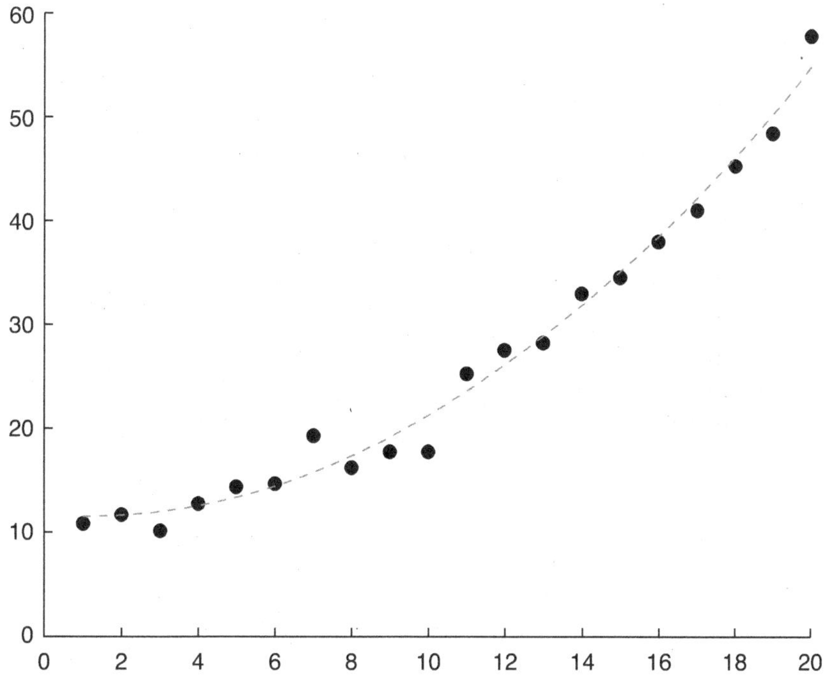

Figure 7.8

8 Functions

MATLAB provides a number of functions for carrying out routine operations when appropriate inputs are given. Familiar examples are `sum` and `mean`. This chapter concerns the way built-in functions work and how you can write functions of your own.

8.1 Understanding Size, Length, and Numel

8.1.1 Unsolved Problem Comment

To understand functions, it's useful to explore how built-in MATLAB functions work. This first problem is about MATLAB's `size`, `length`, and `numel` functions.

Regarding `size`, the first argument provided to the `size` function is the name of the variable whose size is being evaluated. If there is no second argument, `size` gives the number of rows followed by the number of columns. If a second argument is given after the variable name, and if that second input is the number 1, the `size` function gives the first output it normally would (output #1)—in other words, the number of rows. Alternatively, if a second argument is given after the variable name and the second input is the number 2, the `size` function gives the second output it normally would (output #2)—in other words, the number of columns.

The `length` function yields the larger of the number of rows and columns. My advice is to be very careful about the `length` function. If you create a `for` loop, for example, that runs from an initial value (typically 1) up to the length of a variable of interest, you may be in for a rude surprise if you think `length` is the number of rows, for example, but the number of rows is actually less than the number of columns (or vice versa, if you think `length` is the number of columns, say, but the number of columns is less than the number of rows). In the present program, you decide to check for yourself whether `length` equals the larger of the first and second elements of the output of size.

You also inquire into the `numel` function. This function yields the total number of elements in a matrix. You decide to check this by testing whether the output of `numel` equals the product of the first and second elements of the output of size. Something weird happens. The number of elements obtained via `numel` and `prod` are different.

8.1.2 Unsolved Problem Code

```
clear all
close all
commandwindow
clc
```

```
M(1:10,1:2)=rand
disp(' ')
disp('Size, Rows, Columns')
size(M)
size(M,1)
size(M,2)
disp(' ')
disp('Number of elements via numel and product')
numel(M)
prod(size(M,1),size(M,2))
disp(' ')
disp('Length and larger of the two size elements')
length(M)
max(size(M))
disp('Smaller of the two size elements')
min(size(M))
```

8.1.3 Unsolved Problem Output

```
M =
      0.31808         0.31808
      0.31808         0.31808
      0.31808         0.31808
      0.31808         0.31808
      0.31808         0.31808
      0.31808         0.31808
      0.31808         0.31808
      0.31808         0.31808
      0.31808         0.31808
      0.31808         0.31808

Size, Rows, Columns
ans =
    10     2
ans =
    10
ans =
     2

Number of elements via numel and product
ans =
    20
ans =
    10

Length and larger of the two size elements
ans =
    10
ans =
    10
```

188 *Functions*

```
Smaller of the two size elements
ans =
     2
```

8.1.4 Solved Problem Comment

It turns out that the `prod` function doesn't compute the product, at least in the way that was expected. There is another function that does multiply as expected, namely, `times`. I thought `prod` would work and was surprised that it didn't (or didn't in the way he expected). He then thought there probably was a MATLAB function for simple multiplication and found `times` by typing 'help *' in the command window.

8.1.5 Solved Problem Code

```
clear all
close all
commandwindow
clc

M(1:10,1:2)=rand
disp(' ')
disp('Size, Rows,Columns')
size(M)
size(M,1)
size(M,2)
disp(' ')
disp('Number of elements via numel, multiplication, and times rather than prod.')
numel(M)
% prod(size(M,1),size(M,2)) % now commented out
size(M,1)*size(M,2)
times(size(M,1),size(M,2))
disp(' ')
disp('Length and larger of the two size elements')
length(M)
max(size(M))
disp('Smaller of the two size elements')
min(size(M))
```

8.1.6 Solved Problem Output

```
M =
      0.26178      0.26178
      0.26178      0.26178
      0.26178      0.26178
      0.26178      0.26178
      0.26178      0.26178
      0.26178      0.26178
      0.26178      0.26178
      0.26178      0.26178
      0.26178      0.26178
```

```
         0.26178      0.26178
         0.26178      0.26178

Size, Rows,Columns
ans =
    10     2
ans =
    10
ans =
     2

Number of elements via numel, multiplication, and times rather
than prod.
ans =
    20
ans =
    20
ans =
    20

Length and larger of the two size elements
ans =
    10
ans =
    10
Smaller of the two size elements
ans =
     2
```

8.2 Discovering Features of Mean

8.2.1 Unsolved Problem Comment

It is important to use 'help' or 'doc' to discover (or rediscover) what built-in functions afford, as in this example with the `mean` function.

Leading up to this example, I'll share with you that for a fairly long time, I thought the only way to compute the mean of a set of numbers containing a NaN value when one hoped to get the mean of the non-NaN values was to use the `nanmean` function, which comes with MATLAB's statistics toolbox. However, it turns out that you don't need `nanmean` because MATLAB's `mean` function can take an optional argument called `omitnan`. When you include `omitnan` (in quotes), the `mean` function omits all NaN values in computing the mean.

What makes this point noteworthy can be expressed in the form of a confession. Because I used `mean` for a very long time, I hadn't looked at help about it for several years. Only when I was preparing lecture notes about the `mean` function did I discover that this function can take an argument that defines the way it deals with NaN values, as shown here. NaN values can either be omitted or included, depending on a specification for the `mean` function.

The lesson here is to go back on occasion and look up functions after you think you've gotten to know all their properties. Chances are you were in a hurry when you first looked up a function,

190 *Functions*

probably because you had some task to complete by a deadline and weren't inclined to read all the possibilities the function afforded.

An even deeper lesson might be considered as well, though it goes beyond the bounds of computing. When you think you know something or someone so well that you haven't reexamined them for a long time, maybe there's more there than you remembered.

Lofty remarks aside, in the program below there is a mismatch between the two values generated in the last output, though there shouldn't be.

8.2.2 Unsolved Problem Code

```
clear all
close all
commandwindow
clc

max_rows=4;
max_cols=4;
j=0;
summary=[];
for n_rows=2:2:max_rows
    for n_rows=2:2:max_rows
        for n_cols=2:2:max_cols
            X(1:n_rows,1:n_cols)=n_rows+n_cols;
        end
    end
end

% Set the last value in the matrix to NaN
X(n_rows,n_cols)=NaN
disp(' ')
disp('Means of each column without any special argument')
[mean(mean(X,1)) mean(mean(X,2))]
disp(' ')
disp('Means of each column using nanmean')
[nanmean(nanmean(X,1)) nanmean(nanmean(X,2))]
disp('Means of each column with omitnan')
[mean(mean(X,1),'omitnan') mean(mean(X,2),'includenan')]
```

8.2.3 Unsolved Problem Output

```
X =
     8     8     8     8
     8     8     8     8
     8     8     8     8
     8     8     8   NaN

Means of each column without any special argument
ans =
   NaN    NaN
```

```
Means of each column using nanmean
ans =
     8      8
Means of each column with omitnan
ans =
     8    NaN
```

8.2.4 Solved Problem Comment

The last line contained an unexpected mismatch because an incorrect argument was provided to mean when NaN values were supposed to be included. The incorrect argument was 'includenan'. This argument shows that the mean function returns a mean of NaN when at least one value that is supplied to it is NaN.

The take-home message is to take the time to acquaint and reacquaint yourself with the affordances of functions. Also, recognize that a seeming problem with a function can be turned to your advantage. In this case, if you want to check whether there is a NaN value in a data set, you can take its simple mean. If the function returns NaN, that means there is a NaN value in the data set. That can be useful if you have a huge data set and need to check for any "NaN-y" goats in the herd.

8.2.5 Solved Problem Code

```
clear all
close all
commandwindow
clc

max_rows=4;
max_cols=4;
j=0;
summary=[];
for n_rows=2:2:max_rows
    for n_rows=2:2:max_rows
        for n_cols=2:2:max_cols
            X(1:n_rows,1:n_cols)=n_rows+n_cols;
        end
    end
end

% Set the last value in the matrix to NaN
X(n_rows,n_cols)=NaN
disp(' ')
disp('Means of each column without any special argument')
[mean(mean(X,1)) mean(mean(X,2))]
disp(' ')
disp('Means of each column using nanmean')
[nanmean(nanmean(X,1)) nanmean(nanmean(X,2))]
disp(' ')
disp('Means of each column with omitnan')
[mean(mean(X,1),'omitnan') mean(mean(X,2),'omitnan')]
```

8.2.6 Solved Problem Output

```
M =
      0.26178      0.26178
      0.26178      0.26178
      0.26178      0.26178
      0.26178      0.26178
      0.26178      0.26178
      0.26178      0.26178
      0.26178      0.26178
      0.26178      0.26178
      0.26178      0.26178 X =
      8     8     8     8
      8     8     8     8
      8     8     8     8
      8     8     8    NaN
```

Means of each column without any special argument
```
ans =
    NaN    NaN
```

Means of each column using nanmean
```
ans =
     8     8
```

Means of each column with omitnan
```
ans =
     8     8
```

8.3 Messing With a Built-In Function: ginput Loses Crosshairs in david_ginput

8.3.1 Unsolved Problem Comment

Here is a program designed to see whether participants learn to anticipate future positions when they tap on boxes appearing at predictable locations. The question is whether they tap at different places within a box depending on where the next box will be. The boxes appear successively at the following locations per presentation cycle:

1. South
2. North
3. Northwest
4. Southwest
5. South
6. North
7. Northeast
8. Southeast.

This sequence of eight locations (n_locations=8) is repeated in n_cycles. The main scientific question is whether participants will tap in the North location more to the west (left) when the next tap will be in the Northwest box, and more to the east (right) when the next tap will be in the Northeast box. They should only do this if they have learned the sequence. The number of times the sequence is presented, n_cycles, is important in this regard.

The problem is that the ginput function, which is used to record where participants click on the screen, shows crosshairs. This is tolerable, but it really slows people down, and the crosshairs can be distracting. The present program illustrates the problem. The program runs perfectly well, but is suboptimal from a human-factors perspective because it is so slow and because the crosshairs are so visually obtrusive. Because of this, the number of cycles in which the n_locations are shown (n_cycles) is smaller than one would like. It is the smallest value possible to be able to pick up some learning. Ideally, one shouldn't have to modify one's experimental design in a fundamental way like this to accommodate a technical limitation that is transparently trivial.

8.3.2 *Unsolved Problem Code*

```
clear all
close all
commandwindow
clc

n_locations=8; % number of box locations
n_cycles=2;  % number of cycles in which the n_locations are shown
% value of n_cycles is the smallest value possible to pick up some learning
% and is low because the crosshairs make responding so tedious ... would
% like to be able to go much faster
box_marker_size=80; % size of the box
point_marker_size=8; % size of the points used to graph the results

% basic sequence of locations
x=[ 0  0 -1 -1  0  0  1  1];
y=[-1  1  1 -1 -1  1  1 -1];

% basic sequence replicated for the n_cycles
xc=[]; yc=[];
for c=1:n_cycles
    xc=[xc x];
    yc=[yc y];
end
xc; % did not have semi-colon at first so it could be checked
during development
yc; % did not have semi-colon at first so it could be checked
during development

figure(1)
j=0; % counter for events
for c=1:n_cycles
    for i=1:n_locations
        j=j+1;
```

194 Functions

```
        plot(xc(j),yc(j),'ks','markersize',box_marker_size)
        tic
        axis([-1 1 -1 1]*2);   % set limits of the graph
        axis off    % don't show the x or y axis
        [xg(j) yg(j)]=ginput(1);   % record the click location 1 time per event
        t(j)=toc;  % record the time of the response
    end
end
close

figure(2)
plot(xg,yg,'k.-','markersize',point_marker_size)

figure(3)
hold on
plot(xg,'r.-','markersize',point_marker_size)
plot(yg,'b.-','markersize',point_marker_size)
legend('xg','yg','location','northwest')

% Plot the second through the last times. Omit the first time since it
% includes getting started (a different kind of event).
figure(4)
plot(t(2:end),'bo-')
xlabel('Response')
ylabel('Time (s)')

% Gather x values in the north box before heading west and east and do a t
% test on those two samples
x_before_heading_west=xg(2:8:end)
x_before_heading_east=xg(4:8:end)
[h,p] = ttest(x_before_heading_west,x_before_heading_east,'Alpha',0.05)

disp('Mean and std of x_before_heading_west and of x_before_heading_east')
[mean(x_before_heading_west) std(x_before_heading_west) ...
mean(x_before_heading_east) std(x_before_heading_east)]
```

8.3.3 Unsolved Problem Output

[The series of displays with boxes at the various locations – South, North, Northwest, Southwest, South, North, Northeast, Southeast – will not be shown, and neither will the crosshairs placed in each box to allow the program to continue.]

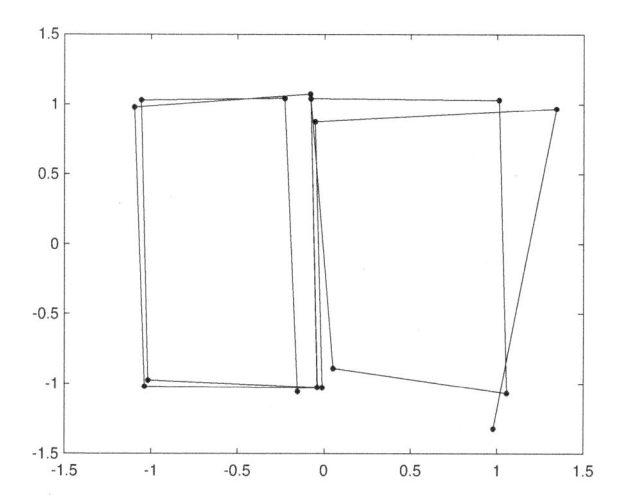

Figure 8.1

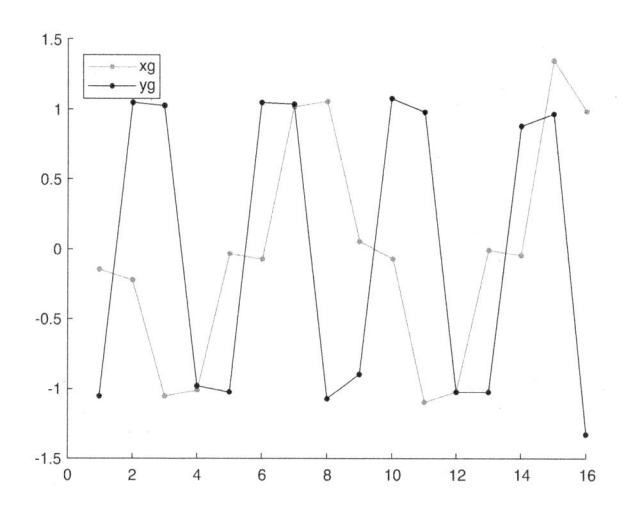

Figure 8.2

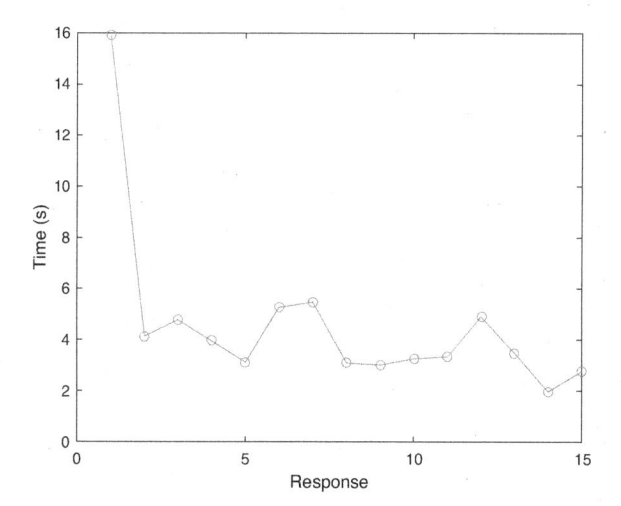

Figure 8.3

8.3.4 Solved Problem Comment

I hoped there would be a way to turn off the crosshairs in ginput. I wanted subjects in my psychology experiments to be able to tap on the screen without a cursor appearing. After failing to find a simple function argument to do this, perhaps along the lines of ('crosshairs','on') or ('crosshairs','off'), I opened ginput by simply typing open ginput on the command line. Seeing it open and knowing I would poke around the program and mess with it, I immediately saved a new version with a different name: david_ginput. I renamed it this way before I knew whether I would be able to find what I wanted to change because I didn't want to accidentally mess up the program. I searched for the word crosshair and found this command: set(crossHair, 'Visible', 'on'). I changed this one line to set(crossHair, 'Visible', 'off'), and added a comment that I had done so. By then saving david_ginput and calling that function, I could have my subjects hit targets with their finger or a stylus and not see (or have to deal with) crosshairs. People could respond much more quickly.

To get this to work yourself, go through the same editing process and either save the function as david_ginput, whereupon you can run the code below as is, or save it with a better name that makes sense for you and change the name of your custom ginput program in the code below.

Of course, you can take a similar approach with other functions. As a reminder, open the function, immediately save it with a new name (hopefully not identical to any other MATLAB function, so go with something idiosyncratic or funky), look for the part you want to change, change it as necessary, and then save the function.

8.3.5 Solved Problem Code

The foregoing code is not reproduced because it had just one small change. After david_ginput was saved, where the previous code had ginput, the new code simply had david_ginput.

8.3.6 Solved Problem Output

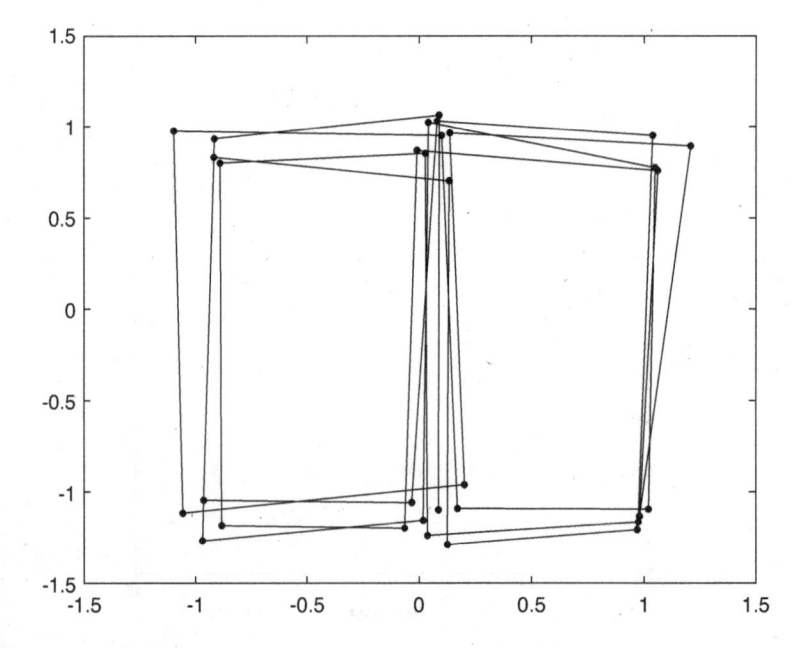

Figure 8.4

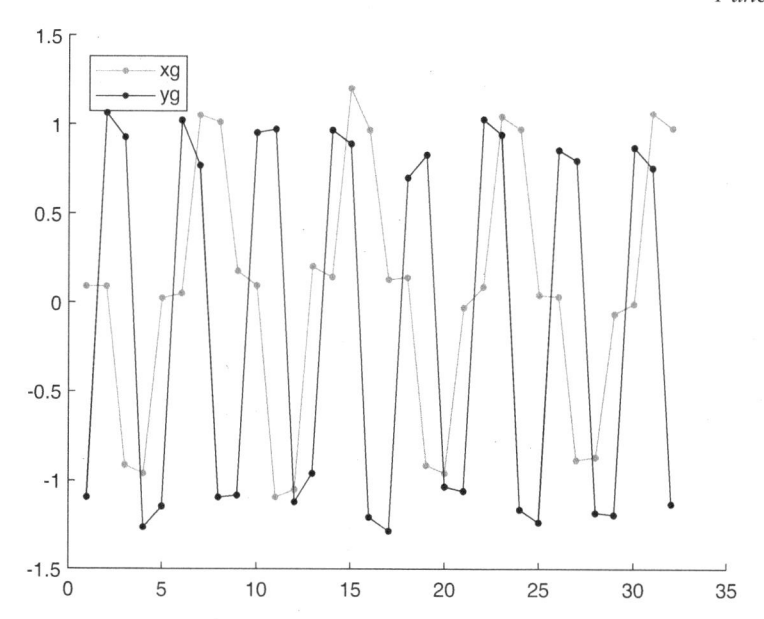

Figure 8.5

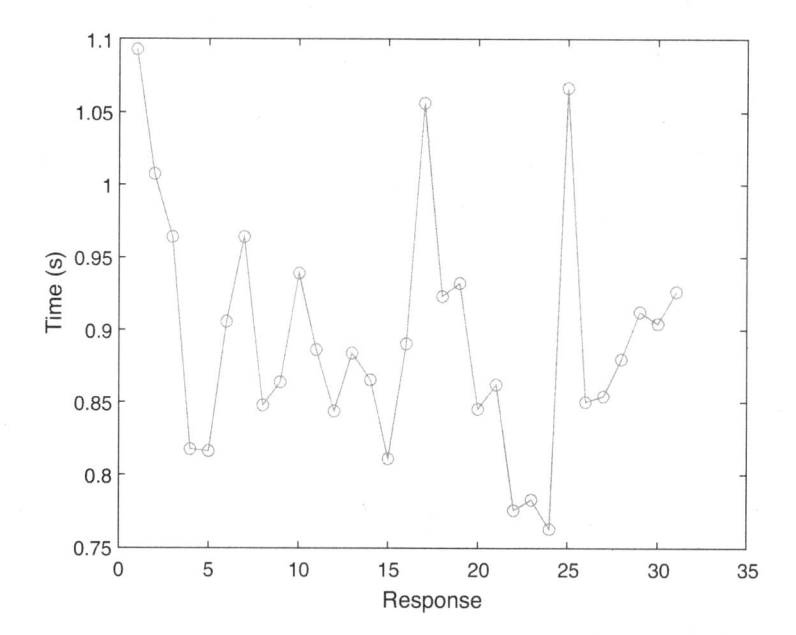

Figure 8.6

8.4 Using Separate Names for Variables and Functions: Avoiding 'Text' as Output for xlsread

8.4.1 Unsolved Problem Comment

This is the example discussed in Chapter 1. The aim is to read text from Excel and then plot the results in a graph using the text command. The data in the Excel spreadsheet come

198 Functions

from Problem 7.9. The program doesn't work. Instead of showing text in the graph, a single point is plotted and an error message is displayed.

8.4.2 Unsolved Problem Code

```
clear all
close all
commandwindow
clc

[nums text raw]=xlsread('David_Week_7_Excel_Relationships_03.xlsx')
whos
fig_number=1;
set(gcf,'position',[1 41 1280 611.2]);
hold on
axis([0 1 0 1])
text_x_shift=.005;

for i=1:size(nums,1)
    plot(nums(i,1),nums(i,2),'.','markersize',18)
    text(nums(i,1)+text_x_shift,nums(i,2),num2str(text{i+1,4}),...,
        'horizontalalignment','left','fontsize',12)
end
plot([0 1],[0 1],'k-')
axis([0 1 0 1])
grid on
box on
xlabel('Sender''s Desire To Send')
ylabel('Receiver''s Desire to Receive')
```

8.4.3 Unsolved Problem Output

```
nums =
           0.1           0.2            1
          0.85          0.78            1
           0.5          0.45            1
           0.2          0.33            1
text =
  5×4 cell array
    'Sender's Desire to …'    'Receiver's Desire t…'    'Relationship Quality'    'Message'
    ''                        ''                        ''                        'Your jokes aren't t…'
    ''                        ''                        ''                        'You're so cute.'
    ''                        ''                        ''                        'You should take a v…'
    ''                        ''                        ''                        'I forgive you.'
```

```
raw =
  5×4 cell array
    'Sender's Desire to …'   'Receiver's Desire to…'   'Relationship
Quality'      'Message'
    [                0.1]    [                     0.2]   [
1]     'Your jokes aren't t…'
    [               0.85]    [                    0.78]   [
1]     'You're so cute.'
    [                0.5]    [                    0.45]   [
1]     'You should take a v…'
    [                0.2]    [                    0.33]   [
1]     'I forgive you.'
  Name       Size            Bytes  Class     Attributes

  nums       4x3                96  double
  raw        5x4              2662  cell
  text       5x4              2566  cell
```

Subscript indices must either be real positive integers or logicals.

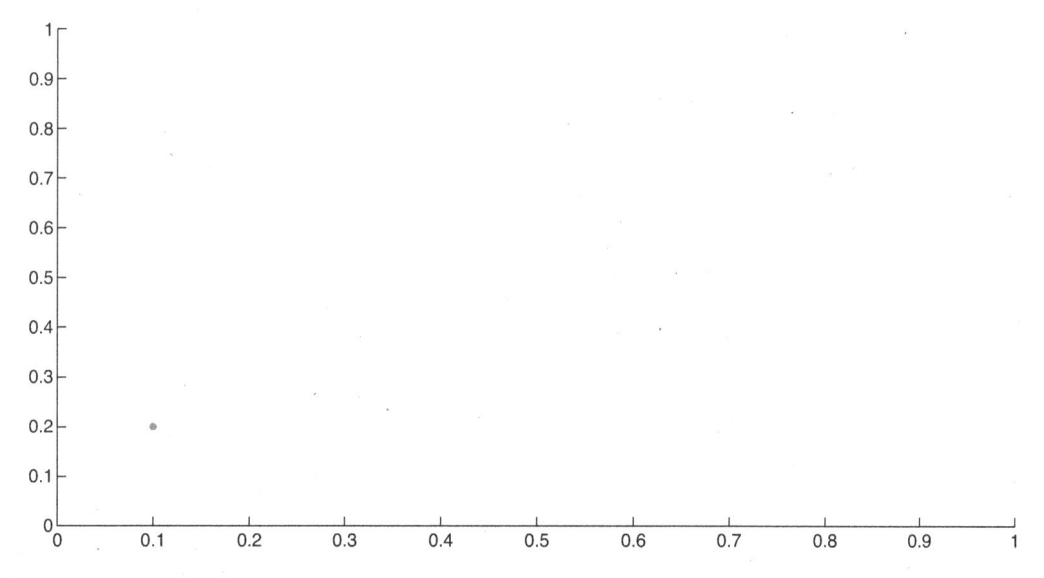

Figure 8.7

8.4.4 Solved Problem Comment

The problem is that the word 'text' is used in the second output of xlsread and then also with num2str, and also in connection with plotting. But text is a built-in function. Changing text to txt in the line with xlsread and in the line with num2str solves the problem.

The take-home message is that sometimes top-down processing can mess things up. Here, because I was thinking that the second output argument of xlsread is of type text, I entered the word text in the second output of xlsread and then, as it happened, I called the text command to produce the graph I wanted. MATLAB came back with an error which made no sense at the time. I spent a long time (several minutes) trying to understand what was wrong. It turned out that I had

200   *Functions*

used a reserved word in a place where it mattered. If I had typed txt or even my_dog_Fido as the name of the second output of xlsread, there would have been no problem.

8.4.5   Solved Problem Code

```
clear all
close all
commandwindow
clc

[nums txt raw]=xlsread('David_Week_7_Excel_Relationships_03.xlsx')
whos
fig_number=1;
set(gcf,'position',[1 41 1280 611.]);
hold on
axis([0 1 0 1])
text_x_shift=.005;
for i=1:size(nums,1)
    plot(nums(i,1),nums(i,2),'.','markersize',18)
    text(nums(i,1)+text_x_shift,nums(i,2),num2str(txt{i+1,4}),...
        'horizontalalignment','left','fontsize',12)
end
plot([0 1],[0 1],'k-')
axis([0 1 0 1])
grid on
box on
xlabel('Sender''s Desire To Send')
ylabel('Receiver''s Desire to Receive')
```

8.4.6   Solved Problem Output

```
nums =
          0.1            0.2              1
          0.85           0.78             1
          0.5            0.45             1
          0.2            0.33             1
txt =
  5×4 cell array
    'Sender's Desire to …'   'Receiver's Desire to…'   'Relationship
Quality'      'Message'
      ''                          ''                          ''
'Your jokes aren't t…'
      ''                          ''                          ''
'You're so cute.'
      ''                          ''                          ''
'You should take a v…'
      ''                          ''                          ''
'I forgive you.'
raw =
  5×4 cell array
```

```
    'Sender's Desire to …'   'Receiver's Desire to…'   'Relationship
Quality'      'Message'
    [                0.1]   [                  0.2]   [
1]     'Your jokes aren't t…'
    [               0.85]   [                 0.78]   [
1]     'You're so cute.'
    [                0.5]   [                 0.45]   [
1]     'You should take a v…'
    [                0.2]   [                 0.33]   [
1]     'I forgive you.'
  Name          Size              Bytes    Class      Attributes

  nums          4x3                  96    double
  raw           5x4                2662    cell
  txt           5x4                2566    cell
```

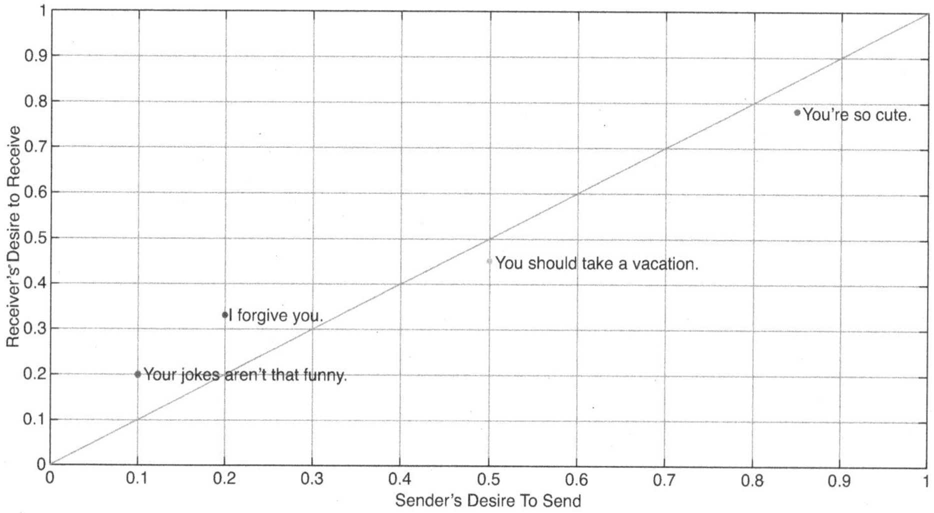

Figure 8.8

8.5 Understanding When Functions Are Not Helpful

8.5.1 Unsolved Problem Comment

All through this book, virtually every program starts with the same four lines of code:

```
clear all
close all
commandwindow
clc
```

As stated in Chapter 1, these four lines clear all variables, close all figure windows, open the command window, and clear whatever is already in the command window.

It would be helpful to avoid having to include these four lines of code all the time and instead to be able to issue one command to do all four things at once. Here is a function designed for this purpose. It has been saved on its own so it can be called by other programs.

202 Functions

```
function stop_typing_four_commands
clear all
close all
commandwindow
clc
```

The function is tested by clearing the deck in the usual way. Then a value is assigned to one variable, x. After that, the function is called with the aim of clearing the variable. The variable is tested by inquiring into its value. However, the variable does not become undefined, as it should if it were cleared. The value is still there. Something is wrong.

8.5.2 Unsolved Problem Code

```
clear all
close all
commandwindow
clc

disp('Value before calling stop_typing_four_commands')
x=1

stop_typing_four_commands
disp('Value after calling stop_typing_four_commands. x should be undefined.')
x
```

8.5.3 Unsolved Problem Output

```
Value after calling stop_typing_four_commands. x should be undefined.
x =

     1
```

8.5.4 Solved Problem Comment

The function doesn't do what's expected because it clears all the variables, which it should, but those variables are *local* to that function, which was not taken into account. All variables are cleared *within* the function, but that action has no effect *outside* the function.

One way to solve this problem is to use global variables, but that approach is more trouble than it's worth for this application. A simpler solution is not to use a function at all, but just to create another program that is called by the main program.

The called program that I have written is stored on my computer with the file name david_housekeeping. I use my first name for my own personal file management (as in david_ginput above). You may wish to do something analogous.

The new program is shown below. The first line is commented and has two percent signs to mark the start of the section. Recall from Section 1.3 that this is how I think programs should typically begin. Then ordinary comments follow, led by single percent signs. The next three lines are executable commands and so are not commented; they don't start with percent signs.

```
%% david_housekeeping
%
```

```
%  A stand-alone program to clear all variables, close all figure windows,
%  open the commandwindow, and clear all contents of the commandwindow.
%
   clear all
   close all
   commandwindow
   clc
```

When the program is called, it works. At the end of the test, the output says x is undefined, as it should. The error message is the one that is sought.

8.5.5 Solved Problem Code

```
clear all
close all
commandwindow
clc

disp('Value before calling david_housekeeping')
x=1

david_housekeeping
disp('Value after calling david_housekeeping. x should be undefined.')
x
```

8.5.6 Solved Problem Output

```
Value after calling david_housekeeping. x should be undefined.
Undefined function or variable 'x'.
```

8.6 Starting Functions With the Word 'Function'

8.6.1 Unsolved Problem Comment

Here is a function and call to that function. The function is supposed to yield a Boolean (true or false) value corresponding to whether any element of the matrix called candidates is in the matrix called full_set. Optionally, the function can generate a matrix called how_many, which lists how many instances of each element in candidates are in full_set. The option is exercised by including how_many (preceded by a comma) in the output list. The function is for use with numbers. The function is commented here because it resides outside the program.

There is a problem, however. Following the illustrative call, an error message appears.

8.6.2 Unsolved Problem Code

[Here is the called function]

```
[truth,how_many]=david_is_in_how_often(candidates,full_set)
number_of_input_arguments = nargin;   % just for interest's sake
number_of_output_arguments = nargout; % just for interest's sake
```

204 Functions

```
how_many(1:size(candidates,1),1:size(candidates,2))=0;
for ca=1:size(candidates,1) % for all the rows of candidates
    for ra=1:size(candidates,2) % for all the columns per row of candidates
        for cf=1:size(full_set,1) % for all the rows of full_set
            for rf=1:size(full_set,2)   % for all the columns of full_set
                if candidates(ca,ra)==full_set(cf,rf)
                    how_many(ca,ra)=how_many(ca,ra)+1;
                end
            end
        end
    end
end
if sum(sum(how_many))==0
    truth=0;
else
    truth=1;
end
return
```

. . .

[Here is the call to the function.]

```
clear all
close all
commandwindow
clc

candidates=[2 3; 4 5;17 18]
full_set=[1:2]
[truth,how_many]=david_is_in_how_often(candidates,full_set)
```

8.6.3 Unsolved Problem Output

```
Undefined function or variable 'candidates'.
```

8.6.4 Solved Problem Comment

The function was badly formatted. Just one word was missing: the word `function` at the very start. MATLAB requires functions to start with the word `function`. The well-formatted first line of the function is shown here. The call to the function is the same as above. The output correctly indicates that it is true that at least one element of candidates is in full_set. When it comes to how_many, the output also correctly shows a 1 for the first row and first column of candidates, indicating that the number 2 appeared one time in full_set. No other elements of candidates appeared in full_set and all other values are 0, as they should be.

8.6.5 Solved Problem Code

[Here is the correctly written opening line of the called function. The rest of the function and the call to it are not repeated here.]

```
function [truth,how_many]=david_is_in_how_often(candidates,full_set)
```

8.6.6 Solved Problem Output

```
candidates =
     2     3
     4     5
    17    18
full_set =
     1     2
truth =
     1
how_many =
     1     0
     0     0
     0     0
```

8.7 Calling Functions Correctly

8.7.1 Unsolved Problem Comment

For a function to be useful, it must be called correctly. Here is a function for finding the Euclidean distance over any number of points in any number of dimensions (e.g., over three points in 3D space). It turns out that the Pythagorean theorem, well known to schoolchildren for finding the Euclidean distance between *two* points, generalizes to *more* than two points no matter how many dimensions there are. As it happens, surprising to some, is that the Euclidean distance is the sum of the squared distances raised to the 1/2 power, not raised to the 1/n power when the integer n exceeds 2. In any case, the new function introduced here doesn't work properly when called. It yields a Euclidean distance, *ed*, of 0 when it clearly should not.

8.7.2 Unsolved Problem Code

[Here is the function that is called.]

```
function ed = david_euclid_dist_any_D(M)
% Find the Euclidean distance over points in any number of dimensions.
% The columns of M are the dimensions (e.g., "x" for col 1, "y" for col 2,
% etc), and the rows >=2 are the successive points.
for row=1:size(M,1)
    if row==1
        ssq=0;
    else
        ssq=ssq+sum((M(row,:)- M(row-1,:)).^2);
    end
 end
 ed = sqrt(ssq);
```

[And here is the call to the function.]

```
clear all
close all
commandwindow
clc
```

206 Functions

```
M=[0 1 2 1 2 3 2 3 4];
david_euclid_dist_any_D(M)
```

8.7.3 Unsolved Problem Output

```
ans =
     0
```

8.7.4 Solved Problem Comment

The error was in the way the function was called, not in the function itself—though, ideally, the function should have only allowed for "legal" inputs. Here you see the original function properly called. The correction is actually not in the call itself but in the structuring of the input to the function. The variable M has semi-colons now to turn M into a 3 × 3 matrix; before, it was a 1 × 9 matrix After seeing the function with the improved M composition, you see a repaired function that has "idiot-proofing." The improved function is shown here followed by the call to it.

8.7.5 Solved Problem Code

[Here is the better call, with the proper formatting of M.]

```
clear all
close all
commandwindow
clc
clear all
close all
commandwindow
clc

M=[0 1 2; 1 2 3; 2 3 4];
david_euclid_dist_any_D(M)
```

[Here is the repaired function with idiot-proofing.]

```
function ed = david_euclid_dist_any_D_idiot_proofed(points_per_
dimension, n_dimensions, M);
% Find the Euclidean distance for one or more points_per_dimension in one
% or more n_dimensions using the matrix of coordinate values whose columns
% of are the dimensions (e.g., "x" for col 1, "y" for col 2, the first two
% dimensions), and the rows are for the successively listed points. Idiot-
% proofing is provided.

ed=NaN;

if (points_per_dimension>1) & ...
        (n_dimensions>=1) & ...
        (size(M,1)==points_per_dimension) & ...
        (size(M,2)==n_dimensions) & ...
        (size(M,1)>=1)
```

```
        for row=1:size(M,1)
            if row==1
                ssq=0;
            else
                ssq=ssq+sum((M(row,:)- M(row-1,:)).^2);
            end
        end
        ed = sqrt(ssq);
    else
        disp('There is an error in your input to the function.')
        disp(['The value of ed is NaN,'...
            'which indicates that there is a problem ...'
            'in the way you called this function.'])
        disp('Please try again. You might need semi-colons, for example.')
        disp(' ')
        return
end
```

8.7.6 Solved Problem Output

[Here is the output when the original function is properly called.]

```
ans =
      2.4495
```

[Here is the output when M is formatted correctly and then when M is formatted incorrectly.]

```
ed =
      2.4495
There is an error in your input to the function.
The value of ed is NaN,which indicates that there is a problem
in the way you called this function.
Please try again. You might need semi-colons, for example.

ed =
   NaN
```

8.8 Creating and Calling a New Function to Control Ticklabel Formatting

8.8.1 Unsolved Problem Comment

MATLAB does not currently allow you to control the formatting of xticklabel or yticklabel numbers. The formatting that comes automatically isn't terrible, but it may not be ideal in all circumstances. For example, as shown in the left subplot generated here, MATLAB changes the number of values that are displayed to the right of the decimal point depending on the presence of zeros in the last significant figure. It would be helpful to specify the number of digits that appear to the right of the decimal point.

A new function is provided to help with this. If the function worked properly, it would show a graph in the right-side subplot that has the same number of digits to the right of the decimal point

208   Functions

no matter what the xtick value and no matter what the ytick value. The function is shown here followed by a call to it. The function doesn't work.

8.8.2   Unsolved Problem Code

[Here is the function.]

```
function david_axis_labels_function(...
    my_y_label_x, my_y_label_y, my_y_value, ...
    my_x_label_x, my_x_label_y, my_x_value, ...
    left_of_decimal, right_of_decimal)

% function to control the number of digits to the right of the decimal
% point when using the text command to produce xticklabels and yticklabels.
% The function is called for one ticklabel at a time (for one tick mark at
% at time. The inputs to the function are the horizontal position of the
% ytick (my_y_label_x), the vertical position of the ytick (my_y_label_y),
% the number of digits to the left of the decimal point, the actual
% yticklabel value, and then the corresponding values for xticks.

text(my_y_label_x, my_y_label_y,...
    sprintf(['%' num2str(left_of_decimal) '.' ...
    num2str(right_of_decimal) 'f'], my_y_value),...
    'backgroundcolor','none','edgecolor','w','horizontalalignment','right')
text(my_x_label_x, my_x_label_y,...
    sprintf(['%2.' num2str(right_of_decimal) 'f'],...
    my_x_value),...
    'backgroundcolor','none','edgecolor','w','horizontalalignment','center')

return
```

[Here is the program with the call to the function.]

```
close all
clear all
commandwindow
clc

n_ticks=5;
marker_size=9;
for sbp=1:2
    subplot(1,2,sbp)
    axis([0 1 0 1])
    plot([-.25:.25:.75],[-.25:.25:.75],'s-','markersize',marker_size,...
        'markerfacecolor','r','markeredgecolor','k')
    axis([-.5 1 -.5 1])
    hold on
    if sbp==1
        xs=[-.25:.25:.75];
```

```
            ys=[-.25:.25:.75];
            set(gca,'xtick',xs)
            set(gca,'ytick',ys)
        elseif sbp==2
            xs=[-.25:.25:.75];
            ys=[-.25:.25:.75];
            my_y_label_x(1:n_ticks)=-.54;
            my_x_label_x(1:n_ticks)=xs;
            my_x_label_y(1:n_ticks)=-.60;
            set(gca,'xtick',xs)
            set(gca,'ytick',ys)
            set(gca,'xticklabel',[])
            set(gca,'yticklabel',[])
            for i=1:n_ticks
                left_of_decimal=1;
                right_of_decimal=.2;
                david_axis_labels_function(my_y_label_x(i),...
                    ys(i),ys(i),...
                    xs(i),my_x_label_y(i),ys(i),...
                    left_of_decimal, right_of_decimal)
            end
        end
end
```

8.8.3 Unsolved Problem Output

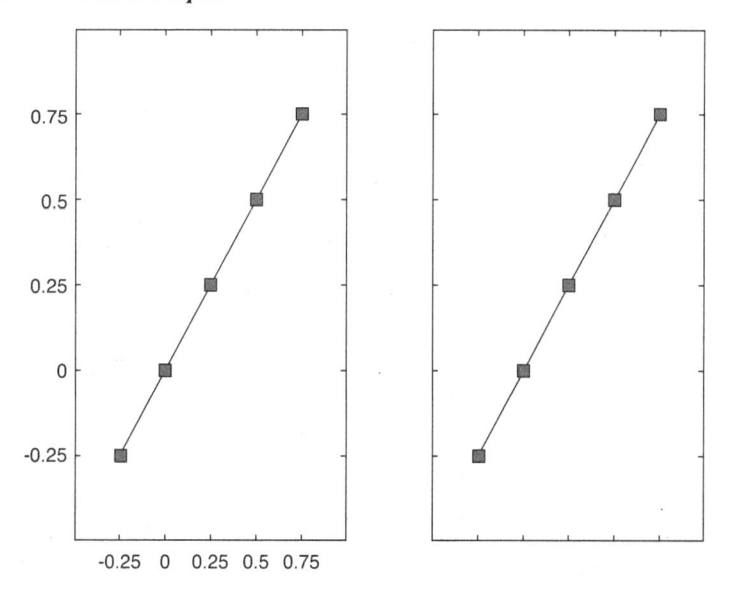

Figure 8.9

8.8.4 Solved Problem Comment

I was thinking of decimal points when I specified the value of right_of_decimal just before calling the function. Because there can't be .2 decimals to the right of the decimal point, the function failed. A low-level lapse of attention caused the problem.

210 *Functions*

To add more information for this example, I enhanced the function to allow for rotation of the numbers along the x and y axis. The new enhanced function is called david_axis_labels_ function_plus_rotations.

8.8.5 Solved Problem Code

```
%% function david_axis_labels_function_plus_rotations
% function to control the number of digits to the right of the decimal
% point when using the text command to produce xticklabels and yticklabels.
% The function is called for one ticklabel at a time (for one tick mark at
% at time. The inputs to the function are the horizontal position of the
% ytick (my_y_label_x), the vertical position of the ytick (my_y_label_y),
% the number of digits to the left of the decimal point, the actual
% yticklabel value, and then the corresponding values for xticks. The
% rotation angles of the numbers along the x and y axes can be controlled
% via rotation_angle_x and rotation_angle_y, respectively.
function david_axis_labels_function_plus_rotations(...
    my_y_label_x, my_y_label_y, my_y_value, ...
    my_x_label_x, my_x_label_y, my_x_value, ...
    left_of_decimal, right_of_decimal,rotation_angle_x,...
    rotation_angle_y)
text(my_y_label_x, my_y_label_y,...
    sprintf(['%' num2str(left_of_decimal) '.' ...
    num2str(right_of_decimal) 'f'], my_y_value),...
    'backgroundcolor','none','edgecolor','w',...
    'horizontalalignment','right',...
    'rotation',rotation_angle_y)
text(my_x_label_x, my_x_label_y,...
    sprintf(['%2.' num2str(right_of_decimal) 'f'],...
    my_x_value),...
    'backgroundcolor','none','edgecolor','w',...
    'horizontalalignment','center', ...
    'rotation',rotation_angle_x)
return
```

[And here is the updated program that calls the enhanced function.]

```
close all
clear all
commandwindow
clc
rotation_angle_x=45;
rotation_angle_y=0;
n_ticks=5;
marker_size=9;
for sbp=1:2
    subplot(1,2,sbp)
    axis([0 1 0 1])
    plot([-.25:.25:.75],[-.25:.25:.75],'s-','markersize',marker_size,...
        'markerfacecolor','r','markeredgecolor','k')
```

```
    axis([-.5 1 -.5 1])
    hold on
    if sbp==1
        xs=[-.25:.25:.75];
        ys=[-.25:.25:.75];
        set(gca,'xtick',xs)
        set(gca,'ytick',ys)
    elseif sbp==2
        xs=[-.25:.25:.75];
        ys=[-.25:.25:.75];
        my_y_label_x(1:n_ticks)=-.54;
        my_x_label_x(1:n_ticks)=xs;
        my_x_label_y(1:n_ticks)=-.60;
        set(gca,'xtick',xs)
        set(gca,'ytick',ys)
        set(gca,'xticklabel',[])
        set(gca,'yticklabel',[])
        for i=1:n_ticks
            left_of_decimal=1;
            right_of_decimal=2;
            david_axis_labels_function_plus_rotations(my_y_label_x(i),...
                ys(i),ys(i),...
                xs(i),my_x_label_y(i),ys(i),...
                left_of_decimal, right_of_decimal,...
                rotation_angle_x, rotation_angle_y)
        end
    end
end
```

8.8.6 Solved Problem Output

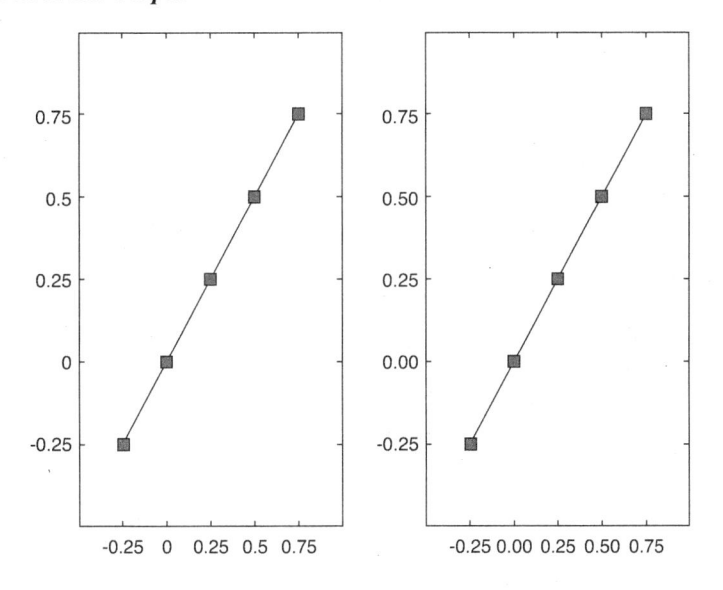

Figure 8.10

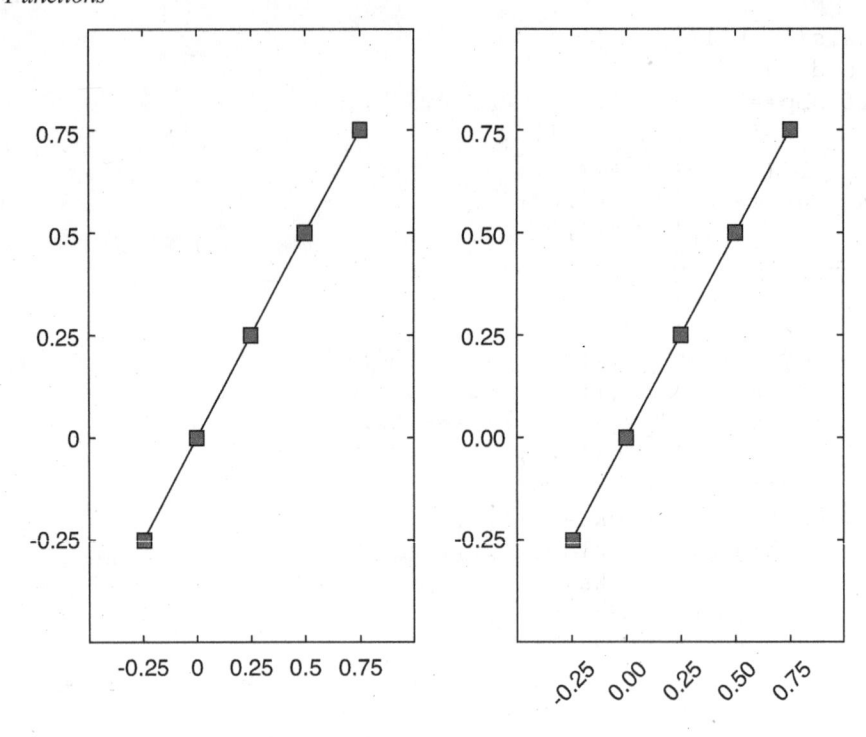

Figure 8.11

8.9 Creating and Calling a New Function to Draw Arrows

8.9.1 Unsolved Problem Comment

As in the last problem, my aim here is to provide a tool that is not currently available in MATLAB, at least to the best of my knowledge. The code is meant to let you draw arrows in a controlled fashion (i.e., to let you control aspects of the arrow beyond its direction and length, which are the only aspects of arrow formation currently possible with MATLAB's quiver function). The new function is called david_arrow. It calls another function called david_angle_find_2, which in turn calls david_euclid_dist. A call to david_arrow is provided, but the call is bad. No arrowhead appears, just a straight line.

8.9.2 Unsolved Problem Code

[Here is david_angle_find_2]

```
function best_angle=david_angle_find_2(x_start,...
x_end,y_start,y_end,n_angles_for_test)
radius=david_euclid_dist(x_start,x_end,y_start,y_end);
angle=linspace(0,2*pi,n_angles_for_test);
best_dist=inf;
for i=1:n_angles_for_test
    candidate_x=x_end + radius*cos(angle(i));
```

```matlab
        candidate_y=y_end + radius*sin(angle(i));
        if david_euclid_dist(x_start,candidate_x,y_start,candidate_y)<best_dist
            best_dist=david_euclid_dist(x_start,candidate_x,y_start,candidate_y);
            best_x=candidate_x;
            best_y=candidate_y;
            best_angle=angle(i);
        end
    end
end
```

[Here is david_euclid_dist]

```matlab
function ed = david_euclid_dist(x1,x2,y1,y2)
ed = sqrt((x1-x2)^2 + (y1-y2)^2)
```

[Here is david_arrow]

```matlab
%% function david_arrow
%   A function to allow for enhanced control of drawn arrows

% A typical call to this function is
% david_arrow(x_start,x_end, ...
% y_start,y_end,arrow_radius,arrow_angle,shaft_descriptor)
% david_housekeeping
% n=1;
% hold on
% x_start(1)=0;
% x_end(1)=1;
% y_start(1)=-1;
% y_end(1)=0;
% for i=1:n
%     if i>1
%         x_start(i)=x_end(i-1);
%         x_end(i)=x_end(i-1)+1;
%         y_start(i)=y_end(i-1);
%         y_end(i)=y_end(i-1)+1;
%     end
%     arrow_radius=.2;
%     arrow_radius_coef=.5;
%     arrow_angle=pi/10;
%     shaft_descriptor='k-';
% david_arrow(x_start(i),…
% x_end(i),y_start(i),y_end(i), …
% arrow_radius,arrow_radius_coef,arrow_angle,shaft_descriptor)
% end

% david_arrow call david_angle_find_2, which in turn calls
% david_euclid_dist
```

214 *Functions*

```
function david_arrow(x_start,x_end,y_start,...
    y_end,arrow_radius,arrow_radius_coef,...
    arrow_angle,shaft_descriptor,n_angles_for_test)

best_angle=david_angle_find_2(x_start,x_end,y_start,y_end,n_angles_for_test);
hold on
plot([x_start,x_end],[y_start,y_end],shaft_descriptor)
fill([x_end,...
    x_end+arrow_radius*cos(best_angle-arrow_angle),...
    x_end+arrow_radius_coef*arrow_radius*cos(best_angle),...
    x_end+arrow_radius*cos(best_angle+arrow_angle),x_end],...
    [y_end,...
    y_end+arrow_radius*sin(best_angle-arrow_angle),...
    y_end+arrow_radius_coef*arrow_radius*sin(best_angle), ...
    y_end+arrow_radius*sin(best_angle+arrow_angle),y_end],...
    [.82 .82 .82]); %'k');
```

[Here is the program that calls david_arrow]

```
close all
clear all
commandwindow
clc

n=1;
hold on
x_start(1)=0;
x_end(1)=1;
y_start(1)=-1;
y_end(1)=0;
n_angles_for_test=3600;
for i=1:n
    if i>1
        x_start(i)=x_end(i-1);
        x_end(i)=x_end(i-1)+1;
        y_start(i)=y_end(i-1);
        y_end(i)=y_end(i-1)+1;
    end
    arrow_radius=.2;
    arrow_radius_coef=.5;
    arrow_angle=pi;
    shaft_descriptor='k-';
    david_arrow(x_start(i),x_end(i),...
        y_start(i),y_end(i),arrow_radius,arrow_radius_coef,...
        arrow_angle,shaft_descriptor,n_angles_for_test)
end
```

8.9.3 Unsolved Problem Output

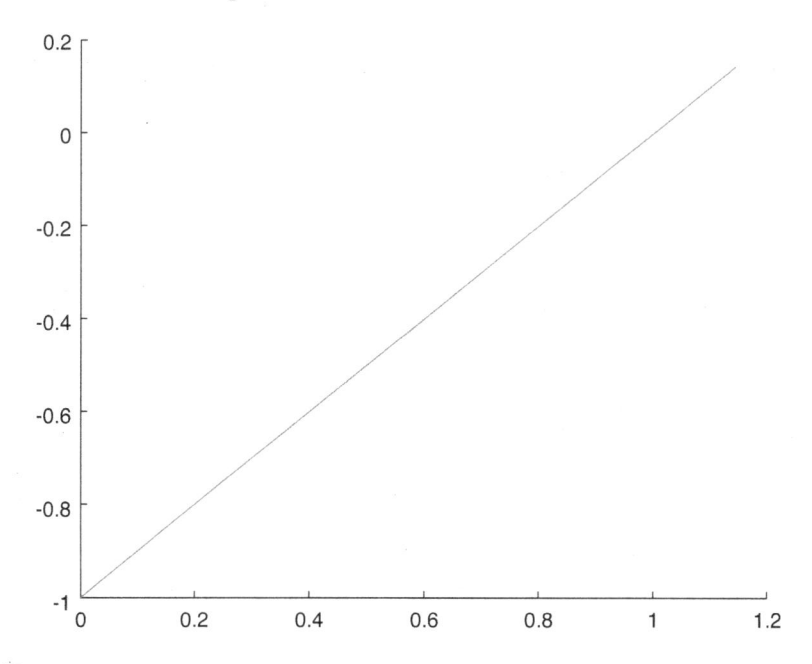

Figure 8.12

8.9.4 Solved Problem Comment

Improper input values were supplied. This could have been prevented with more complete commenting in the new (main) function. I goofed while making version 2, which I saved, but went on to a more successful version 3, which is shown here.

8.9.5 Solved Problem Code

```
%% function david_arrow_3

% A function to draw arrows with adjustable starting positions (x_start and
% y_start), with adjustable ending positions (x_end and y_end), with an
% adjustable arrow head size (arrow_radius), with an adjustable degree of
% "backtracking" to go from the ends of the arrow-head lines back to the
% main arrow by an amount proportional to the lengths of the arrow-head
% lines (arrow_radius_coefficient), with an adjustable angle for the
% arrow-head lines to jut out from the arrow end (arrow_angle), with an
% adjustable graphics descriptor for the lines forming the border of the
% arrow (shaft_descriptor), and the number of angles used to find the best
% angle for the arrow-head lines, though other more direct methods could be
% used for this (n_angles_for_test).

% A typical call to this function is
% david_arrow_3(x_start,x_end,...
% y_start,y_end,arrow_radius,arrow_angle,shaft_descriptor)
% david_housekeeping n=1; hold on x_start(1)=0; x_end(1)=1; y_start(1)=-1;
```

Functions

```
%   y_end(1)=0;
%   for i=1:n
%       if i>1
%           x_start(i)=x_end(i-1); x_end(i)=x_end(i-1)+1;
%           y_start(i)=y_end(i-1); y_end(i)=y_end(i-1)+1;
%       end
%   arrow_radius=.2; arrow_radius_coef=.5; arrow_angle=pi/10;
%   shaft_descriptor='k-';
%   david_arrow(x_start(i),...
%   x_end(i),y_start(i),...
%   y_end(i),arrow_radius,arrow_radius_coef,arrow_angle,shaft_descriptor)
%   end

% This function calls david_angle_find_2, which in turn calls
% david_euclid_dist

function
david_arrow_3(x_start,x_end,y_start,y_end,arrow_radius,arrow_radius_
coef,...
    arrow_angle,shaft_descriptor,arrow_color,n_angles_for_test)

best_angle=david_angle_find_2(x_start,x_end,y_start,y_end,n_
angles_for_test);

hold on
plot([x_start,x_end],[y_start,y_end],shaft_descriptor)
fill([x_end,...
    x_end+arrow_radius*cos(best_angle-arrow_angle),...
    x_end+arrow_radius_coef*arrow_radius*cos(best_angle),...
    x_end+arrow_radius*cos(best_angle+arrow_angle),x_end],...
    [y_end,...
    y_end+arrow_radius*sin(best_angle-arrow_angle),...
    y_end+arrow_radius_coef*arrow_radius*sin(best_angle),...
    y_end+arrow_radius*sin(best_angle+arrow_angle),y_end],...
    arrow_color);
return
```

[Here is the program that calls the revised function.]

```
clear all
close all
commandwindow
clc

n=1;
hold on
x_start(1)=0;
x_end(1)=1;
y_start(1)=-1;
y_end(1)=0;
```

```
n_angles_for_test=3600;
for i=1:n
    if i>1
        x_start(i)=x_end(i-1);
        x_end(i)=x_end(i-1)+1;
        y_start(i)=y_end(i-1);
        y_end(i)=y_end(i-1)+1;
    end
    arrow_radius=.2;
    arrow_radius_coef=.5;
    arrow_angle=pi/10;
    shaft_descriptor='k-';
    arrow_color=[.8 .2 .5]; % red, green, blue, proportions
    david_arrow_3(x_start(i),x_end(i),...
    y_start(i),y_end(i),arrow_radius,arrow_radius_coef,...
    arrow_angle,shaft_descriptor,arrow_color,n_angles_for_test)
end
```

8.9.6 Solved Problem Output

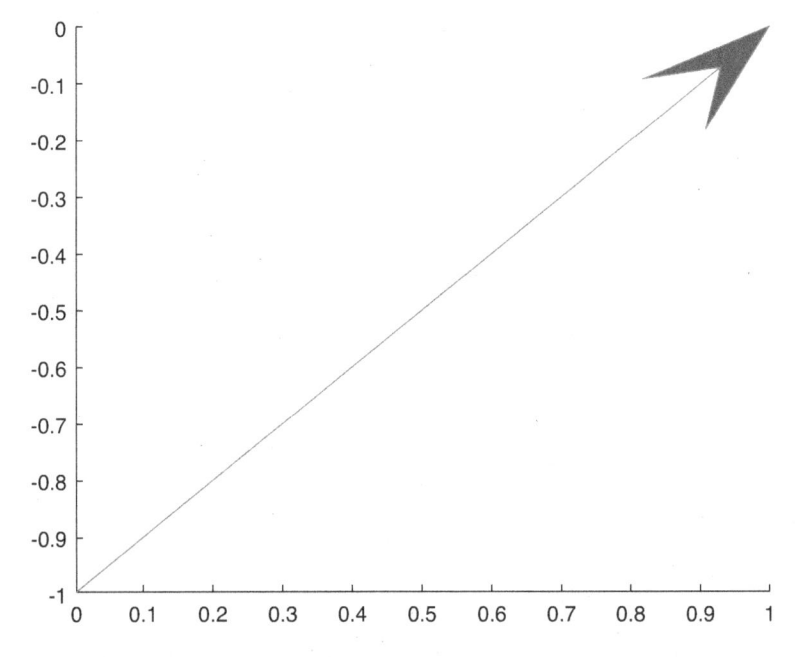

Figure 8.13

8.10 Calling Programs or Functions Remotely Using Eval

8.10.1 Unsolved Problem Comment

Suppose you want to call one program or function from another deep inside a program, but the programs or functions that are available change over time. You might not want to dig deep into the program to change the programs or functions that are called. A function that can be helpful here is `eval`. As its name implies, this function evaluates.

218 *Functions*

The present example illustrates this approach. In the example, you can name a user whose favorite shape, color, and size are given in another program, along with their name (Bob_Criteria or Betty_Criteria). Which program is called depends on the variable assigned to the user. Unfortunately, your evaluation of eval might not be very high in this first use of it.

8.10.2 *Unsolved Problem Code*

[Here are the two criteria programs.]

```
%% Betty_Criteria
favorite_shape='p';
favorite_color='b';
favorite_size=44;

%% Bob_Criteria
favorite_shape='s';
favorite_color='r';
favorite_size=18;
```

[Here is the program that is supposed to use the criteria programs.]

```
clear all
close all
commandwindow
clc

user='Betty';
switch user
    case 'Bob'
        eval(Bob_Criteria);
    case 'Betty'
        eval(Betty_Criteria);
end

max_n=10;
hold on
axis off
for i=1:max_n
    x(i)=randi(max_n,1);
    y(i)=randi(max_n,1);
    plot(x,y,[favorite_color,favorite_shape],'markersize',favorite_size)
end
```

8.10.3 *Unsolved Problem Output*

Attempt to execute SCRIPT Betty_Criteria as a function:

C:\Users\David_A_Rosenbaum\Documents\Dumb Backup Begun 06-01-18\MATLAB BLUES\Betty_Criteria.m

8.10.4 Solved Problem Comment

The problem was that eval must take a string as its input.

8.10.5 Solved Problem Code

```
clear all
close all
commandwindow
clc

user='Betty';
switch user
    case 'Bob'
        eval('Bob_Criteria');
    case 'Betty'
        eval('Betty_Criteria');
    case 'Justin'
        eval('Justin_Criteria')
end
max_n=10;
hold on
axis off
for i=1:max_n
    x(i)=randi(max_n,1);
    y(i)=randi(max_n,1);
    plot(x,y,[favorite_color, favorite_shape],'markersize',favorite_size)
end
```

8.10.6 Solved Problem Output

Figure 8.14

9 Graphics

An earlier chapter, Chapter 5, focused on Plotting. The present chapter (the last one in this book), focuses on graphics more generally. Plotting is addressed again, but now in connection with more advanced or specialized issues. Other topics covered here include forming and coloring shapes, plotting in 3D (including controlling the perspective from which 3D plots are viewed), and animation.

9.1 Ordering Legends

9.1.1 Unsolved Problem Comment

The first program shows a legend, but the top-down ordering of legend entries doesn't map well onto the top-down ordering of corresponding curves. It would be preferable to have better human factors.

9.1.2 Unsolved Problem Code

```
clear all
close all
commandwindow
clc

mfc=['b';'w';'r'];    % markerfacecolor array
hold on
for i=1:3
    for j=1:3
        d(i,j)=i+j;
    end
    plot(d(i,:),...
        'k-o','markerfacecolor',mfc(i),'displayname',['x = ' num2str(i)])
end
legend ('show','location','northwest')
set(gca,'xtick',[1:3])
xlim([0 4])
ylim([min(min(d))-1 max(max(d))+1])
xlabel('x')
ylabel('y')
```

9.1.3 Unsolved Problem Output

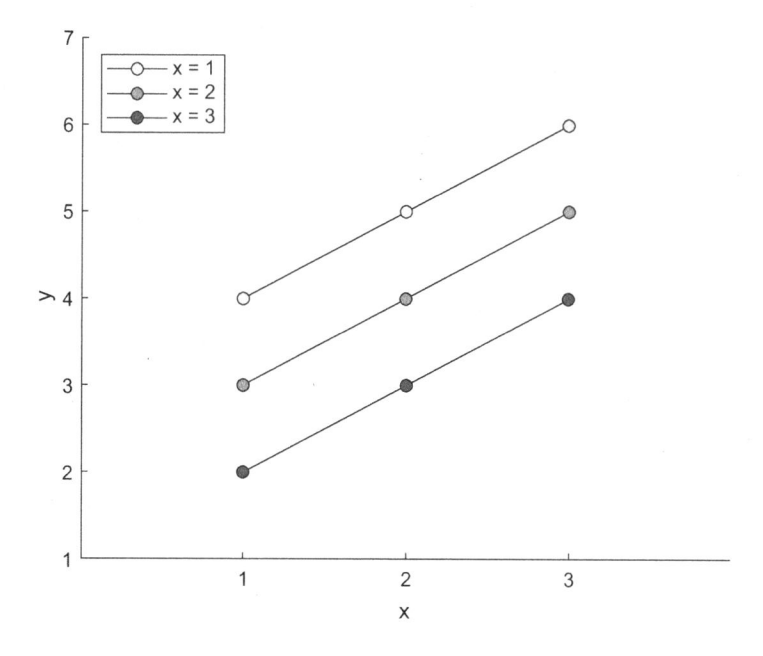

Figure 9.1

9.1.4 Solved Problem Comment

Legend entries are generally produced from top to bottom in the order corresponding to how their corresponding curves were formed. Therefore, to get a better mapping, the highest curve should be plotted first and the lowest curve should be plotted last. This can be done easily by changing for i=1:3 to for i=3:-1:1.

9.1.5 Solved Problem Code

```
clear all
close all
commandwindow
clc
mfc=['b';'w';'r']; % markerfacecolor array
hold on
for i=3:-1:1
    for j=1:3
        d(i,j)=i+j;
    end
        plot(d(i,:),...
        'k-o','markerfacecolor',mfc(i),'displayname',['x = ' num2str(i)])
end
legend ('show','location','northwest')
set(gca,'xtick',[1:3])
xlim([0 4])
```

```
ylim([min(min(d))-1 max(max(d))+1])
xlabel('x')
ylabel('y')
```

9.1.6 Solved Problem Output

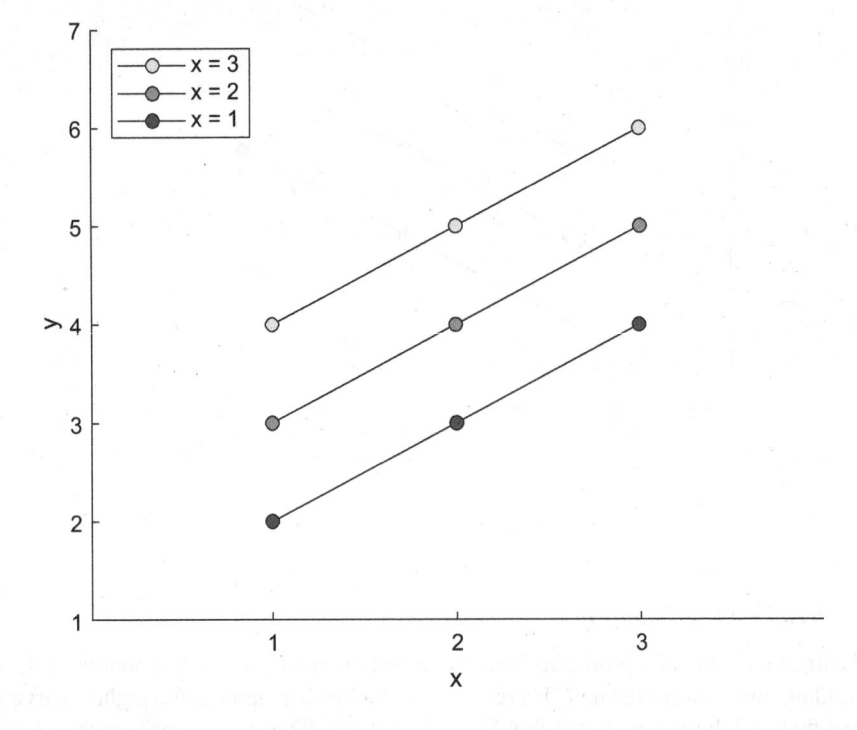

Figure 9.2

9.2 Showing Legends for Some Curves But Not Others, and Showing Subscripts

9.2.1 Unsolved Problem Comment

In the present example, you have three curves but want to refer to only two of the curves in the legend. The middle curve, made up of light gray dashes, shows a theoretical outcome, in contrast to the two other curves, which are made up of solid red and blue curves showing data (albeit fictional data). The outcome is not what you expect. You think that by omitting the display name for one of the curves, that will keep it from being referred to in the legend, but MATLAB creates a legend name for it anyway.

Aside from the issue of how to control legends (solved in the next version), this program shows some math for generating logistic curves. Logistic curves are typically used to describe the probability of one outcome rather than another. Here it's the probability that people judge task B to be easier than task A depending on the number of times each task must be done. Three logistic curves are shown for three groups. The curves appear at different horizontal locations, reflecting differences in how hard the groups find task B to be relative to task A.

Finally, this program shows how to get subscripts: underscore.

9.2.2 Unsolved Problem Code

```
clear all
close all
commandwindow
clc

x=[-6:.01:6]; % a range of values to generate a logistic curve
x_shift=[-2 0 2];
alpha=1;
for i=1:3
    y=(1+exp(alpha*(x_shift(i)-x))).^-1; % logistic curve
    hold on % to plot more than one curve in the graph
    if i==1
        plot(x,y,'b-','linewidth',2,'displayname','A easier than B')
    elseif i==2
        % plot(x,y,'g-','linewidth',2,'displayname','A as easy as B')
        plot(x,y,'--','linewidth',2,'color',[1 1 1]*.6)
    elseif i==3
        plot(x,y,'r-','linewidth',2,'displayname','A harder than B')
    end
end
set(gca,'xticklabel',num2str(linspace(0,1,7)',2));
ylabel('p(B judged easier than A)')
xlabel('n_AA / (n_AA + n_BB)')
grid on
box on
legend ('show','location','northwest')
```

9.2.3 Unsolved Problem Output

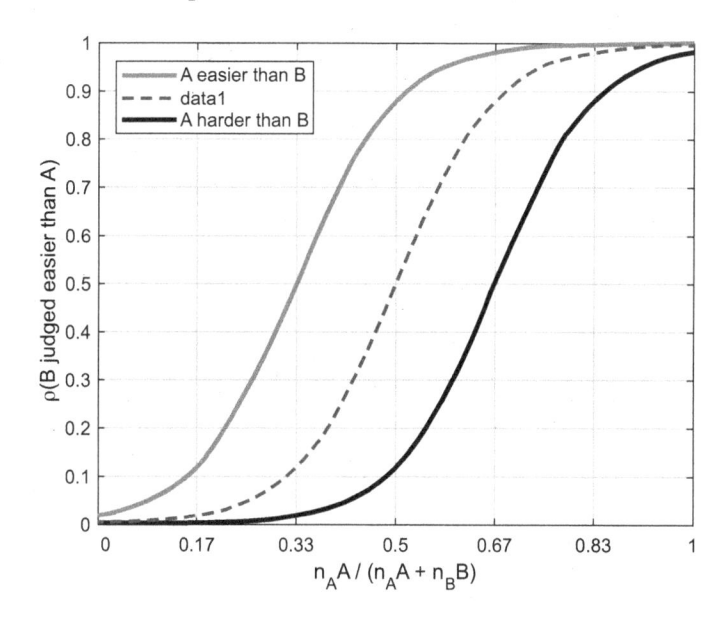

Figure 9.3

9.2.4 Solved Problem Comment

The problem of omitting the legend for the middle curve is solved by assigning the three plots to three variables, arbitrarily called p1, p2, and p3, and then using just two of these variables in the legend call.

Note that the text in the legend call is surrounded by curly braces because the numbers of characters in the text strings for the different legend lines differ. Rather than count the characters in the text strings to check whether they are the same or not, and so whether you need curly braces or not, my advice is always to use curly braces in this context.

9.2.5 Solved Problem Code

```
clear all
close all
commandwindow
clc

x=[-6:.01:6]; % a range of values to generate a logistic curve
x_shift=[-2 0 2];
alpha=1;
for i=1:3
    y=(1+exp(alpha*(x_shift(i)-x))).^-1; % logistic curve
    hold on % to plot more than one curve in the graph
    if i==1
        p1=plot(x,y,'b-','linewidth',2)
    elseif i==2
        p2=plot(x,y,'--','linewidth',2,'color',[1 1 1]*.6)
    elseif i==3
        p3=plot(x,y,'r-','linewidth',2)
    end
end
set(gca,'xticklabel',num2str(linspace(0,1,7)',2));

want_3=false; % grant the option of showing legend for three
curves or two (p1 and p3 in particular)
if want_3
  legend([p1 p2 p3],...
         {'A easier than B';'A as easy as B';...
         'A harder than B'},'location','east')
else
    legend([p1 p3],{'A easier than B';'A harder than B'},'location','east')
end

ylabel('p(B judged easier than A)')
xlabel('n_AA / (n_AA + n_BB)')
grid on
box on
set(legend,'location','northwest')
```

9.2.6 Solved Problem Output

```
p1 =
  Line with properties:
```

```
                Color: [0 0 1]
            LineStyle: '-'
            LineWidth: 2
               Marker: 'none'
           MarkerSize: 6
      MarkerFaceColor: 'none'
                XData: [1×1201 double]
                YData: [1×1201 double]
                ZData: [1×0 double]

  Show all properties
p2 = 
  Line with properties:

                Color: [0.6 0.6 0.6]
            LineStyle: '--'
            LineWidth: 2
               Marker: 'none'
           MarkerSize: 6
      MarkerFaceColor: 'none'
                XData: [1×1201 double]
                YData: [1×1201 double]
                ZData: [1×0 double]

  Show all properties
p3 = 
  Line with properties:

                Color: [1 0 0]
            LineStyle: '-'
            LineWidth: 2
               Marker: 'none'
           MarkerSize: 6
      MarkerFaceColor: 'none'
                XData: [1×1201 double]
                YData: [1×1201 double]
                ZData: [1×0 double]

  Show all properties
```

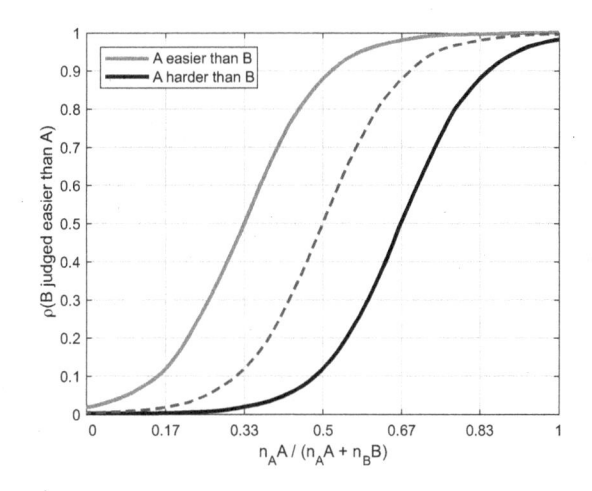

Figure 9.4

9.3 Adding Italics and Symbols to Graphs

9.3.1 Unsolved Problem Comment

Italics and symbols are sometimes desired in graphs. Here an attempt is made to use italicized alpha instead of x, and to use italicized beta instead of y. The result isn't what's expected, however. The characters al appear in front of the alpha on the x-axis and in front of the beta on the y-axis.

9.3.2 Unsolved Problem Code

```
clear all
close all
commandwindow
clc

mfc=['b';'w';'r']; % markerfacecolor array
hold on
for i=3:-1:1
    for j=1:3
        d(i,j)=i+j;
    end
    plot(d(i,:), ...
    'k-o','markerfacecolor',mfc(i),'displayname',['\ital \alpha = ' num2str(i)])
end
legend ('show','location','northwest')
set(gca,'xtick',[1:3])
xlim([0 4])
ylim([min(min(d))-1 max(max(d))+1])
fs=16; % fontsize
xlabel('\ital \alpha','fontsize',fs,'fontweight','bold')
ylabel('\ital \beta','fontsize',fs,'fontweight','bold')
```

9.3.3 Unsolved Problem Output

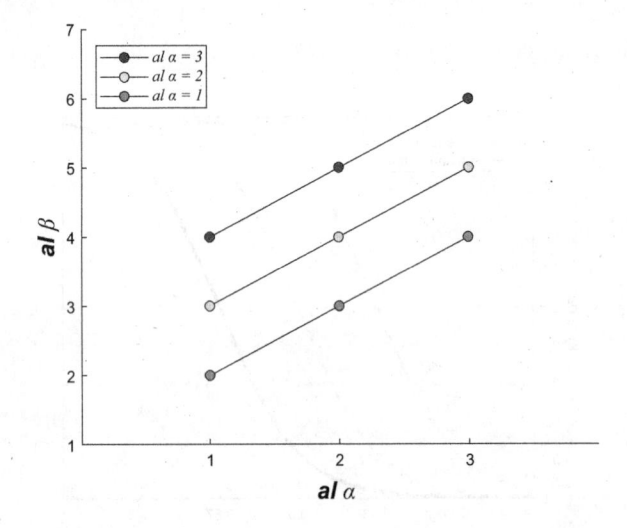

Figure 9.5

9.3.4 Solved Problem Comment

MATLAB requires `\it` for italics as shown in the penultimate line, though you can also (or instead) say `'fontangle','ital'`, as shown in the last line.

9.3.5 Solved Problem Code

```
clear all
close all
commandwindow
clc

mfc=['b';'w';'r'];   % markerfacecolor array
hold on
for i=3:-1:1
    for j=1:3
        d(i,j)=i+j;
    end
    plot(d(i,:), ...
    'k-o','markerfacecolor',mfc(i),'displayname',['\it \alpha = '
num2str(i)])
end
legend ('show','location','northwest')
set(gca,'xtick',[1:3])
xlim([0 4])
ylim([min(min(d))-1 max(max(d))+1])
fs=16; % fontsize
xlabel('\it \alpha','fontsize',fs,'fontweight','bold')
ylabel('\beta','fontsize',fs,'fontweight','bold','fontangle','ital')
```

9.3.6 Solved Problem Output

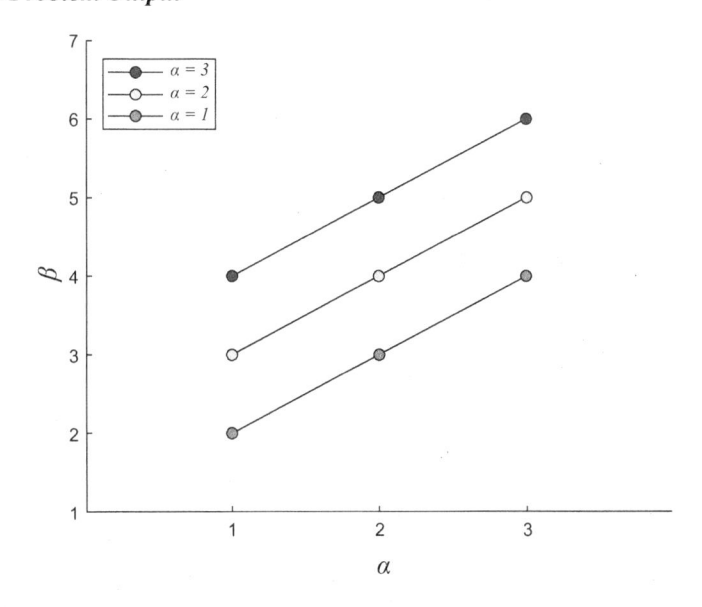

Figure 9.6

9.4 Sequencing Points for Graphs

9.4.1 Unsolved Problem Comment

Suppose that every day you collect two data points. One, whose samples will be plotted on the x-axis, consists of the absolute values of numbers drawn at random from a Gaussian (normal or bell-shaped) distribution. The other, to be plotted on the y-axis, consists of the values just referred to, plus the absolute value of another value drawn at random from the same Gaussian (normal or bell-shaped) distribution, multiplied by stdev. You would like to look at the data with lines between the observed points but with no "backtracks" between them. You would like to plot the data so the successive points are inconsistent with the day-to-day passage of time.

To pursue this goal (one that I have had to pursue on several occasions, albeit not in exactly this context), you look at the data in the first subplot in a way that is likely to show backtracks, and you try to look at the data in the second subplot in a way that ideally should not. The second subplot looks good. All of the backtracks have been removed. However, the values along the x-axis betray a problem. The values along the x-axis are larger than the values along the y-axis, though the y values were based on sums of absolute values. In addition, the correlation between x and y is different in the two subplots, though they must be the same if the identical data are being plotted in different ways.

9.4.2 Unsolved Problem Code

```
clear all
close all
commandwindow
clc

n=20;
stdev=.15;
ms=3; % markersize
r(1:20,1:2)=NaN;
for i=1:n
    g=abs(randn); h=abs(randn);
    r(i,1:2)=[g g+(h*stdev)];
end
r
disp(' ')
subplot(1,2,1)
plot(r(1:n,1),r(1:n,2),'ko-','markersize',ms,...
    'markerfacecolor','w')
c=corrcoef(r(1:n,1),r(1:n,2));
XL=xlim
YL=ylim
% show correlation only with value to right of the decimal
text(XL(1)+.1*(XL(2)-XL(1)), YL(1)+.9*(YL(2)-YL(1)), ['r = '
num2str(c(1,2),2)]);
```

```
subplot(1,2,2)
plot(1:n,r(1:n,2),'ko-','markersize',ms,...
    'markerfacecolor','w')
c=corrcoef(1:n,r(1:n,2));
XL=xlim
YL=ylim
% show correlation only with value to right of the decimal
text(XL(1)+.1*(XL(2)-XL(1)), YL(1)+.9*(YL(2)-YL(1)), ['r = '
num2str(c(1,2),2)]);
```

9.4.3 Unsolved Problem Output

```
r =
        0.49766      0.63828
         1.1557       1.2261
         1.0044       1.1334
        0.33439      0.58241
        0.69688      0.86521
        0.80636       0.8714
         0.4114      0.63338
         1.3316       1.3545
         1.6773       1.6786
         1.7784       2.0319
        0.29139      0.43005
        0.72224      0.81402
        0.83499      0.98695
        0.49905      0.50517
        0.14448      0.18983
        0.73846      0.82103
         1.0645       1.3503
        0.16657      0.19623
        0.22074      0.48666
         1.2329       1.5125


XL =
     0     2
YL =
              0       2.5
XL =
     0    20
YL =
                      2.5
```

230 Graphics

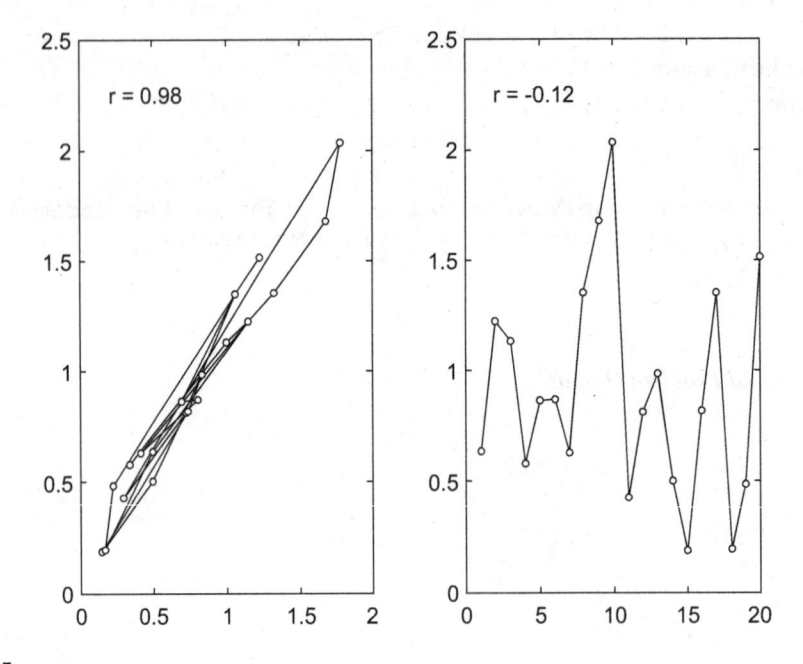

Figure 9.7

9.4.4 Solved Problem Comment

The second subplot was free of backtracks because the x-axis showed the day (or sample) numbers. Hence, the two random variables were not being plotted against each other. The problem can be solved by sorting r with respect to column 1 from smallest to largest to produce the new matrix sr, and then plotting the second column of sr along the y-axis versus the first column of sr along the x-axis. The correlations are now identical, as they must be.

9.4.5 Solved Problem Code

```
clear all
close all
commandwindow
clc

n=20;
stdev=.15;
ms=3; % markersize
r(1:20,1:2)=NaN;
for i=1:n
    g=abs(randn); h=abs(randn);
    r(i,1:2)=[g g+(h*stdev)];
end
```

```
r
disp(' ')
subplot(1,2,1)
plot(r(1:n,1),r(1:n,2),'ko-','markersize',ms,...
    'markerfacecolor','w')
c=corrcoef(r(1:n,1),r(1:n,2));
XL=xlim
YL=ylim
% show correlation only with value to right of the decimal
text(XL(1)+.1*(XL(2)-XL(1)), YL(1)+.9*(YL(2)-YL(1)), ['r = '
num2str(c(1,2),2)]);

subplot(1,2,2)
sr=sortrows(r,1);
plot(sr(1:n,1),sr(1:n,2),'ko-','markersize',ms,...
    'markerfacecolor','w')
c=corrcoef(r(1:n,1),r(1:n,2));
XL=xlim
YL=ylim
% show correlation only with value to right of the decimal
text(XL(1)+.1*(XL(2)-XL(1)), YL(1)+.9*(YL(2)-YL(1)), ['r = '
num2str(c(1,2),2)]);
```

9.4.6 Solved Problem Output

```
r =
      0.22035        0.35665
      0.59117        0.62582
       1.7478         1.7582
      0.92698         1.0857
      0.22248         0.3311
      0.80841        0.94377
     0.067267        0.17821
      0.39678        0.53714
       2.2572         2.4105
      0.17188        0.22407
       1.1484         1.2444
      0.60495        0.64772
      0.69522        0.71119
       1.1257         1.2415
      0.41113        0.46921
        1.644         1.6885
       1.7397         1.9194
      0.63708        0.78959
       1.1291         1.2125
      0.75136        0.99807


XL =
      0        3
```

```
232    Graphics
YL =
                0               2.5
XL =
        0       3
YL =
                0               2.5
```

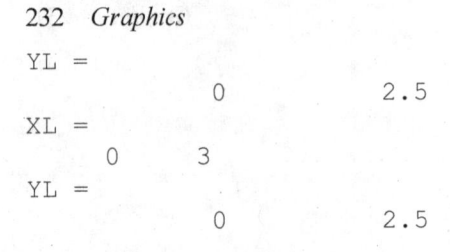

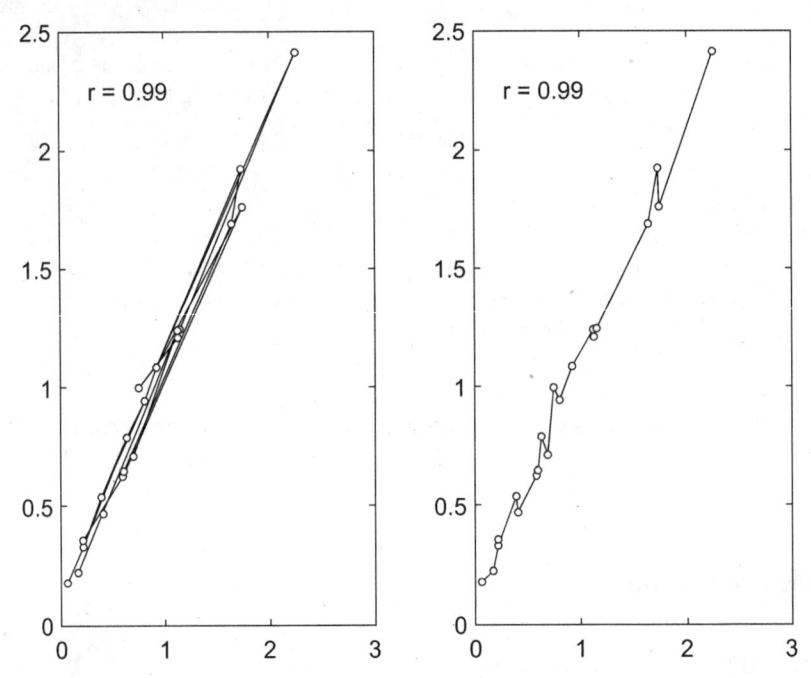

Figure 9.8

9.5 Naming Rather Than Numbering Figures, and Filling n-tagons

9.5.1 Unsolved Problem Comment

Figures can be named, which can help identify them, especially when there are many of them. Figure numbers can be included optionally, as shown here. In this case, as an exercise, the aim is to include figure numbers only for figures showing polygons with odd numbers of corners. Everything looks good until you count the number of corners.

9.5.2 Unsolved Problem Code

```
clear all
close all
commandwindow
clc

polygon_text(4).pt='Square';
polygon_text(5).pt='Pentagon';
polygon_text(6).pt='Hexagon';
font_size=18;
```

```
for n_corners=4:6
    angle=linspace(0,2*pi,n_corners);
    if rem(n_corners,2)==1
        number_title_status='on';
    else
        number_title_status='off';
    end
    fg=figure('name',['n_corners = ', ...
        num2str(n_corners)],'numbertitle',number_title_status)
    hold on
    fill(cos(angle),sin(angle),'w')
    plot(cos(angle),sin(angle),'o','markerfacecolor','y',...
        'markeredgecolor','b','markersize',14)
    text(0,0,polygon_text(n_corners).pt,...
        'horizontalalignment','center', ...
        'fontsize',font_size)
    axis equal
    axis off
end
```

9.5.3 Unsolved Problem Output

```
fg =
  Figure (1: n_corners = 4) with properties:

      Number: 1
        Name: 'n_corners = 4'
       Color: [0.94 0.94 0.94]
    Position: [360 198 560 420]
       Units: 'pixels'

  Show all properties
fg =
  Figure (2: n_corners = 5) with properties:

      Number: 2
        Name: 'n_corners = 5'
       Color: [0.94 0.94 0.94]
    Position: [360 198 560 420]
       Units: 'pixels'

  Show all properties
fg =
  Figure (3: n_corners = 6) with properties:

      Number: 3
        Name: 'n_corners = 6'
       Color: [0.94 0.94 0.94]
    Position: [360 198 560 420]
       Units: 'pixels'

  Show all properties
```

234   *Graphics*

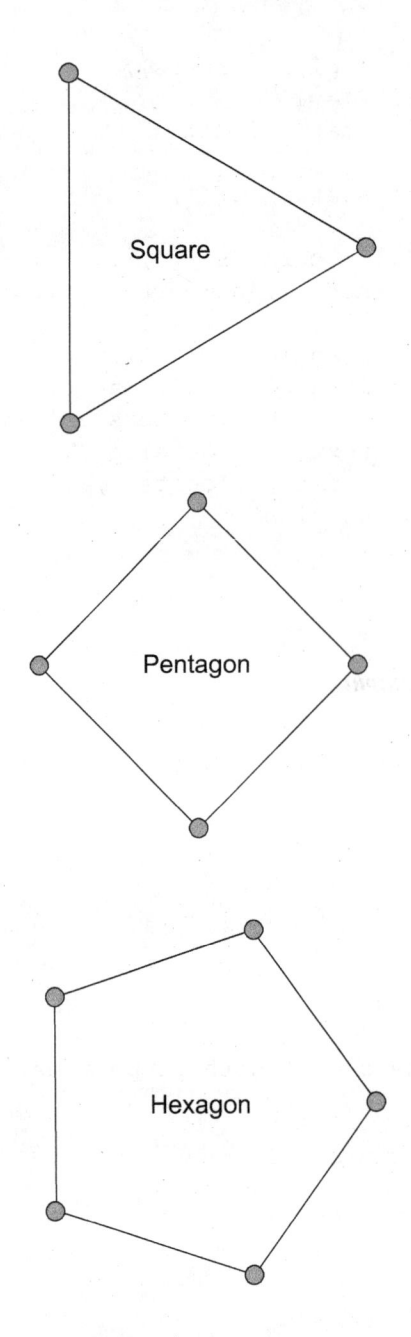

Figure 9.9

9.5.4   *Solved Problem Comment*

The `fill` command runs from the first named value per dimension to the last named value, but if the first and last named values are the same, as they are if they are 0 radians and 2*pi radians, the number of observed corners will be one less than the number of vertices called for. The value of n_corners must therefore be increased by 1 in the specification of angle.

9.5.5 Solved Problem Code

```
clear all
close all
commandwindow
clc

polygon_text(4).pt='Square';
polygon_text(5).pt='Pentagon';
polygon_text(6).pt='Hexagon';
font_size=18;

for n_corners=4:6
    angle=linspace(0,2*pi,n_corners+1);
    if rem(n_corners,2)==0
        number_title_status='off';
    else
        number_title_status='on';
    end
    fg=figure('name',['n_corners = ', ...
        num2str(n_corners)],'numbertitle',number_title_status)
    hold on
    fill(cos(angle),sin(angle),'w')
    plot(cos(angle),sin(angle),'o','markerfacecolor','y',...
        'markeredgecolor','b','markersize',14)
    text(0,0,polygon_text(n_corners).pt,...
        'horizontalalignment','center', ...
        'fontsize',font_size)
    axis equal
    axis off
end
```

9.5.6 Solved Problem Output

```
fg =
  Figure (1: n_corners = 4) with properties:

      Number: 1
        Name: 'n_corners = 4'
       Color: [0.94 0.94 0.94]
    Position: [360 198 560 420]
       Units: 'pixels'

  Show all properties
fg =
  Figure (2: n_corners = 5) with properties:

      Number: 2
        Name: 'n_corners = 5'
       Color: [0.94 0.94 0.94]
    Position: [360 198 560 420]
       Units: 'pixels'

  Show all properties
```

236 *Graphics*

```
fg =
  Figure (3: n_corners = 6) with properties:

      Number: 3
        Name: 'n_corners = 6'
       Color: [0.94 0.94 0.94]
    Position: [360 198 560 420]
       Units: 'pixels'

  Show all properties
```

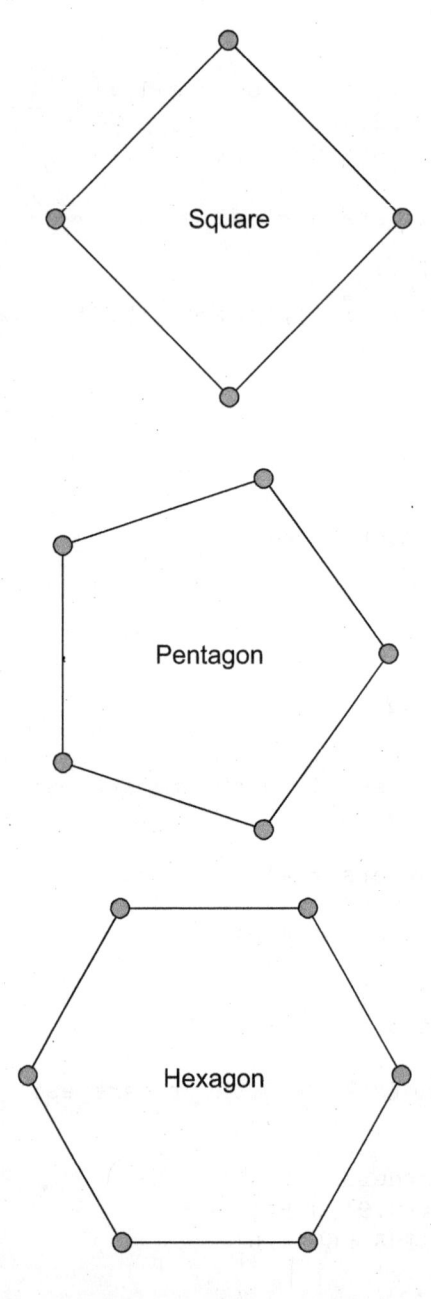

Figure 9.10

9.6 Rotating Text, Overlaying Text on Arrows, and More Plotting

9.6.1 Problem Comment

This program is one I wrote while exploring multinomial models in decision-making. In these models, one seeks to infer from observed data what series of inner decisions led to the final, overt decision. The observed data include the probabilities of various choices and their latencies (how long they took). Because the present program is pretty long, only its solved version is presented here.

The main innovation in the program pertains to the diagram generated at the end. The diagram shows the underlying choice model I was led to. I could have generated it in PowerPoint or some other program, but I elected to program it in MATLAB. It turned out that this posed some challenges. The biggest was having text appear "in front" of arrows (or MATLAB's quiver). In fact, I ended up having quite a bit of email with Mathworks technical support, who said there is no way to put an opaque background behind text. As a result, I developed a work-around.

This program uses `text`, which has been used before in this book, but here more features are used, like ital and rotation. It was necessary to use rotation of the text to overlay it on oblique arrows. However, the arrow shaft went through the arrow. After a while, I learned that there is no way to have a colored background, like a white background, behind text such that the background hides what it's on top of. Someone might want to write an add-on to fix this. Meanwhile, as a work-around, I "interrupted" the black arrow with a white line where the text would go.

Another function used here is `quiver`. This is one of the arrow functions provided by Mathworks. Unlike the david_arrow function introduced in the last chapter, which lets you fill in the arrow head, `quiver` does not.

Because this program has many elements that may be of use to others, it's reproduced here in its entirety. The program is not the most efficient code possible, but I think it's more important to feel in control of one's code than to have it always be as streamlined as possible.

The technical aim of the program is to illustrate multinomial modeling with a two-stage model in which there is some probability of deciding "yes" or "no" in stage 1, and some probability of deciding "yes" or "no" in stage 2 given that "yes" or "no" was decided in the first stage. The latter two probabilities, the probability of deciding "yes" or "no" in stage 2 given that "yes" or "no" was decided in stage 1, can be the same but needn't be.

Assume that the model emits a global "yes" if stage 1 and stage 2 both yield positive decisions, or it emits a global "no" if stage 1 and stage 2 both yield negative decisions, or it emits a global "maybe" if stage 1 yields a positive decision and stage 2 yields a negative decision or vice versa. A way to think about the process is generating predictions about the probabilities of the three response types by drawing a marble at random and seeing what its value is relative to a target value. For example, if p(Yes) at stage 1 is .7 and rand yields a value less than or equal to .7, the response at that stage is "yes"; otherwise it is "no."

A further aim is to generate predictions about reaction times (RTs) by saying that RTs decrease the farther the randomly drawn number is from the target value.

Here a is the probability of "yes" at level 1, b is the probability of "yes" at level 2 given "yes" at level 1, c is the probability of "yes" at level 2 given "no" at level 1, and s is the number of simulations per combination of a, b, and c.

9.6.2 Problem Code

```
clear all
close all
```

Graphics

```
commandwindow
clc

a=.9   % probability of yes at level 1
b=.9   % probability of yes at level 2 if said yes at level 1
c=.2   % probability of yes at level 2 if said no at level 1

s=1000;      % number of simulations
alpha=10;    % exponent for bump used to generate (RTs 10 makes a hump
with flat edges)
k=1*10^8;    % constant for bump used to generate RTs
min_RT=200;  % another constant for bump used to generate RTs
brighten=.80; % for bar graphs

%%% Run simulations and get summaries
summary_1=[];
for ai=1:size(a,2)
    for bi=1:size(b,2)
        for ci=1:size(c,2)
            for si=1:s

                % level 1
                rand_draw_1(si,1)=rand;
                if rand_draw_1(si,1)<a(ai)
                    response_1(si,1)=1;
                else
                    response_1(si,1)=0;
                end
                p_for_bump_1(si,1)=.5*((rand_draw_1(si,1)-a(ai))+1);
% bring range from -1 1 to 0 1
                q_for_bump_1(si,1)=1-p_for_bump_1(si,1);
                RT_1(si,1)=min_RT+...
                    k*((p_for_bump_1(si,1)^alpha)* ...
                    (q_for_bump_1(si,1)^alpha));

                % level 2 if yes at level 1
                rand_draw_2(si,1)=rand;
                if rand_draw_2(si,1)<b(bi)
                    response_2(si,1)=1;
                else
                    response_2(si,1)=0;
                end
                p_for_bump_2(si,1)=...
                    .5*((rand_draw_2(si,1)-b(bi))+1);
                    % bring range from -1 1 to 0 1
                q_for_bump_2(si,1)=1-p_for_bump_2(si,1);
                RT_2(si,1)= ...
                    min_RT+k*((p_for_bump_2(si,1)^alpha)* ...
                    (q_for_bump_2(si,1)^alpha));

                % level 2 if no at level 1
                rand_draw_3(si,1)=rand;
```

```
                    if rand_draw_3(si,1)<c(ci)
                        response_3(si,1)=1;
                    else
                        response_3(si,1)=0;
                    end
                    p_for_bump_3(si,1)= ...
                        .5*((rand_draw_3(si,1)-c(ci))+1);
                        % bring range from -1 1 to 0 1
                    q_for_bump_3(si,1)=1-p_for_bump_3(si,1);
                    RT_3(si,1)=min_RT+k*((p_for_bump_3(si,1)^alpha)* ...
                        (q_for_bump_3(si,1)^alpha));

                end
            end
        end
end

% summary of level 1
summary_1=[rand_draw_1 p_for_bump_1 q_for_bump_1 response_1
RT_1];
mean(summary_1)
figure(1)
subplot(2,1,1)
hist(summary_1(:,end))
colormap([1 1 1]*brighten)
title(['Level 1 RTs  (p = ',num2str(a(ai),2),')']);
subplot(2,1,2)
% plot(summary_1(:,1),summary_1(:,end),'k.') % just doing this left holes,
% so sortrows and use line instead
data_of_interest=summary_1(:,[1 end]);
data_of_interest=sortrows(data_of_interest,1);
plot(data_of_interest(:,1),data_of_interest(:,2),'k-','linewidth',1.2);

% summary of level 2
summary_2=[rand_draw_2 p_for_bump_2 q_for_bump_2 response_2 RT_2];
mean(summary_2)
figure(2)
subplot(2,1,1)
hist(summary_2(:,end))
colormap([1 1 1]*brighten)
title(...
    ['Level 2 RTs if Yes at Level 1 (p = ',num2str(b(bi),2),')']);
subplot(2,1,2)
plot(summary_2(:,1),summary_2(:,end),'k.')  % just doing this left holes,
% so sortrows and use line instead
clear data_of_interest
data_of_interest=summary_2(:,[1 end]);
data_of_interest=sortrows(data_of_interest,1);
plot(data_of_interest(:,1),data_of_interest(:,2), ...
    'k-','linewidth',1.2);
```

```
% summary of level 3
summary_3=[rand_draw_3 p_for_bump_3 q_for_bump_3 response_3 RT_3];
mean(summary_3)
figure(3)
subplot(2,1,1)
hist(summary_3(:,end))
colormap([1 1 1]*brighten)
title(...
    ['Level 3 RTs if Yes at Level 1 (p = ',num2str(c(ci),2),')']);
subplot(2,1,2)
plot(summary_3(:,1),summary_3(:,end),'k.') % just doing this left holes,
% so sortrows and use line instead
clear data_of_interest
data_of_interest=summary_3(:,[1 end]);
data_of_interest=sortrows(data_of_interest,1);
plot(data_of_interest(:,1),data_of_interest(:,2),'k-','linewidth',1.2);

%%% Combine the summaries to get responses and RTs per simulation.
% Have three possible composite responses: yes, no, and maybe.
% RTs can be gotten for each composite response. Because the sizes of the
% three summaries are identical, we can use the size of any to set the
% length of the for loop.
yes_summary=[];
maybe_summary=[];
no_summary=[];
for si=1:size(summary_1,1)
    if summary_1(si,4)==1 & summary_2(si,4)==1  % yes at both levels
        yes_summary=[yes_summary; summary_1(si,5)+summary_2(si,5)];
    elseif summary_1(si,4)==0 & summary_3(si,4)==0  % no at both levels
        no_summary=[no_summary; summary_1(si,5)+summary_2(si,5)];
    elseif summary_1(si,4)==1 & summary_2(si,4)==0  % yes, then no
        maybe_summary=[maybe_summary; summary_1(si,5)+summary_2(si,5)];
    elseif summary_1(si,4)==0 & summary_3(si,4)==1  % no then yes
        maybe_summary=[maybe_summary; summary_1(si,5)+summary_3(si,5)];
    end
end
yes_summary;
size(yes_summary)
proportion_yes=size(yes_summary)/sum([size(yes_summary),...
    size(maybe_summary),size(no_summary)])
no_summary;
size(no_summary)
proportion_no=size(no_summary)/sum([size(yes_summary), ...
    size(maybe_summary),size(no_summary)])
maybe_summary;
size(maybe_summary)
proportion_maybe=size(maybe_summary)/sum([size(yes_summary),...
    size(maybe_summary),size(no_summary)])
```

```
%%% Plot RTs for Yes, Maybe, and No
figure(4)
text_height=.6*max([mean(yes_summary),...
    mean(maybe_summary),mean(no_summary)]);
fs=12; % fontsize
hold on
bar(1,mean(yes_summary))
errorbar(1,mean(yes_summary),std(yes_summary),'k-')
text(1,text_height,num2str(proportion_yes(1), ...
    '%2.2f'),'fontsize',fs,'horizontalalignment','center')
bar(2,mean(maybe_summary))
errorbar(2,mean(maybe_summary),std(maybe_summary),'k-')
text(2,text_height,num2str(proportion_maybe(1), ...
    '%2.2f'),'fontsize',fs,'horizontalalignment','center')
bar(3,mean(no_summary))
errorbar(3,mean(no_summary),std(no_summary),'k-')
text(3,text_height,num2str(proportion_no(1), ...
    '%2.2f'),'fontsize',fs,'horizontalalignment','center')
colormap([1 1 1].*brighten)
set(gca,'ytick',[0:100:600])
ylabel('RT (ms)')
set(gca,'xtick',[1 2 3])
set(gca,'xticklabel',{'Yes';'Maybe';'No'})  % use braces because
these words are of different length
box on

%%% Plot RT as a function of proportion
figure(5)
ms=11;
legend_font_size=12;
hold on
clear x y
x=[proportion_no(1),proportion_yes(1),proportion_maybe(1)];
y=[mean(no_summary),mean(yes_summary),mean(maybe_summary)];
% Plot the three points in the order below so legend words are arranged
% this way from top to bottom for good stimulus-response compatibility
plot(x(1),y(1),'ko','markersize',ms,...
    'markerfacecolor','r','displayname','No');
plot(x(3),y(3),'ko','markersize',ms, ...
    'markerfacecolor','b','displayname','Maybe');
plot(x(2),y(2),'ko','markersize',ms,...
    'markerfacecolor','g','displayname','Yes');
legend('show','location','northeast')
get(legend) % print this out to see which aspects of legend can be specified
set(legend,'FontSize',legend_font_size,'color','w')
xlabel('Proportion')
ylabel('RT (ms)')
grid on
box on
xlim([0 1])
```

242 *Graphics*

```matlab
%%% Diagram the choice probabilities
x_prop=1/5;
y_prop=1/5;
figure(6)
hold on
n=6;
hold on
arrow_length=[.65 .50]  % need two arrow lengths for the two stages;
otherwise the arrows collide
arrow_angle_yes=pi/4;
arrow_angle_no=-arrow_angle_yes;
ms=18; % markersize
mh=.6; % maxheadsize for quiver
fs=11; % fontsize
horiz_text_shift=.01;

x_start(1)=0;
y_start(1)=0;
x_end(1)=x_start(1)+cos(arrow_angle_yes)*arrow_length(1);
y_end(1)=y_start(1)+sin(arrow_angle_yes)*arrow_length(1);
x_start(2)=0;
y_start(2)=0;
x_end(2)=x_start(1)+cos(arrow_angle_no)*arrow_length(1);
y_end(2)=y_start(1)+sin(arrow_angle_no)*arrow_length(1);
x_start(3)=x_end(1);
y_start(3)=y_end(1);
x_end(3)=x_start(3)+cos(arrow_angle_yes)*arrow_length(2);
y_end(3)=y_start(3)+sin(arrow_angle_yes)*arrow_length(2);
x_start(4)=x_end(1);
y_start(4)=y_end(1);
x_end(4)=x_start(4)+cos(arrow_angle_no)*arrow_length(2);
y_end(4)=y_start(4)+sin(arrow_angle_no)*arrow_length(2);
x_start(5)=x_end(2);
y_start(5)=y_end(2);
x_end(5)=x_start(5)+cos(arrow_angle_yes)*arrow_length(2);
y_end(5)=y_start(5)+sin(arrow_angle_yes)*arrow_length(2);
x_start(6)=x_end(2);
y_start(6)=y_end(2);
x_end(6)=x_start(6)+cos(arrow_angle_no)*arrow_length(2);
y_end(6)=y_start(6)+sin(arrow_angle_no)*arrow_length(2);

for i=1:n
    qv=quiver(x_start(i),y_start(i),...
        x_end(i)-x_start(i),y_end(i)-y_start(i),0,'color','k','maxheadsize',mh,...
        'MarkerFaceColor','k')
    x_term=[x_start(i)+x_prop*(x_end(i)-x_start(i)),...
        x_end(i)-x_prop*(x_end(i)-x_start(i))];
    y_term=[y_start(i)+y_prop*(y_end(i)-y_start(i)),...
        y_end(i)-y_prop*(y_end(i)-y_start(i))];
    plot(x_term,y_term,'w');
    plot(x_start(i),y_start(i),'k.','markersize',ms)
```

```
end
axis off
axis equal

% yes level 1
x_start(1)=0;
y_start(1)=0;
x_end(1)=x_start(1)+cos(arrow_angle_yes)*arrow_length(1);
y_end(1)=y_start(1)+sin(arrow_angle_yes)*arrow_length(1);
text(x_start(1)+cos(arrow_angle_yes)*arrow_length(1)/2,...
    y_start(1)+sin(arrow_angle_yes)*arrow_length(1)/2,['p = ' num2str(a)],...
    'horizontalalignment','center','rotation',45);

% no level 1
x_start(2)=0;
y_start(2)=0;
x_end(2)=x_start(1)+cos(arrow_angle_no)*arrow_length(1);
y_end(2)=y_start(1)+sin(arrow_angle_no)*arrow_length(1);
text(x_start(2)+cos(arrow_angle_no)*arrow_length(1)/2,...
    y_start(2)+sin(arrow_angle_no)*arrow_length(1)/2,...
    ['1-p = ' num2str(1-a)],...
    'horizontalalignment','center','rotation',-45);

% yes at level 2 after yes at level 1
x_start(3)=x_end(1);
y_start(3)=y_end(1);
x_end(3)=x_start(3)+cos(arrow_angle_yes)*arrow_length(2);
y_end(3)=y_start(3)+sin(arrow_angle_yes)*arrow_length(2);
text(x_start(3)+cos(arrow_angle_yes)*arrow_length(2)/2,...
    y_start(3)+sin(arrow_angle_yes)*arrow_length(2)/2, ...
    ['p = ' num2str(b)],...
    'horizontalalignment','center','rotation',45);
text(x_end(3)+horiz_text_shift,y_end(3),'Yes', ...
    'fontsize',fs,'fontangle','ital')

% no at level 2 after yes at level 1
x_start(4)=x_end(1);
y_start(4)=y_end(1);
x_end(4)=x_start(4)+cos(arrow_angle_no)*arrow_length(2);
y_end(4)=y_start(4)+sin(arrow_angle_no)*arrow_length(2);
text(x_start(4)+cos(arrow_angle_no)*arrow_length(2)/2,...
    y_start(4)+sin(arrow_angle_no)*arrow_length(2)/2, ...
    ['1-p = ' num2str(1-a)],...
    'horizontalalignment','center','rotation',-45);
text(x_end(4)+horiz_text_shift,y_end(4),'Maybe', ...
    'fontsize',fs,'fontangle','ital')

% yes at level 2 after no at level 1
x_start(5)=x_end(2);
y_start(5)=y_end(2);
x_end(5)=x_start(5)+cos(arrow_angle_yes)*arrow_length(2);
y_end(5)=y_start(5)+sin(arrow_angle_yes)*arrow_length(2);
```

244 Graphics

```
text(x_start(5)+cos(arrow_angle_yes)*arrow_length(2)/2,...
    y_start(5)+sin(arrow_angle_yes)*arrow_length(2)/2,...
    ['p = ' num2str(b)],...
    'horizontalalignment','center','rotation',45);
text(x_end(5)+horiz_text_shift,y_end(5),'Maybe',...
    'fontsize',fs,'fontangle','ital')

% no at level 2 after no at level 1
x_start(6)=x_end(2);
y_start(6)=y_end(2);
x_end(6)=x_start(6)+cos(arrow_angle_no)*arrow_length(2);
y_end(6)=y_start(6)+sin(arrow_angle_no)*arrow_length(2);
text(x_start(6)+cos(arrow_angle_no)*arrow_length(2)/2,...
    y_start(6)+sin(arrow_angle_no)*arrow_length(2)/2, ...
    ['1-p = ' num2str(1-a)],...
    'horizontalalignment','center','rotation',-45,'fontangle','ital');
text(x_end(6)+horiz_text_shift,y_end(6),...
    'No','fontsize',fs,'fontangle','ital')
```

9.6.3 Problem Output

```
a =
         0.9
b =
         0.9
c =
         0.2
ans =
      0.48511      0.29256      0.70744         0.9       233.64
ans =
      0.49374      0.29687      0.70313       0.894        234.2
ans =
       0.5007      0.65035      0.34965         0.2       242.21
ans =
   801     1
proportion_yes =
       0.7986   0.00099701
ans =
    84     1
proportion_no =
      0.083749   0.00099701
ans =
   115     1
proportion_maybe =
       0.11466   0.00099701
            AutoUpdate: 'on'
          BeingDeleted: 'off'
                   Box: 'on'
             BusyAction: 'queue'
          ButtonDownFcn: @bdowncb
              Children: [0×0 GraphicsPlaceholder]
```

```
               Color: [1 1 1]
           CreateFcn: ''
           DeleteFcn: ''
           EdgeColor: [0.15 0.15 0.15]
           FontAngle: 'normal'
            FontName: 'Helvetica'
            FontSize: 9
          FontWeight: 'normal'
    HandleVisibility: 'on'
             HitTest: 'on'
         Interpreter: 'tex'
       Interruptible: 'off'
          ItemHitFcn: @defaultItemHitCallback
           LineWidth: 0.5
            Location: 'northeast'
         Orientation: 'vertical'
              Parent: [1×1 Figure]
        PickableParts: 'visible'
            Position: [0.72512 0.77254 0.15607 0.12048]
            Selected: 'off'
   SelectionHighlight: 'on'
              String: {'No'   'Maybe'   'Yes'}
                 Tag: 'legend'
           TextColor: [0 0 0]
               Title: [1×1 Text]
                Type: 'legend'
        UIContextMenu: [1×1 ContextMenu]
               Units: 'normalized'
            UserData: []
             Visible: 'on'
arrow_length =
        0.65            0.5
qv =
  Quiver with properties:

         Color: [0 0 0]
     LineStyle: '-'
     LineWidth: 0.5
         XData: 0
         YData: 0
         ZData: []
         UData: 0.45962
         VData: 0.45962
         WData: []

  Show all properties
qv =
  Quiver with properties:

         Color: [0 0 0]
     LineStyle: '-'
     LineWidth: 0.5
```

```
          XData: 0
          YData: 0
          ZData: []
          UData: 0.45962
          VData: -0.45962
          WData: []

  Show all properties
qv =
  Quiver with properties:

         Color: [0 0 0]
     LineStyle: '-'
     LineWidth: 0.5
         XData: 0.45962
         YData: 0.45962
         ZData: []
         UData: 0.35355
         VData: 0.35355
         WData: []

  Show all properties
qv =
  Quiver with properties:

         Color: [0 0 0]
     LineStyle: '-'
     LineWidth: 0.5
         XData: 0.45962
         YData: 0.45962
         ZData: []
         UData: 0.35355
         VData: -0.35355
         WData: []

  Show all properties
qv =
  Quiver with properties:

         Color: [0 0 0]
     LineStyle: '-'
     LineWidth: 0.5
         XData: 0.45962
         YData: -0.45962
         ZData: []
         UData: 0.35355
         VData: 0.35355
         WData: []

  Show all properties
qv =
  Quiver with properties:
```

```
     Color: [0 0 0]
 LineStyle: '-'
 LineWidth: 0.5
     XData: 0.45962
     YData: -0.45962
     ZData: []
     UData: 0.35355
     VData: -0.35355
     WData: []
```

Show all properties

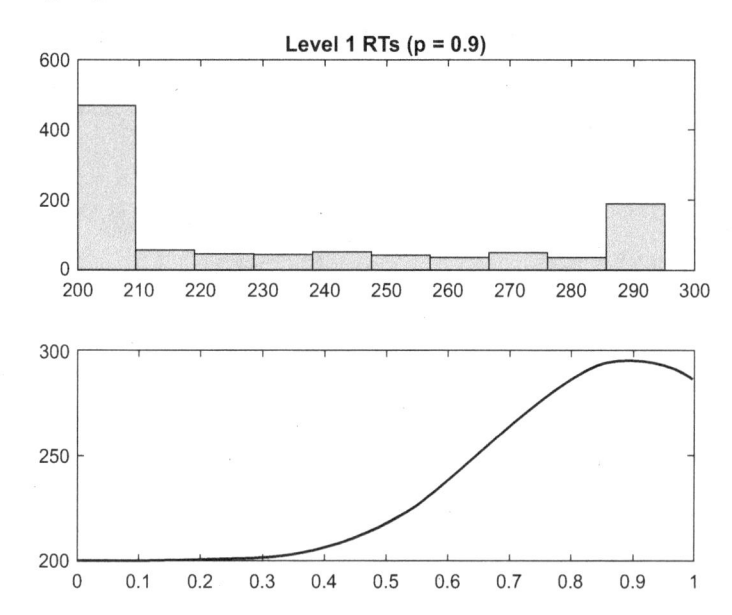

Figure 9.11

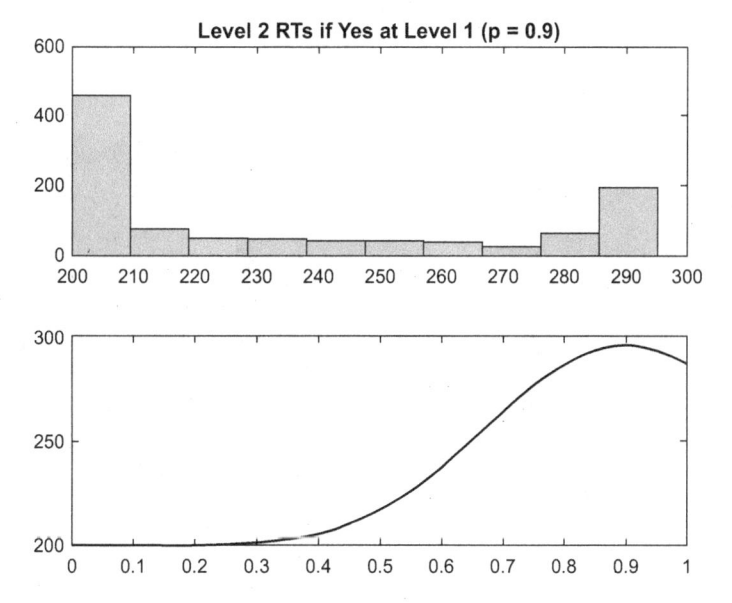

Figure 9.12

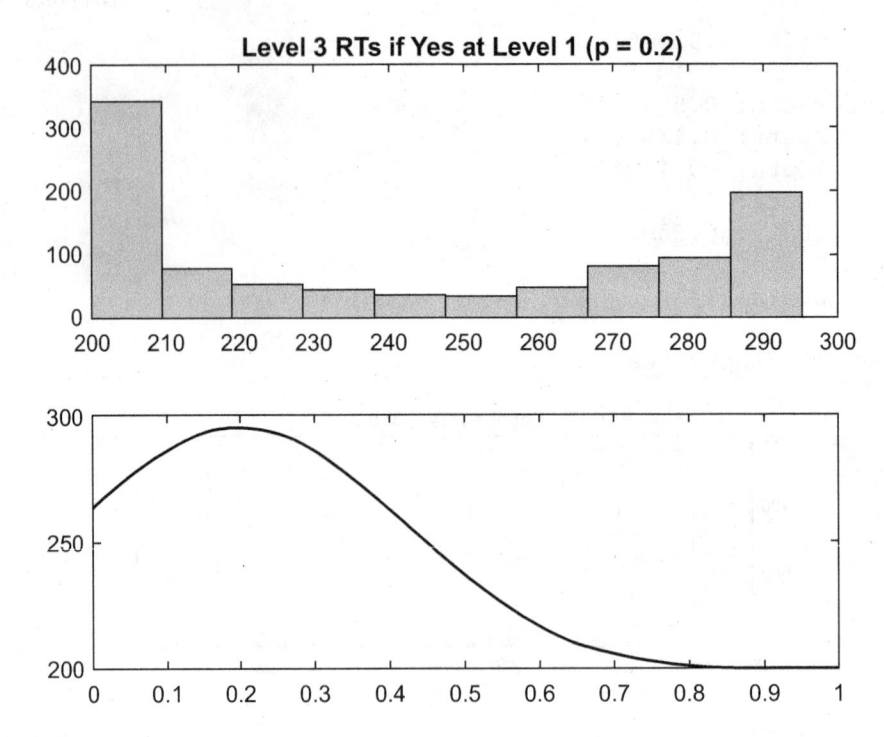

Figure 9.13

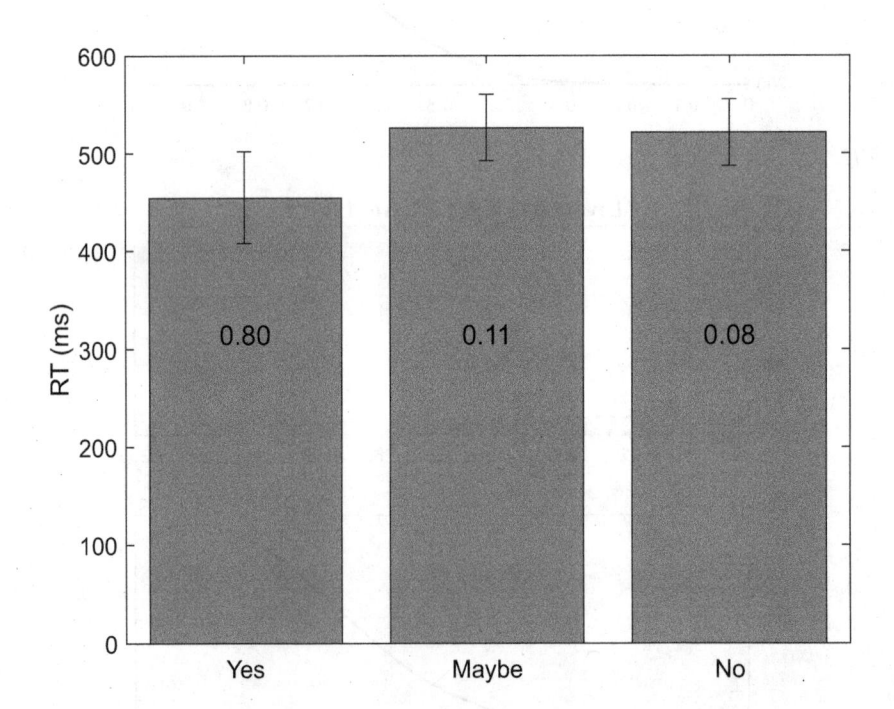

Figure 9.14

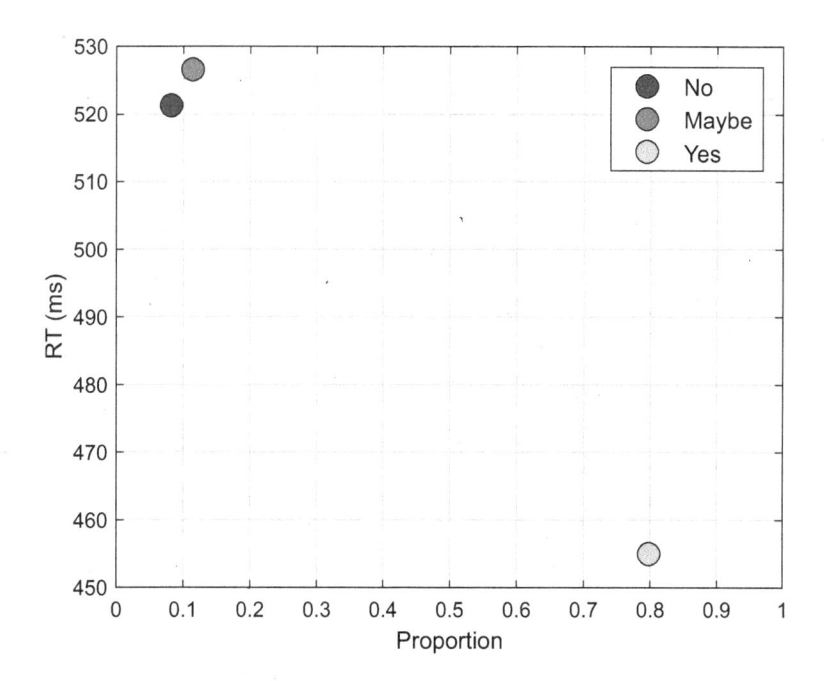

Figure 9.15

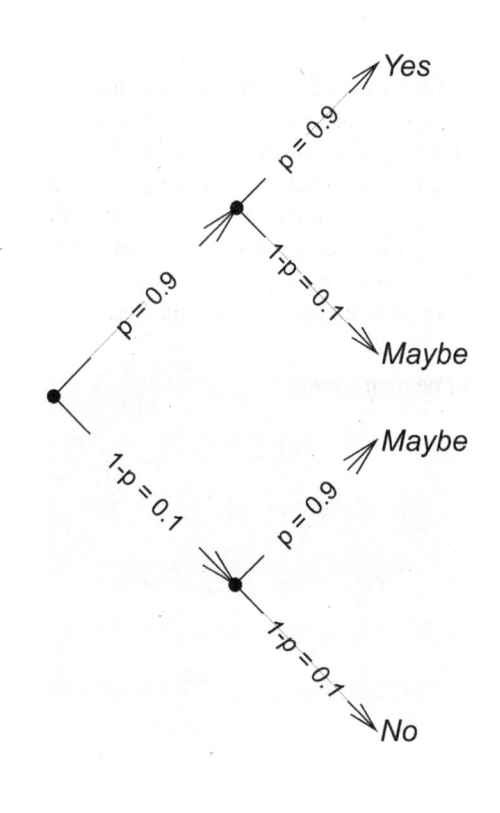

Figure 9.16

250 *Graphics*

9.7 Plotting and Filling in 3D, and Controlling the Camera Angle

9.7.1 Unsolved and Solved Problem Comment

This is a program that illustrates graphing in 3D using the `plot3` and `fill3` commands. The unsolved version fails to show the full 3D rendering because the viewing perspective is suboptimal—from the top down rather than from the side. In this particular case, the top-down view happens to hide critical features, whereas the side view does not.

Because this is a fairly long program and just one added line solves the problem (following the figure(1) command), the unsolved and solved versions are combined here. The unsolved output was generated by commenting the helpful line, which is the line underneath the figure(1) command. The problem was solved by adding a variable called CameraPosition. A suitable set of values for this variable was found by viewing the 3D plot and playing with the turning arrow (an icon visible when the figure window is active) to find a suitable orientation. Once a suitable orientation was found, the `get(gca)` command was used to get the CameraPosition in the command window, and then the good values were added to the program, as seen in the line after figure(1).

A few words about the program will make sense of it, enabling you to draw on parts of the code that might prove useful to you. The program is meant to have human observers judge whether left and right arm positions can be adopted (i.e., are the arm positions anatomically possible?). Surprisingly, there are no existing databases on this topic, as far as I know, so the aim is to develop such a database. This program is a prototype for a larger program to be used with multiple observers and many more trials than the ni=8 iterations used here.

In the program, a torso is created with a front (shown in yellow), a back (shown in gray), a right side (shown in red), and a left side (shown in blue). Left and right shoulder and elbow angles are generated at random. More specifically two components of each angle (azimuth and elevation) are generated randomly. Each set of angles yields candidate elbow and wrist positions in 3-space, with the left arm shown in blue and the right arm shown in red. Participants are supposed to accept the poses by pressing the f key, or to reject the poses by pressing the j key. The poses that are shown are ones that do not let (or should not let) either arm enter or pass through the torso. Decision times are also recorded because they might prove interesting. Decision times might be short when the poses have joint angles at or near the middles of their adoptable ranges (for accepted poses) or when the poses have joint angles far from such angles (for rejected poses), whereas decision times might be long for poses that have joint angles at or near the borders of what's possible.

9.7.2 Unsolved and Solved Problem Code

```
clear all
close all
commandwindow
clc

% Conventions used here for the coordinates
% x == left-right
% y == in-out
% z == up-down

% Point
%   1 left hip front
%   2 left hip back
%   3 left shoulder front
```

```
%  4 left shoulder back
%  5 right hip front
%  6 right hip back
%  7 right shoulder front
%  8 right shoulder back
%  9 left elbow
% 10 left wrist
% 11 right elbow
% 12 right wrist

graph_lim=7;
XMIN=-graph_lim;
XMAX=graph_lim;
YMIN=-graph_lim;
YMAX=graph_lim;
ZMIN=-1;
ZMAX=graph_lim;
np=12; % number of points
r(1:np)=2; % radius from parent point
beta_range=2*pi;   % azimuth
alpha_range=2*pi;  % elevation
delta_prop_length=.001;  % for checking that a limb segment goes into the torso
ni=8; % number of iterations

% assign p values to torso corners
LHF=5;  % left hip front
RHF=6;  % right hip front
RSF=7;  % right shoulder front
LSF=8;  % left shoulder front

LHB=1;  % left hip front
RHB=2;  % right hip front
RSB=3;  % right shoulder front
LSB=4;  % left shoulder front

% assign coordinates to torso corners
x(LHF)=0; y(LHF)=0; z(LHF)=0;   % left hip front
x(RHF)=0; y(RHF)=1; z(RHF)=0;   % right hip front
x(RSF)=0; y(RSF)=1; z(RSF)=3;   % right shoulder front
x(LSF)=0; y(LSF)=0; z(LSF)=3;   % left shoulder front

x(LHB)=1; y(LHB)=0; z(LHB)=0;   % left hip back
x(RHB)=1; y(RHB)=1; z(RHB)=0;   % right hip back
x(RSB)=1; y(RSB)=1; z(RSB)=3;   % right shoulder back
x(LSB)=1; y(LSB)=0; z(LSB)=3;   % left shoulder back

ms=24; % markersize

S=[];  % initialize S, where lots of data will be stored
S_short=[]; % initialize S_short, where less data will be stored
```

252 *Graphics*

```
for i=1:ni

    figure(1)
    set(gca,'CameraPosition',[-68.548 -82.884 34.976]); %the critical line
    hold on
    axis([XMIN XMAX YMIN YMAX ZMIN ZMAX])

    % draw front, back, left, and right sides
    light_blue_color=[.5 .5 .9];

    fill3(x([LHB RHB RSB LSB]),...
        y([LHB RHB RSB LSB]),...
        z([LHB RHB RSB LSB]),'w')    %back
    fill3(x([LHF RHF RSF LSF]),...
        y([LHF RHF RSF LSF]),...
        z([LHF RHF RSF LSF]),'y')    %front
    fill3(x([RHF RHB RSB RSF]),...
        y([RHF RHB RSB RSF]),...
        z([RHF RHB RSB RSF]),'r')    %right
    fill3(x([LHF LHB LSB LSF]),...
        y([LHF LHB LSB LSF]),...
        z([LHF LHB LSB LSF]),...
        light_blue_color) %left

    % Generate possible left and right arm positions that don't enter the
    % torso. Point, p,
    % 9 is left shoulder
    % 10 is left elbow
    % 11 is right shoulder
    % 12 is right elbow

    % initialize counter for number of random samples needed
    intersect_check=0;

    % initialize the bad condition to be escaped
    intersects=true;

    while intersects==true
    % start off on an optimistic foot, have it go bad and try again if needed
        intersects=false;
        for p=9:12
            beta(p)=rand*beta_range;
            alpha(p)=rand*alpha_range;
            if p==9
                origin=LSF;
            elseif p==11
                origin=RSF;
            else
                origin=p-1;
            end
            x(p)=x(origin)+r(origin)*cos(beta(p))*sin(alpha(p));
```

```
            y(p)=y(origin)+r(origin)*cos(beta(p))*cos(alpha(p));
            z(p)=z(origin)+r(origin)*sin(beta(p));

            % Does any segment enter the torso?
            for prop_length=0:delta_prop_length:1
                candidate_x=x(origin)+...
                    prop_length*(x(p)-x(origin));
                candidate_y=y(origin)+...
                    prop_length*(y(p)-y(origin));
                candidate_z=z(origin)+...
                    prop_length*(z(p)-z(origin));

                if ...
                        candidate_x>min(x(1:8)) & ...
                        candidate_x<max(x(1:8)) & ...
                        candidate_y>min(y(1:8)) & ...
                        candidate_y<max(y(1:8)) & ...
                        candidate_z>min(z(1:8)) & ...
                        candidate_z<max(z(1:8))
                    intersects=true;
                end

            end   %for prop_length=0:delta_prop_length:1

    end % for p=9:12
end   %  while intersects==true

% Draw the arms
hold on

plot3(x([LSF 9 10]),y([LSF 9 10]),z([LSF 9 10]),...
    'b.-','markersize',ms)
plot3(x([RSF 11 12]),y([RSF 11 12]),z([RSF 11 12]),...
    'r.-','markersize',ms)
axis([XMIN XMAX YMIN YMAX ZMIN ZMAX])
grid on
xlabel('x')
ylabel('y')
zlabel('z')

% Have user hit j key if posture possible or f key if not. In this
% case, david_ginput is used to suppress the crosshairs, as discussed
% in Problem xxxxxxx. Alternatively, it would be possible to use
% ginput.
b=[]; % the variable for the button press
tic
while isempty(b)
    acceptable_input=false;
    while acceptable_input==false
        [gx gy b]=david_ginput(1);
        if b==106 | b==102    % if b is f (bad) or j (good)
            acceptable_input=true;
            if b==106
```

```
                        status=1;
                elseif b==102
                    status=0;
                end
            end
        end
    end
    S=[S;i x y z alpha beta status toc];
    S_short=[S_short;i beta(9:12) alpha(9:12) status toc];

    % close figure window if more tests to go
    if i<ni
        close
    end

end  % for i=1:ni

S_short

%  Graph the successful (blue) and unsuccessful (red) azimuth-elevation pairs
%  Only need to get one such pair per 2-arm posture since, for now, the
%  right arm has the same shoulder and elbow angles (defined in extrinsic
%  spatial coordinates) as the left arm.

figure(2)
for sb=1:2
    subplot(1,2,sb)
    if sb==1
        title('Shoulder','fontweight','normal')
        relevant_beta_columns=2;
    else
        title('Elbow','fontweight','normal')
        relevant_beta_columns=3;
    end
    ylabel('Elevation (radians)')
    xlabel('Azimuth (radians)')
    axis([0 2*pi 0 2*pi])
    ms=8; % markersize
    box on
    grid on
    hold on
    for si=1:size(S_short,1)
        for col=relevant_beta_columns
            if S_short(si,end-1)==0
                plot(S_short(si,col),S_short(si,col+4),...
                    'r*','markersize',ms);
            elseif S_short(si,end-1)==1
                plot(S_short(si,col),S_short(si,col+4),...
                    'b*','markersize',ms);
            end
        end % for col=2:5
    end % for si=1:size(S_short,1)
end
```

9.7.3 Unsolved Problem Output, Obtained by Commenting the Line After Figure(1)

```
S_short =
  Columns 1 through 8
          1       0.69167      1.6592       2.7356      0.34063
   2.1601      3.6454       2.6082
          2       1.5342       4.1397      0.81191       4.6196
   4.4554     0.74884      0.48989
          3       3.2924      0.63652       4.4651       1.2875
  0.28834      2.9464       3.7784
          4       4.3929       5.0566       1.5162       5.4553
   1.9781      1.1185       3.7368
          5       3.7076       5.9347       2.5091       4.2374
  0.014375     4.9793        5.488
          6       1.0584       2.0523       2.5144       1.0309
   5.4106       2.043       4.7973
          7       1.2632        4.016       2.6382       5.5572
  0.26932      1.5818       1.0797
          8       4.0455       1.3776      0.30676      0.20478
   5.7927        5.56       5.1022
  Columns 9 through 11
       1.6317            1       4.4942
       3.4944            1       67.545
        3.888            0       1.7895
       5.1438            0       1.5006
       1.5228            0       1.4366
       4.3247            0       1.3988
       2.1427            0       1.3491
       2.6078            0       1.5965
```

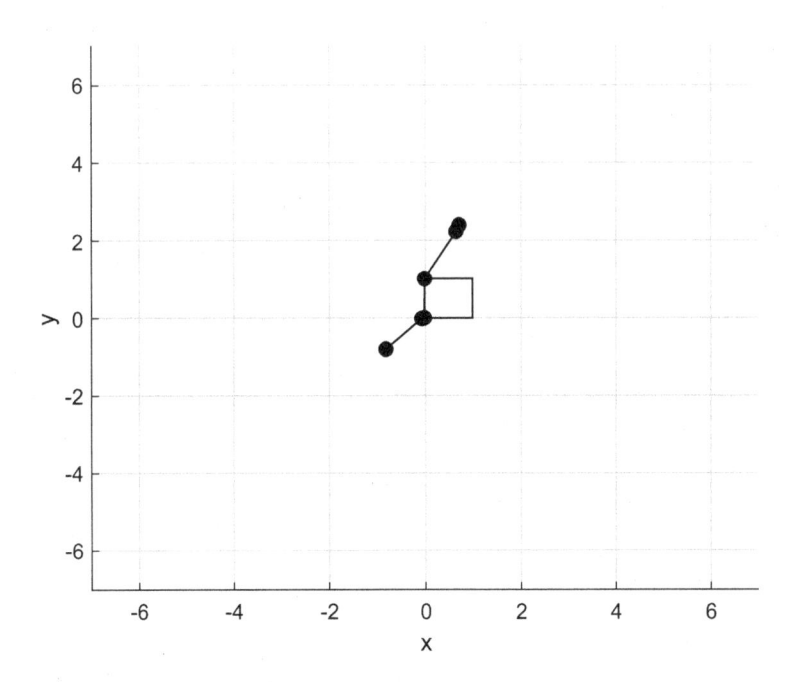

Figure 9.17

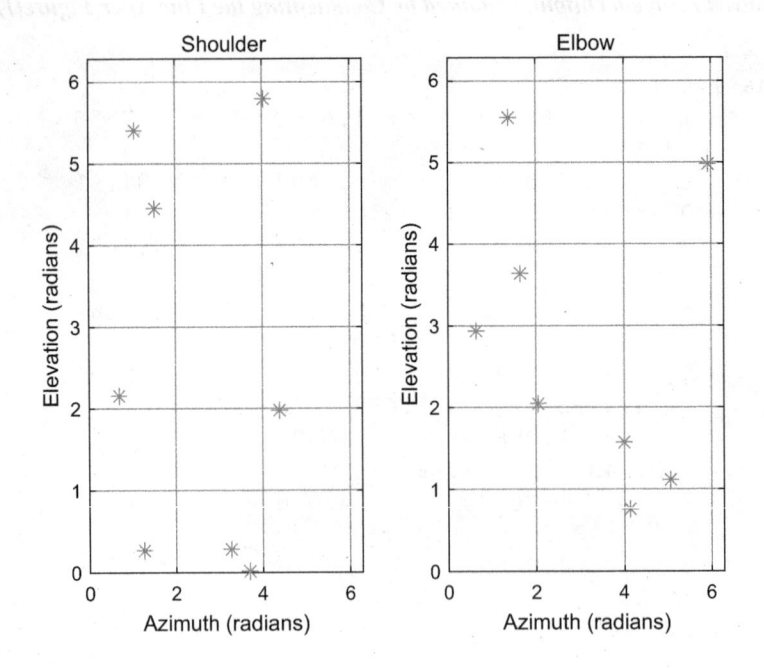

Figure 9.18

9.7.4 Solved Problem Output Obtained by Uncommenting the Line After Figure(1)

```
S_short =
  Columns 1 through 8
          1       6.0807      4.8837      1.4236      5.2041
3.9844     5.6455      0.63628
          2       4.5685      1.8632      3.4538      4.0238
5.8858     1.9616       3.472
          3       1.0127      2.3188      1.4848      5.7133
2.6258     0.50432      6.2476
          4       0.84915     0.33828     5.1665     0.92492
3.4579     4.2509       5.7265
          5       4.9001      3.4506      6.2096      2.2074
3.0613     5.518       0.12034
          6       4.6987      4.3677      5.9762      2.8741
6.0948     1.717        5.7031
          7       1.199       4.8395      2.677       4.2744
5.9821     5.1307       1.8863
          8       5.4776      5.3004      3.0696      2.8713
5.6364     3.0483      0.41051
  Columns 9 through 11
         2.667          1        2.6429
         3.7489         0        3.1546
         4.9687         0        1.5075
         1.9155         0        1.0958
         3.3593         1       75.656
         4.6066         0        4.7337
         5.3942         0        1.2165
         3.742          0        1.3942
```

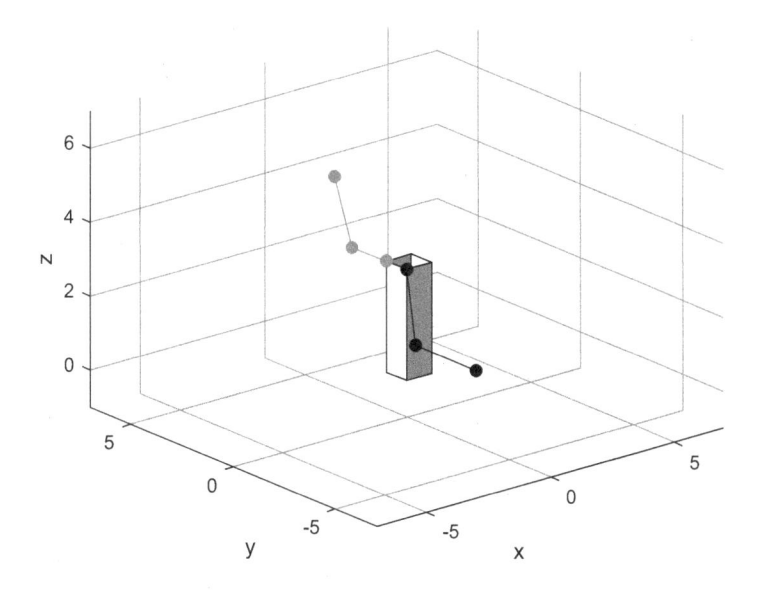

Figure 9.19

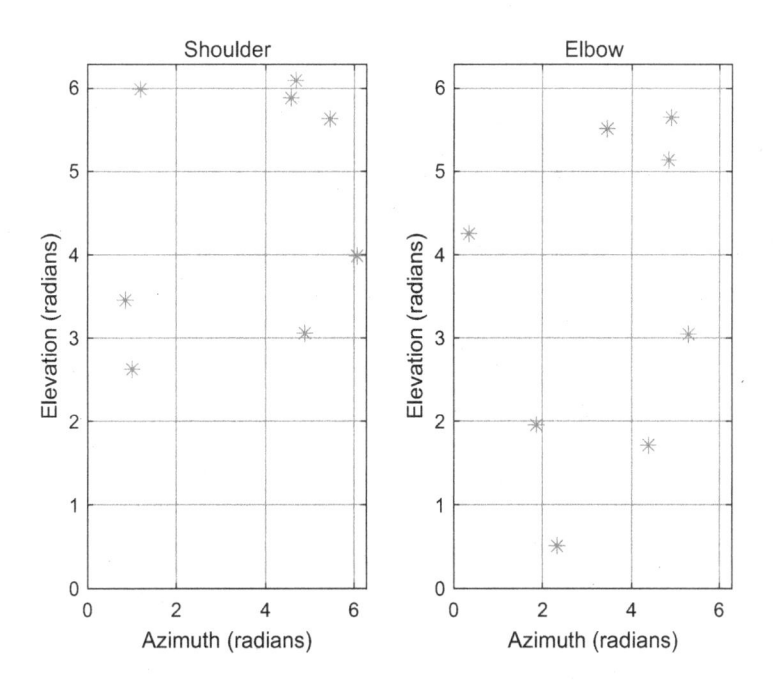

Figure 9.20

9.8 Showing and Then Cropping Images

9.8.1 Unsolved Problem Comment

MATLAB lets you show and manipulate images. The program shown here shows an image on my computer, called 'pic Benny & Papa 10-29-17.JPG' which shows me (Papa) and my grandson (Benny) when Benny was 6 (and Papa was 64). The picture was taken in 2017.

258   *Graphics*

After the image is displayed, the user can click on the corners of an imaginary rectangle centering on the part of the image that is desired. In this case, I clicked on the bottom left and then the top right of the rectangle framing Benny, hoping to see only Benny in the cropped image. However, the image that remained was some other part of the image.

9.8.2   Unsolved Problem Code

```
clear all
close all
commandwindow
clc

pic = imread('pic Benny & Papa 10-29-17.JPG');
image(pic);
axis off
[x y]=ginput(2) % click on the outer corners of the desired frame
kept_part_of_pic = imcrop(pic, [x(1) x(2) y(1) y(2)]);
image(kept_part_of_pic)
axis off
```

9.8.3   Unsolved Problem Output

Figure 9.21

Figure 9.22

Graphics 259

9.8.4 Solved Problem Comment

The imcrop function takes as its input arguments the name of the image being cropped (in this case pic), and a matrix of form RECT, a standard form in MATLAB that includes the following variables (in the order listed here: minimum x, minimum y, width, height). The spatial coordinates passed to imcrop were incorrect before. They are fixed here, making it possible to click on the bottom left and then the top right of the rectangle to frame Benny. Another feature of the fix provided here is that, for any given rectangle, the particular pair of points that is clicked and the order in which the points are clicked doesn't matter, provided the points are the top left and bottom right, or the bottom left and top right. The order of clicking mattered in the previous version. In fact, the reason why the text above said the author clicked on the bottom left and then the top right of the rectangle was to communicate a particular clicking order that would fail. For some orders, one can get lucky and think one's program works in general, though it may not. This is another case where an apparently successful outcome can be misleading.

A final remark about this program is that after the cropping is done, the remaining image is stretched. It can be unstretched by clicking on one side of the figure window and pushing in.

9.8.5 Solved Problem Code

```
clear all
close all
commandwindow
clc

pic = imread('pic Benny & Papa 10-29-17.JPG');
image(pic);
axis off
[x y]=ginput(2)
kept_part_of_pic = imcrop(pic, [min(x) min(y) max(x)-min(x)
max(y)-min(y)]);
image(kept_part_of_pic)
axis off
```

9.8.6 Solved Problem Output

Figure 9.23

260 *Graphics*

Figure 9.24

9.9 Showing Multiple Images and Replacing One of Them

9.9.1 Unsolved Problem Comment

This is a program to show multiple images per figure window. A secondary aim is to click on one image so it is replaced with another. The program, as shown here, calls five stored .jpg files and assigns them to pic(1).pct through pic(5).pct. This version doesn't work, however. Clicking on an image doesn't cause that image to be replaced.

9.9.2 Unsolved Problem Code

```
clear all
close all
commandwindow
clc

pic(1).pct='pic fMRI for blog (02) 08-08-17.jpg';
pic(2).pct='pic Benny & Papa 10-29-17.JPG';
pic(3).pct='pic statues.jpg';
pic(4).pct='pic old-people-in-forest-4928x3264_72022.jpg';
pic(5).pct='pic touch-1661620-2.jpg';

% Show the original four images
figure(1)
for sb=1:4
    ax(sb) = subplot(2,2,sb);
    imshow(pic(sb).pct);
    axis off
    hold on
end
ginput(1)
% clickedAx = gca  % the clicked axes are gca, just confirming that here
axnum = (ismember(ax, gca)); % find the subplot number for the clicked axes
```

```
% In the next figure window, replace the image that was clicked with a new
% image and re-show the images that were not clicked. It turns out to be
% easier to do this in a new figure window than to do it in the same figure
% window because weird image resizing problems arise in the same-window
% case.

figure(2)
for sb=1:4
    ax(sb) = subplot(2,2,sb)
    % if this subplot not the one that was clicked, show same
image as before
    if sb~=axnum
        imshow(pic(sb).pct);
    else
    % if this subplot is the one that was clicked, show
different image
        imshow(pic(5).pct);
    end
    axis off
    hold on
end
```

9.9.3 Unsolved Problem Output

Figure 9.25

262   *Graphics*

9.9.4   Solved Problem Comment

By itself this line of code doesn't work.

```
axnum = (ismember(ax, gca)); % find the subplot number for the clicked axes
```

It needs a find, as shown here in the corrected program.

9.9.5   Solved Problem Code

```
clear all
close all
commandwindow
clc

pic(1).pct='pic fMRI for blog (02) 08-08-17.jpg';
pic(2).pct='pic Benny & Papa 10-29-17.JPG';
pic(3).pct='pic statues.jpg';
pic(4).pct='pic old-people-in-forest-4928x3264_72022.jpg';
pic(5).pct='pic touch-1661620-2.jpg';

% Show the original four images
figure(1)
for sb=1:4
    ax(sb) = subplot(2,2,sb);
    imshow(pic(sb).pct);
    axis off
    hold on
end
ginput(1)
% clickedAx = gca   % the clicked axes are gca, just confirming that here
% Bad (incomplete) code
% axnum = (ismember(ax, gca)); % find the subplot number for the clicked axes
% Good (complete) code
axnum = find(ismember(ax, gca)); % find the subplot number for the clicked axes

% In the next figure window, replace the image that was clicked with a new
% image and re-show the images that were not clicked. It turns out to be
% easier to do this in a new figure window than to do it in the same figure
% window because weird image resizing problems arise in the same-window
% case.

figure(2)
for sb=1:4
    ax(sb) = subplot(2,2,sb)
    if sb~=axnum   % if this subplot not the one that was
clicked, show same image as before
        imshow(pic(sb).pct);
    else % if this subplot is the one that was clicked, show
different image at the subplot
        imshow(pic(5).pct);
    end
```

```
        axis off
        hold on
end
```

9.9.6 Solved Problem Output

Figure 9.26

Figure 9.27

9.10 Keeping Animations From Slowing Down

9.10.1 Unsolved Problem Comment

This program generates an animation, but the animation gets slower and slower as it runs. The output shown here is one frame of the animation, which shows a blue vertical line and a red horizontal line in a circle with a black dot that revolves around the circle. At successive positions, the sine of the angle is plotted in blue (second curve from bottom) and the cosine of the angle is plotted in red (bottom curve). Each time the black dot returns to the zero angle, the sine and cosine functions are reset. The circle makes four revolutions. The times for it to do so are printed out and they grow considerably, reflecting dramatic slowing as the animation continues.

9.10.2 Unsolved Problem Code

```
clear all
close all
commandwindow
clc

n_samples_per_angle=20;
n_cycles=4;
n_all_angles=n_cycles*n_samples_per_angle;
sample_angle=linspace(0,n_cycles*2*pi,n_all_angles);

x_circle_center=0;
y_circle_center=1.5;
line_thickness=1;
trig_line_thickness=line_thickness*1.2;
radius=1;
dot_size=16;
x_bound=3;
y_bound=3;
pause_time=.05;
xlim([-x_bound x_bound]);
ylim([-y_bound y_bound]);
XLim(1:2)=[-x_bound x_bound];
YLim(1:2)=[-y_bound y_bound];
y_for_cosine_graph=-1;
y_for_sine_graph=-2;
T=n_all_angles;
graph_scalar=.25;
n_displays=4;

for dp=1:n_displays
    tic % start timer to record display_time(dp)
    for i=1:n_all_angles
        hold on
        axis equal
        axis off
```

```
% plot circle center
plot(x_circle_center, ...
    y_circle_center, ...
    'k.','markersize',dot_size)

% plot circle
plot(x_circle_center+radius*cos(sample_angle), ...
    y_circle_center+radius*sin(sample_angle),'k-')

%   plot horizontal meridian
plot([x_circle_center + radius*cos(.75*2*pi),...
    x_circle_center + radius*cos(.25*2*pi)],...
    [y_circle_center + radius*sin(.75*2*pi),...
    y_circle_center + radius*sin(.25*2*pi)],'k-')

%   plot vertical meridian
plot([x_circle_center + radius*cos(.5*2*pi),...
    x_circle_center + radius*cos(.0*2*pi)],...
    [y_circle_center + radius*sin(.5*2*pi),...
    y_circle_center + radius*sin(0*2*pi)],'k-')

%    plot line from circle center to current point on circle
plot([x_circle_center x_circle_center + ...
    radius*cos(sample_angle(i))], ...
    [y_circle_center y_circle_center + ...
    radius*sin(sample_angle(i))],'k-')

% plot current point on circle
plot([x_circle_center ...
    x_circle_center+radius*cos(sample_angle(i))], ...
    [y_circle_center ...
    y_circle_center+radius*sin(sample_angle(i))], ...
    'k.','markersize',dot_size)

% plot line from current point on circle to its projection on the
% horizontal meridian
plot([x_circle_center+radius*cos(sample_angle(i)), ...
    x_circle_center+radius*cos(sample_angle(i))], ...
    [y_circle_center+radius*sin(sample_angle(i)), ...
    y_circle_center], ...
    'b--','linewidth',line_thickness);

% plot line from current point on circle to its projection on the
% vertical meridian
plot([x_circle_center+radius*cos(sample_angle(i)), ...
    x_circle_center], ...
    [y_circle_center+radius*sin(sample_angle(i)), ...
    y_circle_center+radius*sin(sample_angle(i))], ...
    'r--','linewidth',line_thickness);
```

266 Graphics

```
            % plot cosine
            plot(-y_bound+(2*y_bound).*[1:i]./T,...
                y_for_cosine_graph+graph_scalar*cos(sample_angle(1:i)),...
                'b--','linewidth',trig_line_thickness)

            % plot sine
            plot(-y_bound+(2*y_bound).*[1:i]./T,...
                y_for_sine_graph+graph_scalar*sin(sample_angle(1:i)),...
                'r--','linewidth',trig_line_thickness)

            pause(pause_time)
            if i<n_all_angles && dp==n_displays
                fill([XLim(1) XLim(2) XLim(2) XLim(1)], ...
                    [YLim(1) YLim(1) YLim(2) YLim(2)],'w')
            end

        end % for i=1:n_all_angles

        display_time(dp)=toc; % stop timer and assign to display_time(dp)

    end % for dp=1:n_displays
    display_time
```

9.10.3 Unsolved Problem Output

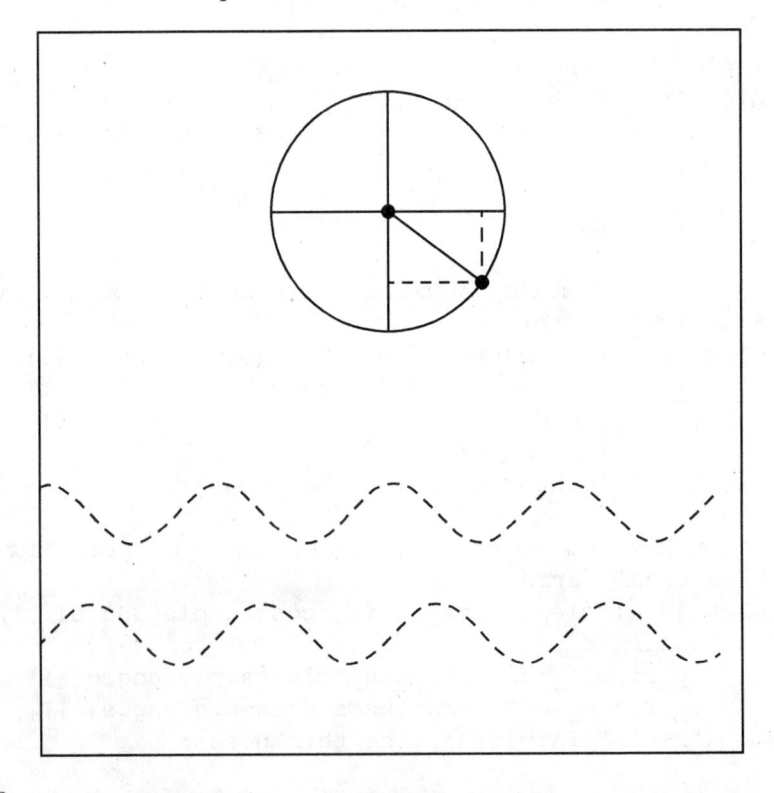

Figure 9.28

```
display_time =
     9.1745         14.129         16.75          19.946
```

9.10.4 Solved Problem Comment

The slowing is caused by the loading of memory as more and more graphics elements are created. Using fill to cover the previously shown items doesn't delete them, and the ever-increasing amount of stored information slows processing.

To solve this problem, use the delete command for each graphics object, stored as such here in association with the plot command. Note that each line of the cos and sin plot are saved as a distinct object so the entire set of cos and sin lines can be deleted with the following commands:

```
delete(P.sinPlot(1:n_all_angles));
delete(P.cosPlot(1:n_all_angles));
```

9.10.5 Solved Problem Code

```
clear all
close all
commandwindow
clc

n_samples_per_angle=20;
n_cycles=4;
n_all_angles=n_cycles*n_samples_per_angle;
sample_angle=linspace(0,n_cycles*2*pi,n_all_angles);

x_circle_center=0;
y_circle_center=1.5;
line_thickness=1;
trig_line_thickness=line_thickness*1.2;
radius=1;
dot_size=16;
x_bound=3;
y_bound=3;
pause_time=.05;
xlim([-x_bound x_bound]);
ylim([-y_bound y_bound]);
XLim(1:2)=[-x_bound x_bound];
YLim(1:2)=[-y_bound y_bound];
y_for_cosine_graph=-1;
y_for_sine_graph=-2;
T=n_all_angles;
graph_scalar=.25;
n_displays=4;

for dp=1:n_displays
tic % start timer to record display_time(dp)
    for i=1:n_all_angles
        hold on
        axis equal
        axis off
```

```matlab
        % plot circle center
        P.cc=plot(x_circle_center, ...
            y_circle_center, ...
            'k.','markersize',dot_size);

        % plot circle
        P.pc=plot(x_circle_center+radius*cos(sample_angle),...
            y_circle_center+radius*sin(sample_angle),'k-');

        %    plot horizontal meridian
        P.hm=plot([x_circle_center + radius*cos(.75*2*pi),...
            x_circle_center + radius*cos(.25*2*pi)],...
            [y_circle_center + radius*sin(.75*2*pi),...
            y_circle_center + radius*sin(.25*2*pi)],'k-');

        %    plot vertical meridian
        P.vm=plot([x_circle_center + radius*cos(.5*2*pi),...
            x_circle_center + radius*cos(.0*2*pi)],...
            [y_circle_center + radius*sin(.5*2*pi),...
            y_circle_center + radius*sin(0*2*pi)],'k-');

        % plot line from circle center to current point on circle
        P.ccp= plot([x_circle_center x_circle_center + ...
            radius*cos(sample_angle(i))], ...
            [y_circle_center y_circle_center + ...
            radius*sin(sample_angle(i))],'k-');

        % plot current point on circle
        P.cuc= plot([x_circle_center x_circle_center + ...
            radius*cos(sample_angle(i))], ...
            [y_circle_center y_circle_center + ...
            radius*sin(sample_angle(i))], ...
            'k.','markersize',dot_size);

        % plot line from current point on circle to its projection on the
        % horizontal meridian
        P.c2h=plot([x_circle_center+radius*cos(sample_angle(i)), ...
            x_circle_center+radius*cos(sample_angle(i))], ...
            [y_circle_center+radius*sin(sample_angle(i)), ...
            y_circle_center], ...
            'b--','linewidth',line_thickness);

        % plot line from current point on circle to its projection on the
        % vertical meridian
        P.c2v= plot([x_circle_center+radius*cos(sample_angle(i)), ...
            x_circle_center], ...
            [y_circle_center+radius*sin(sample_angle(i)),...
            y_circle_center+radius*sin(sample_angle(i))], ...
            'r--','linewidth',line_thickness);
```

```
        % Plot cosine
        P.cosPlot(i)= plot(-y_bound+(2*y_bound).*[1:i]./T,...
            y_for_cosine_graph+graph_scalar*cos(sample_angle(1:i)),...
            'b--','linewidth',trig_line_thickness);

        % Plot sine
        P.sinPlot(i)=plot(-y_bound+(2*y_bound).*[1:i]./T,...
            y_for_sine_graph+graph_scalar*sin(sample_angle(1:i)),...
            'r--','linewidth',trig_line_thickness);

        pause(pause_time)
        if i<n_all_angles
            % delete rather than fill
%               delete(P.cc,P.pc); % can't delete more than one at a time
            delete(P.cc);
            delete(P.pc);
            delete(P.ccp);
            delete(P.cuc);
            delete(P.c2h);
            delete(P.c2v);
            delete(P.hm);
            delete(P.vm);
        elseif i==n_all_angles
            delete(P.sinPlot(1:n_all_angles));
            delete(P.cosPlot(1:n_all_angles));
        end

    end % for i=1:n_all_angles
    display_time(dp)=toc; % stop timer and assign to display_time(dp)

end % for dp=1:n_displays
display_time
```

9.10.6 Solved Problem Output

```
display_time =
       7.3776        6.6587        6.7885        6.6446
```

Index

Note: Page numbers in italics indicate figures on the corresponding pages.

%% (comments) 6–7
3D, plotting and filling in 250–256, *255–257*

adding elements to right side of matrices 12
animations 264–269, *266*
array2table function 122–125
arrows: drawing 212–217, *215, 217*; overlaying text on 237–249, *247–249*
avoiding 'text' as output for xlsread 197–201, *199, 201*

bar graphs 109–112, *111–112*; controlling bars for 113–115, *114–115*; tick labels on 152–153, *152–153*
Bempechat, Janine x

calculations: checking whether two matrices are the same 24–26; discovering and then taking dot product 29–31; getting means 33–35; multiplying matrices 26–27; multiplying matrices element by element 28–29; raising value to a power 32–33; simple summing 23–24; standard deviation 37–40; understanding what you "mean" 35–37
camera angle control 250–256, *255–257*
cells: assigning values to positions of 156–157; seeing contents of 150–152; used to allow for figure titles with different numbers of characters per row 154–155, *154–155*; used to allow for tick labels with different numbers of characters 152–153, *152–153*; used to concatenate double and char variables 148–149
char variables 148–149
colors, plotting 81–85, *83, 85*
columns inserted into matrices 19–20
command window, printing the value of variable in 11
contingencies: adding to new matrix if criterion is met 58–61; checking values relative to cutoffs 46–51; creating a Latin square design 61–65; creating a Latin square design for multiple groups 65–70; sorting 51–55; timing program completions in 70–73; using find to save time 73–76; using for statements 44–46; using if statements 41–43; using while 55–58
correctly calling functions 205–207
crashing and the Enter key 4–5
cropping, image 257–259, *258–260*
cutoffs, checking values relative to 46–51

data: creating formatted headers and, for Excel 133–137; formatting printouts of 130–133
data types 147–148; assigning values to cell positions 156–157; creating deeply nested (three-tiered) structure 159–171; printing structure content 171–173; putting structure elements into matrix 157–159; seeing cell contents 150–152; using a structure to graph deeply nested structure with different kinds of fields 173–181, *177, 181*; using cells to allow for figure titles with different numbers of characters per row 154–155, *154–155*; using cells to allow for tick labels with different numbers of characters 152–153, *152–153*; using cells to concatenate double and char variables 148–149; using fit, understanding its fields 182–185, *183, 185*
deeply nested (three-tiered) structure 159–171; using a structure to graph 173–181, *177, 181*
deletion: of column from multi-row matrix 15–16; of elements from one-row array 14–15
disclaimers, MATLAB 10
division of matrices 31–32
.dlm file 125–126
dot product 29–31
double variables 148–149
drawing of arrows 212–217, *215, 217*
Dweck, Carol S. x

email addresses, users' 141–143
Enter key and crashing programs 4–5
Eval function 217–219, *219*
Excel, writing to 119–122; avoiding 'text' as output for xlsread 197–201, *199, 201*; with column headers using array2table function 122–125; creating formatting data and headers for 133–137

figures: clicking on and saving 143–146, *146*; naming rather than numbering 232–236, *234, 236*; titles with different numbers of characters per row on 154–155, *154–155*
find statements 73–76
fit and its fields 182–185, *183, 185*
fitted exponential function 99–105, *102, 106*
for statements 44–46
function names, MATLAB 1–4
functions: avoiding 'text' as output for xlsread 197–201, *199, 201*; correctly calling 205–207; creating and calling new, to control ticklabel formatting 207–211, *209, 211–212*; creating and calling new, to draw arrows 212–217, *215, 217*; discovering features of mean 189–192; ginput Loses Crosshairs in david_ginput 192–196, *195–197*; started with the word 'function' 203–205; understanding not helpful 201–203; understanding size, length, and numel 186–189; using Eval to remotely call programs or 217–219, *219*

ginput Loses Crosshairs in david_ginput 192–196, *195–197*
graphics: adding italics and symbols to 226–227, *226–227*; keeping animations from slowing down in 264–269, *266*; naming rather than numbering figures, and filling n-tagons 232–236, *234, 236*; ordering legends 220–222, *221–222*; plotting and filling in 3D, and controlling camera angle in 250–256, *255–257*; rotating text, overlaying text on arrows, and more plotting of 237–249, *247–249*; sequencing points for 228–232, *230, 232*; showing and then cropping images in 257–259, *258–260*; showing legends for some curve but not others, and showing subscripts 222–225, *223, 225*; showing multiple images and replacing one image 260–263, *261, 263*
graph limits 81–85, *83, 85*
grids 99–105, *102, 106*

if statements 41–43
image(s): showing and then cropping 257–259, *258–260*; showing multiple images and replacing one 260–263, *261, 263*
indexed positions, assigning values to 13
input-output: avoiding overwriting existing files in 126–130; checking users' email addresses in 141–143; clicking on figures and saving figures in 143–146, *146*; creating formatted data and headers for Excel 133–137; formatting data printouts in 130–133; interacting with users via the input function in 137–138; looking for particular inputs in 139–141; writing out and reading back in a .dlm file 125–126; writing to Excel 119–122; writing to Excel with column headers using array2table function 122–125
interaction with users via input function 137–138
italics 226–227, *226–227*

keystroke sequences, useful 7–8

labels, x- and y-axis 85–90, *88, 90*
Latin square design: created for multiple groups 65–70; creating 61–65
legends: ordering of 220–222, *221–222*; plotting 85–90, *88, 90*; shown for some curves but not others 222–225, *223, 225*
length 186–189
letters added with quote marks 5–6

MATLAB: adding letters with quote marks to 5–6; calculations in (*see* calculations); contingencies in (*see* contingencies); data types (*see* data types); disclaimers on use of 10; functions (*see* functions); getting the enter key to stop crashing programs in 4–5; giving a variable a function name in 1–4; input-output (*see* input-output); matrices in (*see* matrices); plotting in (*see* plotting); program pairs, sections they occupy, and importance of %% in 6–7; Publish feature in 8–9; useful keystroke sequences in 7–8; value of using 1
MATLAB for Behavioral Scientists 1
MATLAB for Behavioral Scientists, Second Edition 1
matrices: adding elements to right side of 12; adding matrices to bottom of other 18–19; adding to new, if criterion is met 58–61; assigning values to indexed positions in 13; checking number of values in 17–18; checking two identical or different 24–26; deleting column from multi-row 15–16; deleting elements from one-row array in 14–15; discovering and then taking dot product of 29–31; dividing 31–32; giving variables acceptable names in 13–14; inserting columns into 19–20; multiplying 26–29; printing the value of variable in command window 11; putting structure elements into 157–159; switching positions of elements in 20–22
mean(s) 33–35; discovering features of 189–192; understanding 35–37
multiple curves, plotting 79–80, *80–81*
multiple groups, creating a Latin square for 65–70
multiplication of matrices 26–27; element by element 28–29
multi-row matrix, deletion of column from 15–16

names, acceptable variable 13–14
naming rather than numbering figures 232–236, *234, 236*
n-tagons 232–236, *234, 236*
number of values in matrices 17–18
numel 186–189

one-row array, deleting elements from 14–15
ordering of legends 220–222, *221–222*
overwriting existing files, avoiding 126–130

plotting: adding power function curves, legends, and labels for x- and y-axes 85–90, *88, 90*; adding text, a grid, and a fitted exponential function 99–105, *102, 106*; adding titles and comparing power versus exponential functions 106–108, *107, 109*; bar graphs 109–112, *111–112*; controlling bars for bar graphs and xtick labels 113–115, *114–115*; controlling colors, point shapes, graph limits, and standard error bars 81–85, *83, 85*; defining terms for 77–78, *78–79*; and filling in 3D, and controlling camera angle 250–256, *255–257*; rotating text, overlaying text on arrows, and more 237–249, *247–249*; showing multiple curves 79–80, *80–81*; subplots 90–98, *94, 98*; thinking clearly while "bar hopping" 116–118, *117–118*; tick labels 152–153, *152–153*
point shapes, plotting 81–85, *83, 85*
power function curves 85–90, *88, 90*
power versus exponential functions, comparison of 106–108, *107, 109*
printing: structure contents 171–173; value of variable in command window 11
printouts, formatting of data 130–133
program completions, timing 70–73
program pairs 6–7
Publish feature, MATLAB 8–9
Python xiii

quote marks 5–6

raising values to a power 32–33
R Blues xiii
Rosenbaum, David A. xi, 1
rotating of text 237–249, *247–249*

sequences, keystroke 7–8
sequencing points for graphs 228–232, *230, 232*
Shepard, Roger 99
simple summing 23–24
size 186–189
sorting 51–55
standard deviations 37–40
standard error bars 81–85, *83, 85*
structure contents, printing of 171–173
structure elements put into matrices 157–159
subplots 90–98, *94, 98*
subscripts 222–225, *223, 225*
summing, simple 23–24
switching positions of elements in matrices 20–22
symbols 226–227, *226–227*

text: graph 99–105, *102, 106*; overlayed on arrows 237–249, *247–249*; rotating 237–249, *247–249*
tick labels 152–153, *152–153*; creating and calling new function to control 207–211, *209, 211–212*
time saving using find 73–76
timing program completions 70–73
titles, graph 106–108, *107, 109*

users' email addresses 141–143

variables: giving acceptable names to 13–14; using cells to concatenate double and char 148–149; value of, printed in command window 11
Vaughan, Jonathan xi, xiv, 1

while statements 55–58
writing out and reading back in a .dlm file 125–126
Wyble, Brad i, xi, xiv, 1

xtick labels 113–115, *114–115*